WE, THE DIVIDED

WE, THE DIVIDED

*Ethos, Politics and Culture in
Post-war Italy, 1943–2006*

REMO BODEI

Translated by
Jeremy Parzen & Aaron Thomas

AGINCOURT PRESS
NEW YORK ⌘ 2006

This translation copyright © 2006 by Aaron Thomas and Agincourt Press

First published in Italian as *Il noi diviso. Ethos e idee dell'Italia repubblicana*
© 1998 by Giulio Einaudi editore s.p.a., Turin.

All rights reserved. Except for brief passages for the purposes of criticism and review, no part of this publication may be reproduced or transmitted in any form or by any electronic or mechanical means (including electronic, mechanical, photocopying, recording, or information storage and retrieval) without prior written permission from the publisher.

First published 2006
Printed in the United States of America
ISBN 978-1-946328-59-5 paperback

Book design and typesetting: Yuko Sawamoto
Back cover photo: Erik Powell / PowellVisual

AGINCOURT PRESS
P.O. Box 1039
Cooper Station
New York, NY 10003
www.agincourtpress.org

In memory of my brother, Romolo (1940–1997),
comrade and witness to this voyage in time.

CONTENTS

INTRODUCTION	9
1 The Solitary Choice	16
2 Post-War Ethos and Sentiment	33
3 Territories of the Imaginary	50
4 Philosophizing in a Divided World	74
5 Home and Society	91
6 Youth and the Irreality Principle	105
7 *Krisis*	121
8 How the "Ethical Party" Became Corrupt and Died	134
9 The Search for Roots	158
POSTSCRIPT · Eight Years Later	174

INTRODUCTION

Any attempt to make sense of the ideals adopted by Italians and the collective choices they have taken in the half-century or more since the establishment of the Italian Republic at the end of World War II is more than ambitious: it is almost a desperate endeavor. In approaching such broad-ranging questions, the risk of falling into generic formulations and of overlooking essential aspects is always looming. In order to avoid such shortcomings, at least in part, a different perspective is needed–a fresh montage of materials and concepts that have been patiently selected and developed.

I have pursued this objective through a twofold strategy of containment. First, I have attempted to compare the values and expectations of Italian society with the ideas and projects of Italian philosophy during this period, which I have examined exclusively from the point of view of its implications and indirect consequences in the field of ethics. Second, in order to avoid flattening the philosophical theories against the backdrop of the historical events from which they emerged and, at the same time, to avoid detaching them completely from that context (as if they were born by parthenogenesis), I have adopted a procedure that disaggregates and re-composes the data in a way analogous to the technique employed by Pointillist painters. In their paintings, isolated dots of different colors, optically pure, are grouped together on the canvas in order to produce (from a distance, by means of retinal fusion) a different color, whose luminous intensity is much greater than what could be obtained by mixing colors on the palette. Thus, in works by the artists Segantini or Pellizza da Volpedo, for example, one can see how small brushstrokes of yellow placed next to brushstrokes of blue combine and form–as one moves away from the painting–a green much more brilliant than what could be produced by directly mixing the two colors.[1]

When applied to our field, this strategy has various advantages. It allows us to compare different and heterogeneous phenomena that are not necessarily or directly correlated (but which have occurred in the same period and geographical area) without conflating them. Indeed, the contrary is true: the various elements can be isolated and placed in tension with each other. Viewing these contrasting elements synoptically and from a distance not only sharpens the clarity of the individual phenomenon itself, but simultaneously avoids both the trap of some varieties of historicism, which view ideas solely as a function of their immediate historical and political context, as well as the opposite pitfall of seeing ideas as completely detached from events, fluctuating widely in empty space. Thus, "facts" and "ideas" can be studied in a way that does not violate their different systems of logic or flatten their dephased rhythms.

This "Pointillist" method also makes it possible to study closely the discontinuities that lie in the interstices between points of "color." So that "Pointillism" does not degenerate into banal impressionism, this approach purposefully renders visible the lacunae in the exposition. Consequently, our method creates the need for further research that will fill in the gaps through appropriate "enlargements" and sectional close-ups; the tools for such closer and more targeted historical and conceptual analysis are provided in the notes. This method offers a sort of bifocal lens that offers gradations in the potential pleasure of research and further study, and allows the text to expand upon itself in proportion to reader's willingness to dig deeper (the text is, however, entirely autonomous with respect to the notes and can even be disassembled "monochromatically" into historical and philosophical sections). This process invites the reader to accompany and to supplement my own narration with his or her own memories, reflections and criticism. Given that each one of us is inevitably subject to our own privileged perspectives–since we live inside a system of opinions and feelings that seem clear to us as, as long as we remain immersed in them–a similar realization regarding the predilection towards advancing our own point of view characterizes the horizon of studies, which always has the

---

[1] See Remo Bodei, "Un paradigma 'fin de siècle': dividere e contrapporre" in Gabriella Belli and Franco Rella, eds., *L'età del divisionismo* (Milan: Electa, 1990), pp. 137-53.

potential to be enlarged but is intrinsically impassable in any inquiry into collective phenomena, especially if it deals with events and concepts that belong in part to the public domain.

The criterion adopted here allows us to open a window onto the limitless mass of thoughts and choices that have involved millions of individuals, each one situated legitimately at the center of his or her own spatial and temporal horizon. The untidy diversity of these distinct points of view is made even more fragmentary by the complexity of Italian history, whose vicissitudes inevitably become more blurry the closer they are to the present and the closer the observer approaches, viewing each point separately to the detriment of the whole.

Such a Pointillist approach, finally, constitutes a useful antidote to the troublesome sensation of *déjà vu* that derives—for those who set themselves the task of studying such problems in depth—from the proliferation of writings dealing with many facets of Italian history, society and philosophy in the post-World War II era (especially the years 1943–1945). Pairing and juxtaposing facts and ideas that we do not usually see together produces, on the one hand, a reciprocal "transcoloration" along the spectrum of implications and allusions, and, on the other hand, a healthy dose of estrangement (which is amplified by the additional chromatic filter of ethics, which allows us to see, in a different light, even that which otherwise is already well-known). In the space of just a few pages, by means of intermittent flashes or by bringing together elements which are familiar when taken separately, some phenomena occasionally display additional and unexpected nuances. In order to delimit the expectations of the reader and to give a sense of the aim to be pursued, I will begin with a preliminary clarification of some of the terms used in the title and employed frequently in the text. With regard to the Italians, the "we" which is "divided" should be understood primarily as it is in "*divisionismo*," the Italian term for the divisionism or Pointillism just described (and later employed throughout the text). Although it does not exclude the possibility, the term does not necessarily refer to the notion of a poisonous laceration that—whether produced by nature or out of historical necessity—pits Italians against each other; nor does the term imply a hidden evil that purportedly corrodes national identity. This expression does not echo, except as a tenuous allusion, the anguished verses of Italy's national anthem, the *Inno di Mameli*, which cries that "we are not a people, because we are divided." In fact, to the extent that they do not degenerate into particularism or open and bloody secession, divisions and contrasting historical memories can even represent a resource, a stimulus that supports the internal dynamic of Italian society.

By the word *ethos*, I mean the set of customs, norms and models of behavior (not always conscious or always commendable) that guide the actions of individuals within a determinate historical community. Well aware of the wear and tear that terms like "ideals" and "values" have suffered, I do not attribute to them any sublime or apologetic meaning. But neither do I consider them to be empty vessels or vacant terms, buying into the obstinate disenchantment and bitter cynicism of those who presume that they understand the prose of the world and know that these highfalutin terms are laughable when used with reference to Italy. When adequately understood, "ideals" and "values"–or rather the models and criteria of choice held to be most desirable–offer a key to codes of conduct and shared life plans, which are appreciated above all in moments of emergency, when they mark clear watersheds in people's effective behavior. They indicate the guiding principles and forms that shape, to varying degrees, the meaning of an individual's or group's actions, often without their explicit knowledge. By the same token, not all values and ideals are equally dignified or acceptable, nor are they equally good for all of the elements of one extended society, composed of a mosaic of smaller societies and inserted, on a larger scale, in the framework of other communities scattered over the surface of the entire planet. Even *omertà*, the Mafia's code of silence, is a value, as is revenge (*vendetta*) in what is left of the code of honor of the Barbargia region in Sardinia. Courage, consistency, honesty, decency, individual unselfishness in the service of a cause and willingness to pay personally for one's convictions and actions all involve modes of behavior whose excellence or exceptionality is recognized even outside the more restricted community within which these "values" are practiced. In their own way, they are "virtues" which demand involuntary respect from those who do not accept their specific motivations and aims, and who might even fight against them in the name of ends which they judge to be superior, like freedom, justice or equality.

The ethos of a people does not form, consequently, a compact or monolithic slab of marble devoid of internal fractures or veining. It contains multiple articulations and stratifications, which I have tried to bring into relief, although often using a "coring" method to extract an indicative sample: the state (with its public administration, the armed forces, the Carabinieri, the police, diplomacy, education system, and the courts), the Church (with its hierarchies), society (with its political parties, centers of economic power, unions, professional and trade associations, local traditions), the family (and the roles it performs), and criminal organizations (with its own rules and rites). Each institution or group constitutes both a particular "issuing bank" or "stock exchange" of ethical values, often in competition with one another, as well as a mechanism to control the strains—and stabilize the stresses—to which these same values are constantly subjected.

The systematic study of these partial ethical systems would open an immense field of investigation in areas that have been only scarcely cultivated and that have never been "tilled" in an intensive or comparative manner. If pursued, their detailed mapping and stratigraphy would cast more light on the morphology of a national history that is itself tortured, splintered and hybridized. They would show, perhaps more than in any other European nation, the ways in which areas of accentuated modernity coexist with residual archaisms, and how diverse historical periods flow into the same river-bed (the behaviors and modes of thinking and feeling observable today are but the surface layer of customs and ideas, whose depth in some areas reaches down almost three thousand years of uninterrupted urban civilization). At the same time, Italians' behavior is nothing but a local variation on universal forms of human conduct.

As a collateral effect, this survey might help to dispel (if there is still any need to do so) the persistent myth of Italy as a country ruled by *commedia dell'arte*, melodrama (sung but not lived firsthand), the strains of mandolins and "amoral familism," where every conflict is feigned or smoothed over, where everything is immobile because it all remains the same and where every discourse on ethics seems like a joke. Undoubtedly, these stereotypes exist for a reason, and partial evidence can be found to back them up. There is, undeniably, a deficit of public spirit among millions of Italians, which has been often noted over the centuries by foreign visitors and deplored by contemporary Anglo-Saxon sociologists as a tenacious attachment to Guicciardini's *particulare*, that is, to interests of family and property, of "blood" and "possessions." There is no point in regretting the fact that one is not different from who one is, nor in giving into the habit of indulgent self-flagellation by focusing on the vices of the Italians and on missed opportunities in the nation's history, such as missing out on the Protestant Reformation. Italians, for better or worse, have already been "made." This does not mean, however, that the negative clichés can be generalized, that a causal connection exists between attachment to one's family and the lack of a civic sense, or that "virtuous minorities," capable of going against the tide in times of emergency, are or have been absent.

The history of Italy is doubtless a succession of terrible vicissitudes and sad, dark periods without redemption, each marked by grief, pain, malaise, arrogance, misdeeds, real and symbolic killings of leaders, violence and impunity. We must descend into this inferno, in which Italians are not alone, in order to reveal their ethos. In just the twentieth century alone they have lived through at least four international wars (Libya, World War I, the African War and World War II, not to mention the Spanish Civil War, the Gulf War and the war in Kosovo), a civil war, twenty years of Fascist dictatorship, a series of political systems from which the adversaries of the various governments in power were rigorously barred, the presence of ferocious illegal organizations that affect everyday life in four of Italy's regions, massacres of innocent citizens, plots hatched by invisible powers, varieties of terrorism that have actively involved tens of thousands of people, systematic corruption and a dead-end future for millions of young people without work. But taken together, along with the art of making due, even the tenacious and sporadic capacity of many to react to these and other inauspicious conditions has managed to produce effective antibodies.

The itinerary that I have undertaken cannot be reduced to the analysis of a presumed "Italian ideology," nor to a description of Italian "customs" (with which a comparison is nonetheless unavoidable inasmuch as an ethos has to do, by definition, with customs, and customs, in turn, with the indefinable "odor" of those years, associated with myriad habits, traumatic experiences, volatile moods or tenacious worries and passions, even including minor episodes, which memory has saved from oblivion, and objects from daily life that by now are nearly obsolete). In interweaving ideas and events, this book devotes much space to a consideration of Italian philosophical schools, particularly to the most recent and least discussed. They are implicitly evaluated at the points where they form a tangent to, and diverge from, the common ethos. The greatest focus is given to those which, rightly or wrongly (and thus no internal critique of them will be proffered), have most influenced public debate, and have often been translated indirectly into practical programs. But in addition to ideas, which more or less legitimately refer to reality, the collective Italian imagination will be examined here–the tapestry of desires, expectations, projects, hopes and fears. Thus, a "second history" emerges that runs parallel to the official history; it registers both the irresolvable conflicts and the uneasy convergences between the feelings of the majority of Italians and the ideas and programs for action that are developed by the few or spring from restricted circles.

In thinking about what all of us have variously lived through (according to the ways in which each generation is punctuated by the power of events and the gradual disappearance of social actors), the reader is left to insert the trajectory of his or her own life into the common mental and moral landscape, which is crisscrossed and marked by experiences that will never be repeated in the same way.

CHAPTER 1
The Solitary Choice

On One's Own

Symbolically, the roots of the ethos of the Italian Republic can be traced to "five days" that in the course of only five years shaped the face of the nation and left a mark on the experience and historical memory of its inhabitants: July 25, 1943; September 8, 1943; April 25, 1945; June 2, 1946; and January 1, 1948. The most noted and now most controversial date is undoubtedly September 8, 1943, the decisive moment when the Italy's institutions first showed their fragility as they shattered or simply dissolved. It was then that Italians felt largely alone and on their own, for they saw crumble before their eyes the cluster of diverse loyalties and "sentimental convergences" which they had hitherto trusted – such as the affection for one's family, devotion to the Savoy dynasty, loyalty to the state and allegiance to the National Fascist Party. But this moment is also the touchstone for an evaluation of the Italian ethical posture – even as individual motivations may be diverse – during unexpected and catastrophic upheavals.

Following the so-called "reciprocal deception" between the Badoglio government and the Allies on September 8, 1943, all official points of reference suddenly dissolved. With the state's monopoly on the legitimate use of force broken, the majority of Italian adults found themselves desperately alone and forced to bear the responsibility of certain decisions that they never thought they would have to make. They were confronted with a dramatic conflict of values that implicitly struck at the heart of the entire social structure. These dilemmas were made even more painful by the fact that the possible choices lacked the approval of any unanimously recognized authority.

In routine situations, citizens are not asked to express their opinions on the set of norms that regulate civil life nor on the criteria used to distinguish between the just and the unjust, but calamitous events and unexpected power vacuums force them to take clear-cut and comprehensive positions, if for no other reason than that "the obligations toward the state no longer constitute a secure point of reference for individual behavior, since the state is no longer in a position to demand the 'loving sacrifices' upon which it had so often relied."[1]

The double loyalty that most Italians harbored for the diarchy King/Duce had been shattered. The two powers were now separate and mutual enemies, and they could no longer retain the combined affective investment of the past. Each and every person – men still of combat age in particular, but even women and civilians, who would die, by the war's end, in numbers almost equal to those who died in battle – was deprived of this ideal point of reference, and now had to evaluate his or her own specific situation and quickly take stock. The negative examples that came on September 8th from the highest authorities made apparent to everyone that the safeguarding of one's own life and interests was more than legitimate, while some were induced to search for a new order that would put an end to the state of nature provisionally reigning amid the rubble of the civil state. Many, on the one hand, found their conscience confusedly clogged with residual values (an attachment to the past; a sense of "honor" that was understood to entail respect for previous alliances and a desire not to be disparaged for having once again exchanged friends for enemies; a love for country, which was still thought of as the fatherland of Fascism that had sought to give pride to a "dispersed people that has no name"; and a blind faith in the "Duce who will never die"). On the other hand, they were pervaded, in hindsight, by a dim perception of having been fooled (pushed into a war for which they were absolutely unprepared) and struck by the premonition that the tragedy of the present was opening unexplored spaces of freedom and opportunity.

---

1   Claudio Pavone, *Una guerra civile. Saggio storico sulla moralità della Resistenza italiana* (Turin: Bollati Boringhieri, 1991), p. 23. On September 8, 1943, see: Elena Aga-Rossi, *Una nazione allo sbando. L'armistizio italiano del settembre 1943* (Bologna: Il Mulino, 1993); and *idem*, *L'inganno reciproco. L'armistizio tra l'Italia e gli Angloamericani del settembre 1943* (Rome: Ministero per i beni culturali e ambientali, 1993).

Others, deprived of institutional support and temporarily free from the chain of military command, aspired only to whatever peace they could get and carved out, in the meantime, a minimal space of livability for themselves and those dear to them. Thus, they immediately rediscovered the most ancient and protective nucleus of aggregation, and it is to that nucleus – the family – that they returned, as if to a safe port, viewing it as their "only fatherland."[2] In this *nostos*, the fortune or misfortune of the majority was determined by chance, based on geography and the changing front lines. In other words, their fate was decided by whether they found themselves spatially closer to the Germans or the Allies, to the Kingdom of the South or the territory of the emerging Italian Social Republic. In this Italy that was "split in half," occupied *de facto* by more than one foreign army and which saw two Italian armies locked in battle with one another (starting a new historical cycle of limited sovereignty), there was also a variegated "gray zone." Falling into this zone were not only the individuals and groups that used caution and the desire "not to compromise themselves" as their general rule of thumb toward the end of the war, but also the ecclesiastical hierarchies (which functioned as mediators between the combating factions and as protectors of the population during the most difficult moments of bombing, evacuations, German retaliation, the black market and the anonymous denunciation letters), and those who for whatever reason would not resort to arms.[3]

Facing "reality" was painful and provoked bewilderment and fear; it meant, among other things, the discovery of a lack of real autonomy, personal responsibility and solid, collective values. If the traditional absence in Italian history of a culture of interiority, as well as the pull of Fascist propaganda to be a part of the disciplined masses – to "believe, obey and fight" – had eliminated the already weak disposition of many to exercise their own free-

---

2   The family was described in this way, at least as early as August 9, 1943, in a letter that a lieutenant of the Royal Army wrote to his wife. See Pietro Cavallo, *Italiani in guerra. Sentimenti e immagini dal 1940 al 1943* (Bologna: Il Mulino, 1997), p. 384.

3   On the wide role assumed by the Church and the nature of its activities, see: Sergio Cotta, *Aspetti religiosi della Resistenza* (Turin: AIACE, 1977); Jean-Dominique Durand, *L'Église catholique dans la crise de l'Italie (1943–1948)* (Rome: École Française, 1991); and the results of the researches conducted by the Istituto Sturzo presented at the conference *Cattolici, Chiesa, Resistenza* held in Rome in September 1995.

dom,[4] Italy's tortured national history, combined with the recent efforts of Fascism, nonetheless failed to plant strong roots in these communitarian ideals. Making choices is never easy, and Italians were now obliged to ponder the unknown nature of new circumstances and to recover and tap hidden reserves of moral sense, even if only to salvage what was salvageable. Still without sufficiently thought-out convictions, they were exposed to the risk of sacrificing some ideals to the advantage of others, but they could also feel the satisfaction of seeing the positive results of their actions. The fact that those who made clear-cut decisions were in the minority does not reduce the moral weight of their choices; if anything, it increases it. Such was the case of the political exiles who returned after many years, the clandestine organizations operating in Italy during the Fascist regime, the 220,000 known partisans and the more than 600,000 prisoners of war in Germany who refused to fight for the Italian Social Republic. The same must be said, however, of those who adhered to values more difficult to share from a humanitarian point of view, yet who followed their ideals by fighting on the opposing front.[5]

---

4   At the university level, the Fascist mystique had made diffuse blind obedience coupled with a pompous rhetoric. An example of the latter can be found in the pronouncements of a zealous professor in 1940, for whom the fundamental assumption of fascism is "the perfect communion between an incandescent Faith, which is decoupled from reality, and a form of Reason that is detoxified of the egocentric arrogance that the preachers of intellectualistic civilization flatter themselves with and rave about"; see Fidia Gambetti, *Gli anni che scottano* (Milan: Mursia, 1967), p. 284ff.

5   To appreciate the sense and the weight of the values at play, a comprehensive reading of the following volume of letters of those sentenced to death during the Resistance and of the casualties of the Italian Social Republic is indispensible; one must, however, keep in mind the criteria employed by the editors in their choice of letters. See Piero Malvezzi and Giovanni Pirelli, eds., *Lettere dei condannati a morte della Resistenza italiana* (Turin: Einaudi, 1954); and *Lettere dei caduti della Repubblica Sociale Italiana* (Milan, 1960). While in the former we may detect a faith in the unstoppable march of history that will lead to peace, and with this the triumph, variously, of equality, of freedom or of Stalinist Communism, in the latter we find an excitement for battle or the desire to save the honor of the fatherland. With regard to the latter, see for example the undated letter of the twenty-year-old Paolo Carlo Brogi, who wrote "God, see to it that Italy is saved; see to it that shame vanishes from the forehead of its children. If this requires blood, here I am: take my blood and that of anyone who, like me, loves Italy. It will be a joyous sacrifice, and the tears of our mothers will be the dewdrops on the flowers of freedom, the one and only freedom"; *Lettere dei caduti*, p. 92. Even loyalty to the "German ally" was upheld by those fighting for the Italian Social Republic in a curious blend of respect, fear and scorn – including sentiments expressed in the popular song "*Camerata Richard, benvenuto*" (Welcome, Comrade Richard), in which we hear that "today the Earth is crashing, but the two of us form a single soul" – as well as admiration for the efficiency of the German war machine coupled with a veiled disdain for the cruelty of their methods.

The attitude of Admiral Bergamini, commander of the battleship "Roma," provides an example of the heroism in defeat and the sense of duty. The evening of September 8th – the day before the great ship was sunk by the Germans – he addressed the commanders of the Naval Group, communicating the order to hand over the Italian fleet to the Allies:

> Tell this to your men. In their generous hearts, they will find the strength to accept this immense sacrifice… Although this was not the path we envisioned, this is the path we must now take without hesitation, because what counts in the history of a people are not the dreams and hopes and denials of reality, but the conscience of duty fulfilled to the very end, whatever the cost.[6]

It is incorrect to speak of September 8th simply as an inauspicious date that marked the "death of the fatherland" (which April 25, 1945, Liberation Day, could do nothing to resurrect).[7] For, on the one hand, the "fatherland" had been already identified by Fascism with one segment of Italians and, on the other hand, because the temporary institutional void and the division of Italy into two opposing states immediately afterward prevented the identification of a single, common "fatherland." But neither can one say that this date marked the fatherland's glorious resurrection, although it certainly laid some of the groundwork by establishing a break with the past. This newly created equilibrium was nonetheless rendered fragile by the latent division of the parties in the *guerra per bande* (the "group warfare") of the Resistance in the North and the tenuous legitimacy of the institutional and

---

6   Cited in Ferdinando Di Lauro, *Saggi di storia etico-militare* (Rome: [s.n.], 1976), pp. 43–44. Bergamini's message recalls – but with greater force – that of Admiral De Courten cited in Aga-Rossi, *L'inganno reciproco*, pp. 356 and 371. This episode of resolute and responsible acceptance of one's own duty on the part of Bergamini certainly has nothing to do with the controversy over the "flag-waving loyalty of the Navy to the oath" they took or, put differently, to their presumably different behavior of defeat with respect to other armies; see Renzo De Felice, *Mussolini l'alleato. II. La guerra civile* (Turin: Einaudi, 1997), p. 189 n. See also Giorgio Giorgierini, *Da Matapan al Golfo Persico. La Marina militare italiana dal fascismo alla Repubblica* (Milan: Mondadori, 1989), pp. 550ff.

7   See Renzo De Felice, *Rosso e nero*, ed. Pasquale Chessa (Milan: Baldini e Castoldi, 1995) and Ernesto Galli della Loggia, *La morte della patria. La crisi dell'idea di nazione tra Resistenza, antifascismo e Repubblica* (Rome-Bari: Laterza, 1996). According to these authors, this period is a signal of the "ethical and political weakness of the country" and of the citizens' loss of a sense of national belonging. I will discuss this argument at greater length in chapter 9 of this volume. Although the expression "*morte della patria*" (roughly: "death of the fatherland") is drawn from the Sardinian jurist and writer Salvatore Satta, the meaning that he attributes to it is much more complex. See Salvatore Satta, *De profundis*, ed. Remo Bodei (Nuoro: Ilisso, 2003).

political forces in the South (something which did not help to reinforce the unity and homogeneity of the governing classes after the war).

The Dissolution of "We"

It was not so much the "fatherland" that died, but an ideal and practical model of the state, for which Giovanni Gentile's last work, *Genesi e struttura della società* (*Genesis and Structure of Society*) constitutes a solemn testimonial.

After the fall of Fascism, the Sicilian philosopher – who had retired to the Florentine countryside to write – remained loyal to the regime and fully consistent with the ideas he had professed in the past. Just as all that he had hoped for crumbled and a complete institutional collapse seemed immanent, Gentile – in a paradox analogous to that of his fellow Sicilian, Pirandello, at the time of Matteotti's murder – publicly and ostentatiously affirmed his ties to Fascism. Convinced of the necessity to proceed toward a "pacification of the soul," that is, of the need for a renewed "concord" to cement national unity, Gentile traveled on November 17, 1943 to Salò (capital of the Italian Social Republic, on the banks of Lake Garda) to pay a visit to the Duce. Gentile sought, moreover, to combat the most extreme and desperate wing of the incipient Social Republic, which had launched a ferocious campaign of terror against the "traitors" of July 25th and the "felons" of September 8th.

Written in one of the most painful moments in the history of Italy, between August and September 1943 (a period that reminded Gentile of the Battle of Caporetto of 1917, in which the Italian army was routed, provoking the mass desertion or surrender of hundreds of thousands of Italian troops), *Genesis and Structure of Society* represents a heartfelt return to the theme of the "Ethical State" (Fascism was considered an "experiment" in this form of governance). This time, the ethical state was proposed as an antidote to the feared dissolution of the national community, and as an extreme attempt to overcome the discord of the moment and rediscover the force necessary to reconstruct civil life from its shaken foundations. A highly dangerous phase had begun, in which the survival of Italians as a people was at stake. In the arc of a few months, the centuries-long work of building national identity and independence was at risk, and with it the ties of solidarity so laboriously woven, the sense of duty and the awareness of the sacrifices necessary to recover from the present crisis.

This apotheosis of the State was stressed with greater vigor precisely at the moment that its powerlessness became increasingly clear, in a world characterized by the dissolution of all forms of stability. Nonetheless, Gentile insisted on attributing almost divine honors to the state, by linking the caducity of the citizen to the secular eternity of the political sphere. The "ethical state" ends up being superior even to Hobbes' absolutist "mortal God." In fact, the "ethical state" was not limited to enforcing the laws and determining the kinds of behavior and actions consistent with these laws: it dwells within the individual conscience, takes the place of religion and directs the inner self toward absolute values, however immanent and earthly. Gentile thus broke with a long tradition of philosophy that runs from Aristotle – by way of Spinoza – to Hegel. None of these great thinkers posited the state as the culmination of human actions, viewing it as the coronation of human action. Situated above politics for Aristotle, Spinoza and Hegel were, respectively, the contemplative life, wisdom and the "absolute spirit" (art, religion and philosophy).

The ethical state is totalitarian (the noun "totalitarianism" was coined by Gentile in 1925, while the adjective "totalitarian" was coined by Lelio Basso in 1923) because it literally recognizes no superior: *superiorem non recognoscens*. It does not distinguish between the external sphere of public, visible behavior and the internal sphere of deep, invisible convictions. Politics has taken away religion's most potent weapon: the ability to believe, the faith that pushes one to attempt the impossible. Gentile conceived of the role of the state within the individual in the same manner in which Saint Augustine imagined the role of God in every man's soul: as *interior intimo meo* and *superior summo meo*, that is to say, "more intimate to myself than I am to the most intimate part of me" and "higher than my highest faculties" (*Confessions*, III:6,2). Gentile's very vocabulary reveals these Augustinian antecedents inasmuch as he holds that the state is not fulfilled merely in the *inter homines esse*, but lives also – and above all – *in interiore homine*.[8] The illusion that the state is something external to its components would prove disastrous – as he wrote on November 28, 1943, in an article in *Cor-*

---

8   See also Giovanni Gentile, *I fondamenti della filosofia del diritto* (Florence: Sansoni, 1937), pp. 158–59.

riere della Sera entitled "Ricostruire" ("Rebuilding") – when the threat of annihilation of the country made everyone feel as if the life of each individual was at stake, "even though everyone was able in the past to delude himself by believing that it was the state that was in danger rather than he himself."[9]

For a long time, Gentile thought that the conscious mastery of the self – freedom – could not take place without an uninterrupted battle against the moment of alterity – of passivity, of servitude – which cannot be eliminated in any of us. This moment is within us not outside of us, and it is expressed in the will of the individual to escape immediately from that which obliges him to make explicit his connection with the universal, in the relationship between teacher/student, parent/child, master/slave and dominator/dominated. Inasmuch as I am really the state, the state contains an element of alterity with which I must inevitably enter into conflict. Such alterity is represented by an authority that at first seems to limit my freedom, until – and only after a struggle – it proves to be my ally, a substantive part of myself. I arrive finally at understanding the hidden parallelism by which "the individual develops and the State develops" at the same time.[10]

"At the bottom of the 'I', there is a 'We'": this is the constant theme that unfolds in the works of Gentile, if with different variations and accents, and culminates in *Genesis and Structure of Society*. From this "We" burgeons the authority that will set free the "I" who listens to it. At the base of the "I," there is "a sort of original sociality,"[11] that anchors and stabilizes it in its identity, which would otherwise be uncertain and mobile (here we are speaking *ab absurdo* since the individual, even if he wanted to, could never become this "I," a single isolated atom, in Stirner's sense of the Unique). In fact, for Gentile, "the individual is the greatest particularity to the degree that as he is the greatest universality. The more he is himself, the more he is everyone."[12] In other words, the deeper he delves into himself, the more he finds universality that constitutes the *interior intimo meo*. The individual is part of the *societas*, to whose life he contributes.

Everyone has within himself his own *socius*, and every thought is thus a

---

9   Giovanni Gentile, "Ricostruire," *Corriere della sera*, November 28, 1943, quoted in Renzo De Felice, *Autobiografia del fascismo* (Bergamo: Minerva italica, 1978), p. 587.
10 Giovanni Gentile, *Origine e dottrina del fascismo* (Rome: Libreria del littorio, 1934), p. 47.
11 Giovanni Gentile, *Genesi e struttura della società* (Florence: Sansoni, 1955), p. 32.
12 *Ibid.*, p.19.

dialogue, both with oneself and with the other. This *socius*, however, does not represent merely our shadow or our fellow traveler. It is not just in us: it *is* us. Individuality does not consist of a gift of nature or a biological endowment. It is an uninterrupted conquest, a continuous and unstoppable Becoming, in which one connects to the universal while conserving one's own particularity, discovering that the two are one and the same in the process of change: "For this reason the individual – conscience and possession of the universal – does not exist from the beginning; it is not a given. For an individual, it is not enough to be born; rabbits and chickens are also born, but they will never be individuals."[13] Contrary to English liberalism with its origins in natural law, which posits the individual's existence prior to the state – that is, private property of the "I" – Gentile stresses that the "particular individual is a product of the imagination... circumscribed within the extreme limits of birth and death, as well as by the brief confines of its physical person."[14]

Within the concrete dialectic of the "particular" and the "universal" (two abstractions, when considered separately), the individual is not pure freedom, just as the state is not pure constraint. As Gentile maintained:

> The true state... does not limit or constrain, but expands and empowers the personality of the citizen: it does not oppress him, but rather liberates him. Of course, the state is never a perfect state. But every effort made to change the form of the state obeys the same logic that makes every man search for his life in the universal and in freedom. This effort would not be possible, for that matter, if the state were not, even in its imperfection, the very will of the citizen who, unsatisfied, aspires to a more adequate form. The particular will, which contains the force of universal becoming, is the will of all.[15]

The upshot of this is the correspondence between authority and freedom, as well as the axiom which states that obedience to authority increases and exalts one's own freedom: "Authority must not curtail freedom, but neither can freedom pretend that it can do without authority, because neither of the two terms can exist without the other."[16]

---

13   *Ibid.*, p.22.
14   Giovanni Gentile, *Che cos'è il fascismo?* (Florence: Sansoni, 1925), p. 25.
15   Giovanni Gentile, *Introduzione alla filosofia* (Milan: Treves, Treccani, Tumminelli, 1933), p. 187.
16   *Idem, Genesi e struttura della società*, p. 60.

When all is said and done, however, this purported unity of the particular and the universal – of freedom and authority – is dubious. In fact, the nature of the ethical state implies a coercive solidarity: there is an absence of any real autonomy conceded to the "I" by the state. In Macpherson's terminology, Gentile rejects "possessive individualism," that is to say, the idea of a subject isolated from others and master of himself. In more general terms, however, he also rejects the individual's capacity for self-determination and choice: for Gentile, there is no such thing as an "atomistic" individual, nor can there be a society external to the individual. The family, school and state already potentially function as principal agents in the individual's socialization, making possible – or in some cases bringing awareness to – the fact that the "I" belongs to an "undivided We."

The only autonomy that an individual can expect is that of realizing oneself within the community by mystically fusing with it. The culmination of self-realization remains the sacrifice of one's own life for the benefit of the collectivity. The eternity promised to the individual by the ethical state does not imply, however, the immortality of the soul or its transfer to another world, as in the dogma of some religions. Death is a detachment from one's own immediate particularity, and at the highest level it is an abandonment of the self in favor of the social totality, in which it continues to live in an ideal sense. For this reason, it is necessary "to become immortal and not remain attached to the self like an oyster to the reef."[17]

In this way, however, authority ends up suffocating freedom and the "I" is crushed by the "We." Everything is shifted, theoretically, to a higher plane towards the majesty of the state, as well as towards those who, over time, represent it (inasmuch as the empirical side of politics can be recognized theoretically). In this sense, Gentile's doctrine coincides with the ethics of Fascism, which encouraged each citizen's self-denial and self-sacrifice

---

17 *Ibid.*, p. 157. On Gentile's thought, see H. S. Harris, *La filosofia sociale di Giovanni Gentile* (Rome: A. Armando, 1973); Salvatore Natoli, *Giovanni Gentile filosofo europeo* (Turin: Bollati Boringhieri, 1989; Augusto Del Noce, *Giovanni Gentile. Per una interpretazione filosofica della storia contemporanea* (Bologna: Il Mulino, 1990); and Eugenio Garin, "Introduzione a G. Gentile," *Opere filosofiche* (Milan: Garzanti, 1991). On the political and personal aspects of Gentile's life, especially in the final years before his death, see Benedetto Gentile, *Dal discorso agli italiani alla morte, Giovanni Gentile. La vita e il pensiero* (Florence: Sansoni, 1951), vol. IV, pp. 36ff.; Sergio Romano, *Giovanni Gentile. La filosofia al potere* (Milan: Bompiani, 1984); Luciano Canfora, *La sentenza. Concetto Marchesi e Giovanni Gentile* (Palermo: Sellerio, 1985); Giovanni Gentile and Fortunato Pintor, *Carteggio, 1895–1944* (Florence: Le Lettere, 1993); Paolo Simoncelli, *Cantimori, Gentile e la Normale di Pisa* (Milan: Franco Angeli, 1994); and Gabriele Turi, *Giovanni Gentile. Una biografia* (Florence: Giunti, 1995).

for the sake of the regime and the fatherland.

The Restless Conscience

From 1942 to 1945, in the face of events and the dissolution of the ethical state, the need to safeguard individual conscience from the oppressive anonymity of the collective conscience assumed clear political implications, even among Gentile's disciples. For them, the nexus between citizen and state, and between freedom and authority, had been split apart.

The first to defend the notion of an individual who acts without being able to appeal to any principle higher than himself was Cesare Luporini. After having attended Heidegger's courses in Freiburg and having attempted to build a bridge between existentialism and actualism, he took on – in January, 1943, in Bottai's journal *Il Primato* – the question of philosophy as the "conscience of a crisis." In a veiled polemic with Gentile, Luporini distinguished two opposing modes of thinking about the emergency: "on the one hand, the crisis is resolved and pacified by setting itself up on a higher plane than its terms; on the other hand, the crisis is sharpened and exasperated by defining itself in its own antinomical terms."[18] Luporini's choice fell, naturally, on the further deepening of the crisis and the decision to seek one's own authenticity, not in obedience to the ethical state but rather in a "calling," an inarticulate voice that resounds in silence and can be heard only through the emotive modality of restlessness and anxiety. It shows us the paths to freedom by encouraging us – almost forcing us – to take possession of our own destiny and unchain ourselves from habit and acquiescent apathy.

Luporini asserted the irreducibility of the individual to the state and the priority of the "I" over the "We" by both embracing the solitude into which the individual had been pushed by the tragic events and by assuming the existential dimension of contingency, singularity and the finite nature of each individual ("the here and now" in the "implicit centrality" of every conscience). Thus, he indirectly rejected the ideal of individual's supreme sacrifice – at once, automatic and blind – to the state in the manner of Moloch, who considered persons to be *quantités négligeables*. Luporini instead emphasized the individual, both in his connection to the human

---

18 See Bruno Maiorca, ed., *L'esistenzialismo in Italia* (Turin: Paravia, 1993), p. 131.

species in general and in his undeferrable personal responsibility, that is to say, the need for the individual to assume the burden of freedom in a specific "situation," thus resisting the temptation of letting himself be dragged along by the flow of events. It is precisely in the moments of greatest uncertainty that we realize the difference between our actions, which are "unconditioned," and our reactions, which are mimetically conditioned by the behavior and expectations of others. These reactions are "for the most part polluted by a sort of irresponsibility" on the basis of which "we let others decide for us." In such moments:

> A current pulls us and we are abandoned to it. It is the current of common levity, and we let ourselves go: our weight is relieved onto our companions and nullified in movement. But at the moment a hindrance stops us (death, illness, failure), we suddenly realize that we are isolated and alone... It is then that a restlessness reveals itself, a restlessness which brooded under the skin of our easier life and which – we realize – was always present, but noticed just enough so as to flee it... This deep restlessness was an appeal by our being to our own essence; it warned us that we were now alone and that what we hadn't wanted of our own accord was now imposed upon us by the circumstances.[19]

Those who face their duty seriously cannot flee from circumstances. They must force themselves to conquer the conditions and obstacles they encounter along the way, soberly recognizing the nature and level of difficulty of each without believing that it can be overcome by mere force of will, rash exaltation or foolish recklessness.

For many, however, the need to escape the tutelage of the ethical state was accompanied by the corollary need to abandon the bell-jar of the solitary conscience. The remedy was sought through action and political and social commitment, which exempted the individual from the contorted ruminations and inconclusive daydreams of thought by placing him in ef-

---

19   Cesare Luporini, *Situazione e libertà nell'esistenza umana* (Florence: Le Monnier, 1942), pp. 4–5. If distinct echoes of Heidegger can be heard in Luporini's thought – in particular the Heidegger of *Being and Time* (esp. §54ff.) – absent is any will to "be-for-death" in any sacrificial sense. Heidegger, on the other hand, would reaffirm this notion in 1944 – just as the National Socialist regime was coming to an end and recruiting into the army even adolescents – in sacrificing his own life for the fatherland. See Cesare Luporini, "Con Heidegger 1931–1993. Alcune riflessioni, oggi, tra filosofia e politica" in Franco Bianco and Karl-Otto Apel, eds., *Heidegger in discussione* (Milan: Franco Angeli, 1992), pp. 25–49; and S. Poggi, "La finitezza e la filosofia dell'esistenza" in Bruno Accarino, ed., *Il pensiero di Cesare Luporini* (Milan: Feltrinelli, 1996), pp. 76–91.

fective contact with others and with the world. By participating in political activity and in the war (in civil or military groups, clandestine or official), philosophers discovered other forms of community that did not coincide with the state or with a unified party. They were now fighting real battles against a flesh and blood enemy very different from the polemical idols they faced in the "Littoriali della Cultura" (the intellectual competitions held during the Fascist period) or in the pages of literary and philosophical journals. They found themselves, moreover, working and thinking about the future without the illusory protection once promised by Fascist historiography, which until recently had guaranteed certain victory for imperial Italy. History now appeared to be driven by an irresistible storm wind: "There are gales wailing like water-spouts, which we cannot ignore, for eventually they sweep the individual from his table and whisk him into the air." There was, however, no longer room for the private torments of the soul since, "faced with questions of life and death, the last generation does not have time to construct an internal drama: it has found an external drama already perfectly built."[20]

The world now forcefully reclaimed those rights that the conscience, in its demand for existential absoluteness, had attempted to retain after its recent escape from the seduction of the ethical state. The world demanded to be recognized, at the cost of swallowing the pride and self-esteem only recently acquired by the individual, severing his or her imaginary ties to the eternal categories of traditional metaphysics, surrogate of the lost ethics of politics. Some felt that the truth needed to be shown, along with – together and indissolubly – the fragility of the historical world, which exists only inasmuch as it is created, in the "poetical" awareness of the "nothingness of its origins," from the feeling of caducity that suddenly bursts when confronted with a conscience forever lagging behind events. Arturo Massolo registered this in 1944 when he wrote – during the bombing of Livorno, and under the influence of both Gentile and Heidegger – that "the individual is never a dawn: he moves in a world already come to light, the essence of which is hidden from him." It is this state of being that projects him toward the anguished uncertainty of the future, in a fluctuation of appearances that distance him from himself. "Psychologically, this is our punishment: feeling

---

20 Giame Pintor, *Doppio diario 1936–1943* (Turin: Einaudi, 1978), p. 52; *idem*, "Il nuovo romanticismo," *Il Primato*, II (August 16, 1941).

that we do not have full possession of ourselves. From the moment we start living, we live far away from ourselves."[21] The remedy for the present crisis can only be found in the awareness that history is a field of uncertainties where human projects and ideals advance, even as they risk defeat at every moment. And yet, Massolo would assert that the advance of these projects and ideals would have a greater chance of success if those who supported them could organize into political associations capable of backing up their convictions with a critical mass sizable enough to make lasting effects on reality.

In just a few years, the *societas* had thus definitively lost its Archimedean fulcrum *in interiore homine*.[22]

The Rights of Reality

The necessity of a continuous and obstinate confrontation with the real was never doubted by Benedetto Croce, the other tutelary deity of a divided Italy. For him, to indulge in vain regrets and desires to flee the world, to throw – in the manner of Gentilian actualism – "one's heart beyond the obstacle" and breed impotent hopes meant cultivating an attitude of passive cowardice. It was better to take note of the state of things and inventory the damages caused by the war and Fascism in order to bring Italy, as soon as possible, back to civilized Europe, from which it had become detached when it allied itself with Hitler's Germany.[23] After almost half a century of intellectual reign, Croce was still able to exercise decisive moral and political authority in the Kingdom of the South. He served in fact as a

---

21 Arturo Massolo, *Storicità della metafisica* (Florence: F. Le Monnier, 1944), pp. 133–36.

22 Although existentialism would take on forms less dramatic and more critical with the "positive" and "problematic" existentialism of Nicola Abbagnano, the existentialism of this period by and large did not remove itself from history, locking itself in conscience, as did that form of existentialism that Norberto Bobbio would later denounce in reference to Sartre: "Existentialism did not incite one into battle. Rather, the lesson it taught was that one should stand on one's own, desperately aloof with clairvoyant dignity, without getting one's hands dirty or compromising oneself, and without getting involved. One would not fight evil; rather, one would flee from it and, precisely for this reason, one would end up accepting it"; see Norberto Bobbio, "Di un nuovo esistenzialismo," *L'Acropoli*, no. 16 (April 1946), p. 174. For Abbagnano, see his *Introduzione all'esistenzialismo* (Milan: Bompiani, 1942); for a broader treatment of this problem, see Antonio Santucci, *Esistenzialismo e filosofia italiana* (Bologna: Il Mulino, 1967).

23 See Benedetto Croce, "Il dissidio spirituale della Germania con l'Europa" in Benedetto Croce and Thomas Mann, *Lettere 1930–1936* (Naples: F. Pagano, 1991).

privileged mediator between the Italian government and the Allies – especially the English – concerning the agreement that the country would have to accept at the end of the war, following the forced abdication of Vittorio Emanuele III. He recommended, moreover, the formation of a volunteer Italian Freedom Corps, to prevent Italy from being at the complete mercy of the victors.[24] His proven anti-Fascism and his serene balance made him an element of continuity with pre-Fascist Italy, though perhaps less of an intermediary between the former ethical values and those newly ripened in the culminating phases of the war and the Resistance. But even though his moderate liberalism (in which the individual had preeminent value over the masses and the state – far from being ethical, it was only useful) was better received after the war, his political position was less attractive to the major populist parties, which unknowingly followed the Gentilian model aimed at the mobilization of conscience rather than the disenchanted and individualistic Crocean position. For that matter, the tradition of European liberalism has always been very weak in Italy, where the rights of the individual are always preceded by those of the dominant institutions or the phantom souls of the "masses."[25]

It is precisely this fidelity to the world (in the sphere of every individual's responsible choices) that constitutes the nucleus of Croce's ethics and the deepest justification of his "absolute historicism." His ethics call for the recognition of the specificity, the differences, the complexity and the multiple contradictions of the present, resisting the constant allure of a nostalgic return to mythical golden ages or an unchecked rush toward remote future

---

24 Croce himself called for the king's dismissal, arguing publicly on December 20, 1943 that "to assume that Italy should hold on to the present king is like expecting a revived individual to remain embraced to a corpse"; see Benedetto Croce, "Appello ai popoli delle Nazioni Alleate" in *Per la nuova vita d'Italia (1943–1944)*, and reprinted in *Scritti e discorsi politici, 1943–1944* (Bari: Laterza, 1973), p. 43. In order to avoid the possibility that the Allies would humiliate the Italian people as such, Italians must "look at the so-called victors and judge them for what they are. They ought to say to them clearly that we see them as "big" but not "great"; that they might arouse fear like tigers or boa constrictors, but not so much as to warrant admiration as clever spirits or as benefactors of the human spirit"; see Benedetto Croce, "La depredazione dell'Italia, intervista al 'Correio' di San Paolo del Brasile," July 4, 1946, reprinted in *Scritti e discorsi politici, 1943–1947* (Bari: Laterza, 1962), vol. II, p. 322.

25 On the masses, see Benedetto Croce, "Considerazioni sul problema morale del nostro tempo," *Quaderni della "Critica,"* (1945), vol. 1, no. 1, p. 1: "In these times, there is the myth of the 'masses', which according to what is said and believed, evidently push history forward and are the sign of progress: the masses, a mysterious and prodigious force that harbors within itself a hidden and irresistible knowledge and power, which one must devotedly listen to or auscultate in order to passivly receive an echo, as if from the old Sibyl."

utopias. Respecting the rights of reality does not mean honoring whatever exists, but neither does it mean ignoring it. Between these two extremes – the attitude of Sancho Panza (who too readily adapts to the rules of a world that he does not wish to transform) and the visionary idealism of Don Quixote (who swaps the images of stemming from his own desires for reality) – there is, for Croce, a fertile intermediary position represented by effective action. Through action, one can file away at the harshness of a reality that is not immutable but, by its very nature, in a state of perpetual and uncertain transformation. Without giving in to illusion, one must begin, over and over again, to build the new from the ruins of the old, relying only on ourselves. The following passage, worthy of quotation in its entirety, contains an allegory both of Italian history at that moment and the tasks that await all peoples and individuals struck by calamity:

> The bishop of Turin, Maximus, comforted the citizens of Milan, whose homes had been destroyed and churches burned by Attila, by calling on them to consider that God had conceded to the hands of the enemy '*non civitatem quae in vobis est, sed habitacula civitatis, non ecclesiam suam, sed receptacula ecclesae*' [not the city that is in you but the physical structure of that city; not His church, but the container of that church] and the people of Milan with their bishop, although frightened and mournful, '*tamen in libertate perduraba[n]t*' [endured in freedom]. Man will always possess this ideal house or this ideal church, which alone is real, and in it is the only life worthy of humanity. What else can be asked of man? History finds its meaning in ethics... But it is during the moments of truce granted by destructive forces that civilization has woven and rewoven its fabric, lasting for centuries and even millennia between times of episodic and partial destruction, even managing to put together a 'universal history' with a supposed beginning, middle and end. This universal history is, in other words, a finite achievement of worldly and otherworldly perfection, into which has been woven the illusion that human civilization is the formation to which the Universe tends and exalts itself, and for which Nature acts as a pedestal. A painful effort is required to switch to the other vision of human civilization, in which it is seen as a flower that springs from solid rock, plucked and left to die by an adverse rain cloud: its merit does not lie in the eternity that it does not possess, but in the eternal and immortal force of the spirit, which can always produce an eternity that is newer and more intense.[26]

---

26 Benedetto Croce, "La fine della civiltà," *Quaderni della "Critica,"* (1946), vol. 2, no. 6, pp. 6–7.

In order to intervene in events in such a way as to realize the goals set by everyone, Croce held that the most effective tool was a two-tiered moral discipline. At the individual level, this moral discipline had to triumph over various forms of "paralysis of the will": a lack of rooted convictions and the tendency to escape into the "transcendent." At the level of society, it had to overcome transformism, cowardice, chronic weakness and the inconclusive ethics and politics afflicting the governing classes of Italy (which suffered, at least since the times of Crispi, but above all under Mussolini, from some form of "power complex"). Industriousness, moral and intellectual honesty, concreteness and sobriety were the values to which Croce continued to appeal, in a context in which Italy needed, more than ever, to remain at a distance from the new seductions of social justice posed anew and promoted by Italian communists and the Soviet Union.[27]

[27] In his interventions in the post-war political debate, Croce detected a close affinity between fascism and communism; see Antonio Cardini, *Tempi di ferro. "Il Mondo" e l'Italia del dopoguerra* (Bologna: Il Mulino, 1992), pp. 116–20. Croce himself chided Italian communist intellectuals for not having followed Gramsci's model. As he wrote in a book review of Gramsci's *Letters from Prison*, "Allow me to note, without any intention to offend anyone, that today's communist intellectuals depart too much from Gramsci's example, from his openness to truth, no matter where it comes from, from his painstaking accuracy and equanimity, from the kindness and tenderness of his sentiments, from his pure and dignified style"; Benedetto Croce, review of Antonio Gramsci, *Lettere dal carcere*, (Turin: Einaudi, 1947), in *Quaderni della "Critica,"* vol. 3, no. 8 (1947), p. 87. Of the vast literature on Croce, the following works deserve mention, for the purposes of the present discussion: Michele Abbate, *La filosofia di Benedetto Croce e la crisi della società italiana* (Turin: Einaudi, 1957); Sandro Setta, *Croce il liberalismo e l'Italia postfascista* (Rome: Bonacci, 1979); and Gennaro Sasso, *"Per invigilare me stesso". I taccuini di Benedetto Croce* (Bologna: Il Mulino, 1989).

CHAPTER 2
Post-War Ethos and Sentiment

From the Ethical State to the Ethical Party

Symbolically, the story of the Fascist ethical state ended with the Shakespearean image of the Duce, his lover and his entourage obscenely exposed, hanging upside down from hooks at the gas station in Piazzale Loreto, in a fierce and liberating ritual of savage justice and collective self-purification.[1] The ethical state relinquished its place to a lesser god – the "ethical party" – and alongside it a greater one, which we might term the "Ethical Church." The latter – which Gentile and Fascism had attempted to diminish as a competitive "institution for the transmission" of values – had not only survived the war intact, often managing to have its compromises with Mussolini's regime forgotten, but it was even morally and politically strengthened from the moment that the most powerful government party referred to its teachings. The Church was now ready to exercise its role as a protagonist in Italian society, making use of another ancient institution that has served as a substitute in moments of supreme state crises: the family.

Immediately following the war (and at least during the first three decades of Republican Italy), relationships involving loyalty and absolute devotion to a cause no longer tended to be immediately associated with the ideas of the "nation" or the "fatherland." Instead, these relationships appeared to be tied – in a sort of political synecdoche (*pars pro toto*, the part for the whole) – either to only one part of it, i.e. the party in its role as a carrier of broad-based needs; or – in a sort of reversed synecdoche (*totum pro parte*, the whole

---

[1] On Piazzale Loreto and the symbolic meanings it entails, see Sergio Luzzato, *Il corpo del Duce. Un cadavere tra immaginazione, storia e memoria* (Turin: Einaudi, 1998).

for the part) – to the Church, as guarantor, in this historical phase, of otherworldly interests beyond temporal, individual ones. Although they were always in competition with one another and each was far from monolithic, the popular parties inherited from the ethical state some mimetic traces of the party-state. They displayed, in fact, an inclination to transform themselves, for the sake of their members, into a universal, "totalitarian" leader, to which citizens delegated their own individual responsibility. Because of the intrinsic weakness of democratic traditions in Italy and the fact that the mass party developed there under the aegis of Fascism (the National Fascist Party was the only "modern" party with which anyone had any familiarity), the parties represented the main source of collective identity in this period: the division of memories and of the "fatherland" itself (into the two state entities of the Kingdom of the South and the Italian Social Republic from 1943 to 1945) left citizens without any authoritative or unitary points of reference.[2] Driven, moreover, by a desperate need to believe in and anchor themselves to something solid and visible, millions of men and women – their experience still scarred by the international and civil wars, the bombings, the evacuations, the so-called "black bread," the trauma of the change from monarchy to republic and, alongside all of this, the memory of spontaneous help offered and received in those crucial moments – reinvested their hopes in the parties, in the form of a massive, but not total, transference of loyalty from the whole to the parts. In some cases, one part presented itself as a whole, inasmuch as the principal parties – the Italian Communist Party (PCI) and the Christian Democrats (DC) – each referred to ideal, all-encompassing communities, which incorporated and transcended the "fatherland." Although each party appealed to a different ideal community – "proletarian internationalism" for the PCI, Catholic ecumenism for the DC – each was seen as an antidote to nationalistic "sacred egoism."

---

2 On the political parties after the war, see Giorgio Galli, *I partiti politici italiani, 1943–1991* (Milan: Rizzoli, 1991) and Paolo Farneti, *Il sistema dei partiti in Italia, 1946–1979* (Bologna: Il Mulino, 1993). For an account that underlines the "centrifugal forces" within Italian society that challenge the ability of the political parties to control effectively their own members, and which increase the educative and propagandistic functions of the party, see Paolo Pezzino, "Identità deboli e partiti forti. Le radici storiche della crisi italiana," *Storica*, 6 (1996), pp. 55–95, esp. pp. 77ff. Collective memory was also divided in the wake of German and Fascist massacres in some localities, billed as reprisals, something which served to alienate some of the population from the ideals represented by the partisans. For a few exemplary cases, see Leonardo Paggi, *Storia e memoria di un massacro ordinario* (Rome: Manifestolibri, 1996); Giovanni Contini, *Una memoria divisa* (Milan: Rizzoli, 1997); and Paolo Pezzino, *Anatomia di un massacro. Controversia sopra una strage tedesca*, (Bologna: Il Mulino, 1977).

The ethical importance that the mass parties historically claimed for themselves over the course of the twentieth century fostered a conflation of their tasks with the prerogatives of the state, and contained the seeds not only of the subsequent "partitocratic" degeneration of the political system (underway at least as early as the mid-1960s), but in retrospect also of the death of the "ethical parties," which after 1992 would be publicly deprived of their halo. The mass parties, identifying themselves with the state when they were in power and with the betrayed public interest when they were in opposition, ended up, by virtue of the positive role they played, weakening the image of a power *super partes*, a neutral guarantor of all citizens.

With the beginning of the Cold War, even fundamental values began to be subdivided among the different contenders, who claimed to represent one against the other. In this way, anti-communism paralyzed and cast suspicion on all measures to bring justice and social equality, while anti-capitalism and anti-Americanism together cast suspicion on assertions of the rights of individuals and the ideals of freedom, discredited as thin fig-leaves that concealed ruthless class violence. This ideological clash often dulled the sense of participation in a shared experience, and it led to the de-legitimization of any party alliance, even though later it also slowly induced millions of citizens (and herein lies the innovation) to accept political democracy as a place for the impassioned and rational meeting of contradictory opinions. With national and international loyalty divided between love for the tortured, "poor fatherland" and feelings of belonging to movements of global scope, Italian politics became a battle between opposing "ethical agencies."

The divvying up of power began: in essence, the Christian Democrats were the heirs of both the state – in the continuity, practically unscathed, of its infrastructure and the social block that re-solidified around it (industry, bureaucracy, banking, middle classes) – and the defense of the family. In classical terminology, therefore, the Christian Democrats inherited the principle structures of *polis* and *oikos*. The parties of the Left, which did not want or were not able to affect or interrupt the continuity of the state, were left with control of substantial sectors of cultural consensus and a relative hegemony within civil society (which should not be overestimated in light of the enormous power of Catholic culture and sensibility to penetrate the lower and middle classes).³ But while the perspective of the Christian Democrats, as an interclass party, was that of politics as "service" and its practical aspiration was to enter all the folds of society and emulate them, the Italian Communist Party aspired instead to be a "party of workers and of opposition... a party for the masses with characteristics of an elite party or cadre."⁴

The Civil War of the Soul

While Italians were acclimating to the ideological and religious distinctions among citizens, a civil war of the soul exploded. The "iron curtain" was thus drawn even between individuals, within families, between friends and colleagues. At times it took cruel forms, in private continuations of the war after its official conclusion. Between April and July of 1945, thousands of persons were reportedly murdered for political reasons, in addition to those killed in ordinary acts of violence or in personal vendettas (on this theme, Giovanni Guareschi drew a series of cartoons for the review *Candido* entitled "Via Emilia," after the road that leads from Piacenza to Rimini through the region of Emilia-Romagna).⁵ In this context of widespread hostility, however, there were nonetheless cracks through which occasional good will and cooperation filtered, as Guareschi himself depicted in the immediately popular figures of Peppone and Don Camillo.⁶ There was also visible daily compromise between Catholics committed to the "atheist" Left and Communists who married in the Church and had their children baptized. But these were not only manifestations of superficial compromise. Political hatred is not always able to corrode the centuries-old Catholic culture of

---

3   The modern party, which was originally Leninist, is "a formidable invention of twentieth-century social engineering, comparable to the monastic and chivalric orders of medieval Christendom"; E. J. Hobsbawm, *Il secolo breve* (Milan: BUR, 1995), p. 96. On the distinction between ethics and morality, see Remo Bodei, "Remota Justitia: Preliminary Considerations for a Resumption of the Debate of Ethics and Politics," *Praxis International*, vol. 6, no. 2 (July 1986), pp. 124–47.

4   Marcello Flores and Nicola Gallerano, *Sul PCI. Un'interpretazione storica* (Bologna: Il Mulino, 1992), pp. 138–39.

5   See Giovanni Guareschi, *Il mondo Candido 1946–1948* (Milan: BUR, 1991); and G. Crainz, "Il conflitto e la memoria. 'Guerra civile' e 'triangolo della morte'," *Meridiana*, n. 13 (January 1992), pp. 17–55.

6   These events echo, for that matter, a real battle of ideas between a mayor and a parish priest in Correggio; see Marta Boneschi, *Poveri ma belli. I nostri anni cinquanta* (Milan: Mondadori, 1995), pp. 63–64.

mediation or to entangle the fabric of interpersonal relationships: it often leaves free zones, resistant to violence and favorable to accord. Between divergent ethical and political models there remained a line of demarcation that was clear and, in theory, insuperable: on one side were ideals projected toward the future in the name of justice and equality, work for all and the end of exploitation; on the other was the claim of freedom and prosperity for the present with signs of enterprise and cautious acceptance of the economic and political models of the market. Militancy – forged of partisan generosity, proselytism, mobilization, opposition, personal sacrifice and a privileging of the public sphere to the detriment of private life and immediate interests – gave many a reason to live. In this way, one could discover, in the words of Beppe Fenoglio, "how great man can be in his normal, human dimension" – in this case, via his participation, whether direct or indirect, in daily events or collective projects.[7]

Of the bitterness of the nationalistic ideological conflicts that characterized the world before the war, intensity remained only in the conscience of the militants, in the framework of the great simplification of ideas and sentiments concerning the changed global scene, where the decisive struggle lay between two single blocs, the representatives of Good and Evil. Consequently, the new structures of identity – the political parties – did not privilege aspects concerning civil concord, but rather Manichean division, mirroring the division of the world into anti-fascism, anti-capitalism and anti-communism. The parties thus succeeded in consolidating themselves as "ethical powers," institutions which claimed that portion of loyalty and civic spirit which had been stripped from a state that had never really been able to prove itself.

From an ethical perspective, the history of Republican Italy represents the laborious elaboration of rules of cohabitation that arise out of the opposition and mediation between a multiplicity of values and life plans. These rules derived from the combination of at least five characteristic factors. First, there was Fascism, which had politicized large groups of the population, literally driving from their private refuge those who had traditionally been excluded or kept at the margins of politics (children, adolescents, women, peasants, clerical workers). After enveloping them in a multitude

---

7 Beppe Fenoglio, *Il partigiano Johnny* (Turin: Einaudi, 1968), pp. 39–40. See also Danilo Montaldi, *Militanti politici di base* (Turin: Einaudi, 1971), esp. pp. 289–308.

of associations, Fascism pushed them to participate in public demonstrations, to leave the confines of their homes or the worries exclusive to their trades. It sought to give a national conscience to those who lived in isolated communities, especially the rural masses for whom the world ended with the visible horizon of their village, where the echo of great collective events arrived already muffled. The peasants were not only the largest class in numerical terms, but also the most politically "virginal," although they were tied to the "magical world" and to the teachings of the parish and the traveling preachers. Second, there was the split from which Italy emerged after more than two decades of Fascist rule, with the virulence that accompanied the hostility and mutual disrespect between citizens that had fought on opposing fronts. Third, there was the enduring presence in the Italian state of the official center of Catholicism, with the Vatican continuing to enjoy autonomy and privileges in the very heart of Italy's capital. The approval of Article 7 of the Constitution – motivated by the understandable concern to avoid igniting a religious war in the already contentious political environment – allowed the Church to continue to make its weight felt in the political choices faced by the Republic. Fourth, there was the entry of Italy into the United States' political and, in part, cultural sphere of influence, thereby constituting a frontier between the two blocs. Fifth, there was the presence of the strongest, albeit most "liberal," Communist party in the West, which inherited Gramsci's conception of the ethical party as the "Modern Prince" (the educator, on the intellectual and moral level, of the often undisciplined and rebellious masses, like the peasants of Southern Italy).

After the war, the party sections or "cells," the "casa del popolo" (Communist or Socialist community centers), the recreational activities of Sunday schools and parishes, the unions, the sporting events and, later, the festivals organized by the leftist papers *L'Unità*, *Avanti!* or *Amicizia*, promoted and intensified the notion of "popular" participation. Although there was no lack of clientelism and opportunism, the double-edged and contradictory experience of fear (war, bombings, hunger) and hope (rebirth, well-being, a better world) taught many to view and practice politics as a total and jealously exclusive commitment. It was thought that the realization of non-political expectations would only come through political means. In retrospect, such passionate hyper-politicization today would raise some curious eyebrows. In this period of emergency, however, reliance on "ideological amphetamines" appears to have been an unavoidable necessity, required to carry out the exhausting tasks of adapting to new contexts, both domestic and international. It was a common conviction that freedom could be realized within the party, the union or the Church – that is, within "all-encompassing" and protective organizations that, in exchange, required a degree of discipline and obedience analogous to the ethical state. The primacy of politics thus represented, in miniature and in a partial way, the continuation – albeit through democratic means of persuasion – of the Fascist attempt to integrate all citizens into collective life.

The Ethics of State Administration

Some of the consequences of the widespread politicization of both men and women under Fascism were irreversible even in Republican Italy. On the positive side of the ledger, one consequence was the wide participation, often all-encompassing, in events pertaining to the entire national collectivity; on the negative side, however, authoritarian tendencies remained rooted in Italian society along with a conception of the state that, in both the mentality and the practice of everyday life, continued to treat its citizens as subjects. Despite the "demilitarization" of society and the birth of democracy, the ethos of certain categories that formally represent the structure of the state (administered in a Weberian sense by a "rational bureaucracy" and possessing a monopoly on the legitimate use of violence) was not sufficiently revamped.

If we take a panoramic view of the state administration, we see that the "continuity of the state" did not suffer excessive tremors for long. Especially at the higher levels, the *esprit de corps* (or caste sprit, as the case may be) of its "servants" either remained intact or was reluctantly modified. At times, such adherence to the models of the past also had its positive side, as in the case of the ministerial bureaucracy whose spirit of service (combined with a wait-and-see *arrière-pensée* of self-preservation) maintained with "equanimity" the activities of public administration even when the unified Italian state was divided into two warring branches. In 1943, while a small part of the documents of the ministries was transported to Brindisi and then to Salerno, the majority of the remaining papers was sent north from Rome, well-packaged and organized under the supervision of a German functionary. Although Fascism had aided the social climb of bureaucrats and middle-class clerks, political allegiance to the new regime in Salò among functionaries arriving from the capital was negligible:

> during those months, the conscience of many was decisively influenced by the values of neutrality of the administration, which was the fundamental heritage of the Italian bureaucratic tradition left untarnished by the historical experience of Fascism (indeed, on some accounts, the regime had actually helped to root those values even deeper); by the guiding force of hierarchical obedience; and by the sense of substantial continuity before and after September 8th. In the post-war period, one alibi in self-defense (which many did not feel to be an alibi) was heard recurrently: namely, of having exorcized the worst, which assured the survival of the administration and avoided the complete politicization of the bureaucratic activities.[8]

The situation of the armed forces was very different. The army, navy and air force had been greatly scaled back after the Treaty of Paris (where De Gasperi went as a "notary of others' defeats"). They were driven by the memory of a lost war, by the less-than-brilliant Italian military traditions and by their new role in society to keep a low profile in the hopes of future re-legitimization. The Fascist transformation of the army, and of the air force in particular (child of the regime and thus roughly coeval with it), had been based largely on swelling the number of personnel and the extension of certain privileges to the highest levels of the three branches. At any rate, members of the military (both officers and enlisted men) were left with a much stronger sense of nostalgia than that inspired by the fall of the monarchy, an institution that had once enjoyed great respect among the high ranks. The sense of "honor" and "discipline" remained intact within the

---

8 Guido Melis, *Storia dell'amministrazione italiana. 1861–1993* (Bologna: Il Mulino, 1996), p. 393, and for the entire period of the Italian Republic, see pp. 383ff. See also *Storia della società italiana dall'Unità a oggi*, vol. IX: *L'amministrazione centrale*, ed. Sabino Cassese (Turin: Einaudi, 1984). Although the state fell on September 8, certain non-political branches, like the train system, continued to function: "You buy your ticket, they punch it at the entrance, you get on the train. Then the conductor blows his whistle, the engine-driver responds with the hearty whistle of the locomotive, and the train departs. Everything is as it ever was–almost. The state is in ruins, the army disbanded, but the train from Acqui to Alessandria is still functional. It seems absurd. It is as if in the wake of a cataclysm that shook the face of the Earth, one realizes that life continues, that days and nights continue to follow one another." See Giovanni Pesce, *Senza tregua. La guerra dei GAP* (Milan: Rizzoli, 1995), pp. 19–20.

armed forces, especially in the academies, among officers and in the few remaining elite corps; this could be seen in the so-called *corsi di ardimento* or "courage courses" (together with remnants of the Fascist mentality, which could be passed on in part because the political powers were not very concerned with controlling the military). But these values began to lose their prestige among the younger generations. The result was the discrediting, on a social level, of the ethics of sacrifice and obedience, as well as the ascendance of civilian life over the old "glamour of those in uniform." Various factors reduced the sphere of influence of the military ethos: the recognition of conscientious objectors (for which Aldo Capitini had fought); the spreading of pacifist ideologies (beginning with the anti-nuclear movements toward the end of the 1950s); the unwillingness, common among many Western democracies, to accept loss of human life or put their citizens at risk, thus limiting their involvement solely to extreme cases of wars that directly concerned the defense of the nation's borders or its strategic outposts. The entrance into NATO gave the Italian armed forces a decisively politicized role (although they were not completely integrated with the other allied forces on the European chess board, as in the case of the close collaboration between the Americans and the Germans), which changed their territorial placement by heavily concentrating troops for roughly forty years in Northeastern Italy along the so-called "Gorizia Threshold," a critical point in the province of Friuli from which any movement of Warsaw Pact troops coming from Hungary could be halted. In a period much closer to us, other factors helped to change the role of the military with respect to the broader social order: the reduced dislocation of conscripts from their region of origin, which had characterized Italian history from the times of Unification and had aided the partial fusion of North and South, as well as a "new model for defense" that, in light of the changes which had come about with the end of the bipolar world and the need for quick interventions in distant places, pushed towards a greater professionalization of the armed forces and the creation of a permanent nucleus of elite troops (thereby moving the armed forces from a static model to a dynamic one). These changes were not and would not be painless, inasmuch as they imposed greater costs on society for safety and burdened the Italian state with responsibilities in the

Mediterranean and Balkans.[9]

With a smaller loss of prestige, the diplomatic corps was subjected to an analogous downsizing, especially in the period in which Italy – as a member of NATO (1949) and the European Community (1957), but with privileged ties to the United States – was becoming a "sort of strange, imaginary animal in the zoo of international politics, half land animal and half marine life, neither bear nor whale, but rather some kind of 'tri-color amphibian' perennially in search of status rather than a role and of support rather than autonomy, sensitive more to perception that to reality, oscillating between extremes of shyness and defiance."[10] Even with the changes that took place over half a century of Republican history, the ancient split between Italy's vague aspirations for a role as a medium-to-large power and Italy's actual possibilities for intervention and recognition in international affairs apparently had not yet healed in either the diplomatic corps or the military.

The Carabinieri, however, kept a high profile. Founded in 1814 at the beginning of Restoration in the Kingdom of Sardinia, they always had the task of "maintaining order." After initially playing the role of police force,

---

9   For some of the institutional issues, see Aldo D'Alessio, *Esercito e politica in Italia* (Rome: Editori Riuniti, 1974); and Enea Cerquetti, *Le forze armate italiane dal 1945 al 1975. Strutture e dottrine*, (Milan: Feltrinelli, 1975). For more general accounts, see John Whittam, *Storia dell'esercito italiano*, (Milan: Rizzoli, 1979). On the period spanning from World War II to the "restructuring" of the army in the 1950s and later, see Filippo Stefani, *Storia delle dottrine e degli ordinamenti dell'esercito italiano*, 3 vols. (Rome: Stato maggiore dell'Esercito, 1985-1989); Carlo Jean, *Storia delle Forze Armate Italiane. 1945– 1975*, 2 vols. (Milan: Franco Angeli, 1994); idem, *Geopolitica* (Rome-Bari: Laterza, 1995), pp. 245ff; and Virgilio Ilari, *Storia militare della prima Repubblica* (Ancona: Nuove ricerche, 1994). For historical background of the Italian armed forces during the preceding period, see Giorgio Rochat, *L'esercito italiano da Vittorio Veneto a Mussolini* (Bari: Laterza, 1967); Giuseppe Valle, *Storia dell'aeronautica italiana* (Milan, 1946); Giuseppe Santoro, *L'aeronautica italiana nella seconda guerra mondiale*, (Milan: Edizioni Esse, 1957); and Giorgio Bocca, *Storia d'Italia nella guerra fascista. 1940–1943* (Milano: Mondadori, 1977), pp. 83–125. On newspapers in the barracks and authoritarian neo-Fascist mentality through the mid-1970s, see Giancarlo Lehner, *Parola di generale. Neofascismo, analfabetismo e altro nella stampa per le FF. AA.* (Milan: Mazzotta, 1975). This tendency was balanced by the modernization of military discipline and by the partial opening of the armed forces to civil society; see Virgilio Ilari, *Le Forze Armate tra politica e potere 1943–1976* (Florence: Vallecchi, 1979), pp. 70ff. On the relationship between the Italian government, the Italian armed forces, and NATO, see Brunello Vigezzi, ed., *La dimensione atlantica e le relazioni internazionali nel dopoguerra* (Milan: Jaca, 1987) and Salvatore Minolfi, *L'Italia e la NATO. Una politica nelle maglie dell'alleanza* (Naples: CUEN, 1993). On western armies tendency to wage wars that save the greatest number of lives of their own soldiers, see Robert J. Kaplan, *The Ends of the Earth* (New York: Random House, 1996). On Aldo Capitini's non-violent position, see his *L'obiezione di coscienza in Italia* (Manduria: Lacaita, 1959).

10   Carlo Maria Santoro, *La politica estera di una media potenza. L'Italia dall'Unità a oggi* (Bologna: Il Mulino, 1991), p. 10.

based on the model of the French Gendarmerie Nationale, their specific function was soon determined by their capillary extension throughout the entire Italian territory, their installation in almost every little town (today there are 4,664 stations), their roots in society and their reliability. The "ethical foundations" of this "corps of foot soldiers and cavalry, distinguished for their good conduct and wisdom," as defined in the period of its establishment, consisted of loyalty to the institutions and a proclaimed apolitical nature, values that were an integral part of its "mystique" (even if in its history, there have always been episodes of complicity with the ruling classes, from the time of Unification through the "Piano Solo"). During Fascism, the Corps was the "granite column of the State and the Regime," and during the 1930s it counted twenty legions and roughly 50,000 men. Gabriele D'Annunzio called it "the Arm of unshakeable loyalty and silent abnegation." Its loyalty remained, however, with the monarchy instead of the regime – and for this reason the "Ventennio [two decades of Fascism] marked the great comeback for the police forces, which until then held a subordinate position to the Carabinieri but became the main policing agents during the regime."[11] During World War II, the Carabinieri took part in the conflict on a massive scale, militarily orchestrating the arrest of Mussolini and contributing significantly to the Resistance. With the Badoglio government, their numbers grew to 80,000, with 44,000 remaining displaced in the North where they were not generally considered loyal to the government of the Italian Social Republic. In August, 1944, the Germans stormed their barracks and deported some 7,600 Carabinieri to Germany. At the end of the Partisan war, 2,753 Carabinieri had died and 6,521 had been wounded. Rightfully remembered for their courageous deeds were Salvo d'Acquisto, Vittorio Marandola, Fulvio Sbaretti and Alberto La Rocca, who sacrificed their lives to save hostages (in the course of the entire war, 4,618 Carabinieri died, 15,124 were wounded and 578 were lost in action). From 1962 to 1964, under the command of General De Lorenzo, the corps was reorganized and relocated to the cities. In accordance with

---

11 See Gianni Oliva, *Storia dei carabinieri. Immagine dell'Arma, 1814–1992* (Milan: Leonardo, 1992), p. 187. The author underscores his own position as an "external student of the military world" who has to overcome the scarcity of important documentation and the fact that in this field of research "the shortcomings in the debate are blamed on the state's apparatuses of force... Such are the consequences that result from the disinterest that almost always has surrounded military questions in Italy, owing to the Right's instrumental patriotism and the Left's knee-jerk antimilitarism." See also Giorgio Boatti, *L'Arma. I carabinieri da De Lorenzo a Mino: 1962–1967* (Milan: Feltrinelli, 1978).

NATO plans and the "Stay Behind" project, a massive network of telecommunications was set up and the Eleventh Mechanized Brigade was created (with 50,000 men and 130 armored vehicles). In 1964, De Lorenzo was tempted to set into motion the "Piano Solo," a plan that called for the Carabinieri alone ["solo"] to take over the vital nerve centers of the state and of telecommunications, as well as to carry out the internment, at Capo Marrargiu in Sardinia, of thousands of presumed political adversaries who had been preventatively blacklisted. During the years of violent protest and terrorism in Italy, the Carabinieri took center stage, but with a high cost in blood. In the most recent past, as of 1992, the organization was reported to count 112,000 men in its ranks. However, it is not so much their number that establishes the Corps' importance, but rather the collective perception of their role in Italian society. If the negative stereotype of the Carabinieri as plotters of coups d'états prevailed around 1968, today's younger generations seem to have come to accept some of the more traditional values of previous generations and have once again placed their trust in the Corps.[12] To be sure, there has been no return to the wholesome authoritarian lineage of the Marshal portrayed in "*Pane, amore e fantasia*" (Bread, Love and Dreams), which was advanced in the cinema of the 1950s, but the difference between the current attitude toward the Carabinieri and that of a few decades ago couldn't be greater.

While the Carabinieri originated with the Savoy dynasty, the Police Force, which was established in the Kingdom of Sardinia in 1852 under the rubric of "Corpo delle Guardie di Pubblica Sicurezza" and charged with safeguarding the public, has taken on, with time, more of a "Bourbon" cast and become one of the few "industries" in the Mezzogiorno. It has been tied more closely to particular governments in office than to the state as such and is less dependent on connections with political power. Reconstituted after the war without many changes in personnel or methods (in part because its components had not directly participated in the conflict), the Corps had 51,367 active members in 1946 and in 1948 – according to Scelba, who organized the "Celere," Italy's riot police, with the "concept of a rapid and decisive intervention" – its numbers had grown to 150,000,

---

12   Cfr. Antonio de Lillo, "Orientamenti di valore e immagini della società" in Alessandro Cavalli and Antonio de Lillo, eds., *Giovani anni 90* (Bologna: Il Mulino, 1993), pp. 74–75, 92.

although he had rounded up the figure, in excess of its true number.[13] In the frequent encounters between the forces of order and protesters or strikers during the most difficult phases of the Cold War, for about ten years the police – rather than the Carabinieri – took on the fundamental role of repressing and calming down "agitators." The "Carcaterra agreement" of 1954 created an informal division of duties of the two organizations: the Carabinieri were given the countryside and the small towns in the provinces while the police were assigned, along with the Celere, to the cities.[14] Italy's State Police has undergone further significant changes in recent decades, with the creation of a female police force in 1959 and with unionization. Today, the Carabinieri and police coexist even in the cities, although their coordination is still not entirely harmonious.

Despite the obvious differences between state apparatuses, institutional representatives were all slow, relative to other components of civil society, to adapt to the democracy "born out of the Resistance" and to accept its value systems and individual guarantees. For most people (even in the schools, a subject that would merit a separate discussion), the habit of obedience and passive respect for hierarchical order was too strong to allow them to approve of a regime that seemed to undermine law and order by allowing legal, organized political dissent and offering a certificate of legitimacy to the enemies of the "fatherland," who had automatically been singled out as Communists and their allies. The end of Fascism and the progressive alienation of women and young people from religion only sharpened the conviction that the end of the ethics of sacrifice and duty had opened the way for an asymmetrical demand for ever-expanding rights without any corresponding duties, together with the growth of an individualism that rejects the idea of taking risks or making sacrifices for the benefit of the collectivity.

Finding a Bridge

With the end of the war, Italians were affected by both the fallout from the

---

13 See Giuseppe Carlo Marino, *La Repubblica della forza. Mario Scelba e le passioni del suo tempo* (Milan: Franco Angeli, 1995), pp. 52–53.

14 See Angelo D'Orsi, *Il potere repressivo. La polizia* (Milan: Feltrinelli, 1976); Romano Canosa, *La polizia in Italia dal 1945 ad oggi* (Bologna: Il Mulino, 1976); and Guido Corso, *L'ordine pubblico* (Bologna: Il Mulino, 1979).

conflict and altogether new troubles. On the one hand, they needed to reorganize in order to absorb and to assimilate into civilian life the many veterans who were returning from Germany, the United States, Kenya, India and the Soviet Union, as well as the refugees from Italy's ex-colonies, Istria and Dalmatia. On the other hand, they needed to prepare to enter other spheres of internal and international tension. Although the conflicts seemed only potential and less serious (or at least more remote) when compared to those which had just transpired, the expectation of a better future appeared threatened. An overpowering need for normalcy had become intertwined with great fears and great hopes. After Hiroshima and Nagasaki and especially after the Russians' acquisition of the atomic bomb, the nightmare of a nuclear holocaust loomed as a silent threat between the two superpowers following the accords of Teheran, Yalta and Potsdam. Every phenomenon appeared double-edged: the advent of socialism, heralded by some as an element in the pursuit of justice, was feared by others as the theft of property earned by honest people through hard work and daily sacrifice. The arrival of American food and dollars was seen either as a process of enslavement or as generous aid in the liberation of Italy and Europe from misery. The fear of Communism (especially among farmers, small businessmen and the bourgeoisie, and which was more intense in Central and Southern Italy than in the North) and of the reaction against it coexisted as disquieting projections of the long shadows cast by their respective guardian-states. Added to the trepidation in this world was the final threat of the other world, perceived by Catholics involved in politics when the Church began to excommunicate Communists in July, 1949. There were those, however, who courageously went beyond these patterns, seeking to heal the wounds of the war and ease the atmosphere of hate and mutual distrust. This was the case of Don Zeno Saltini, founder of the Nomadelifa, a "city of young people" near Grosseto that took in children mutilated or orphaned in the war, dropouts and victims of poverty and then united them in "families" in which a volunteer played the role of "mother" or "father." This anomalous community, suspected of Communist tendencies by ecclesiastic authorities, was forced to close, ridden with debt, in 1952.

The rupture with the past and the sense of discontinuity and instability were felt with great force. This was particularly true for exiled politicians, whose long absence afforded them a less provincial view from the outside, but who were also largely unaware of many of the changes which the Fascist regime had introduced or which were the product of the simple passage of time. Although the major political leaders, albeit with some amount of confusion due to overlapping yet discontinuous snapshots of society, were quickly able to get involved in these new circumstances, Italy was still struggling to find new faith in itself. While the amount of Italian blood spilled in World War II was much less than in the "Great War," the material and moral damage, the psychological wounds and the grief were immense (nearly every family was mourning its dead or missing and some families would even scatter flowers over the graves of unnamed civilians and unknown soldiers). Even the darkest periods of the "barbaric invasions" paled in comparison to the destruction the cities had suffered in the bombings. In the countryside there remained traces of the shifting frontlines and the lack of farm laborers, which earlier had been conscripted for military service. Buildings and factories could be rebuilt, fields replanted, and lost or damaged works of art restored or found, but the deepest wounds were internal, as seen in the behavior of many, and which the experience of the war failed to heal and only made worse.[15] The young democracy needed to overcome the tendency to disparage all laws and a false, self-righteous rebelliousness inherited (partially) from the previous regime. "Beware," wrote the jurist, activist, politician and public intellectual Piero Calamandrei, "one of the most dangerous diseases and most pathological legacies that Fascism has left Italy is that of discrediting the law."[16] In his attempt to find a way out of the predicament, Calamandrei founded the journal *Il Ponte* (*The Bridge*) in 1945 and presented it as follows: "Our plan is clear from the title and the emblem on the cover. [It is] a bridge [that] has crumbled, and between the two stumps of the columns that remain standing, a girder has been laid to allow men on their way to work to begin crossing again."

The end of the monarchy upset ancient equilibriums (although it ruled the unified state of Italy for just eighty-five years, it had a longstanding tradition in the Kingdoms of the Two Sicilies and Sardinia). Especially in Central and Northern Italy, with the partial exception of Piedmont, feudal values which the monarchy had instilled definitively disappeared: loyalty

---

15 Silvano Lanaro, *Storia dell'Italia repubblicana. Dalla fine della guerra agli anni novanta* (Venice: Marsilio, 1992), pp. 5ff.

16 Piero Calamandrei, "Chiarezza nella Costituzione" in *Scritti e discorsi politici* (Florence: La Nuova Italia, 1966), vol. II, p. 29.

to a living symbol identified with the fatherland (which the centuries-old Savoy dynasty had promised to unify), a hierarchical order sanctified by time and anchored to tradition, as well as the accompanying values of stability and continuity. The vertical axis of the paternal authority of the sovereign in the national monarchist hymn "*Cunservet Deus su Rei*" (God Save the King) was thus transformed into a horizontal and egalitarian one in the Republican anthem, "*Fratelli d'Italia*" (Brothers of Italy). Only in the South did monarchist values continue to survive for decades, remnants of a longstanding attachment of the urban and country plebeians and weakened bourgeoisie to the benevolent image of an authority envisioned as standing above all parties and factions.

Despite Italy's evident success during the period of reconstruction, the wounds healed slowly, in part because 65% of potential industry was destroyed during the war. Many disliked the Italy that had risen from the ruins. The defeated (Fascists and monarchists, who had witnessed the fall of the regime and the disappearance of the last two kings into exile in Egyptian Alexandria and Cascais) as well as the supporters of Giannini's "Uomo Qualunque" ("Ordinary Man") party, viewed Italians, with respect to the recent past, as even more oppressed by oligarchies, threatened by corruption, squeezed by taxes and impoverished by inflation (the cost of living in 1947 was fifty times that of 1938). Thus began, once again, the underground tremors of the classes who felt themselves victims of events and the bullying of the winners. It was the middle class, especially the lower middle class, that made this material and moral unease known and expressed a quiet desire for revenge. The war had brought the "erosion or disappearance of their savings" and had thus eaten away at their respectability, pushing them down the social ladder and dangerously closer to the feared worker, while unscrupulous profit-mongers and deal-makers prospered. With the movements of *sudismo rivendicazionisti* ("Southern restitutionists"), *qualunquismo* ("every-man-for-himself-ism," a populist movement that espoused indifference to and mistrust of the political system) and the monarchical legitimists, there was a gradual "return to order" that culminated (due to other factors as well) in the elections of April 18, 1948.[17]

---

17 See: Angelo Michele Imbriani, *Vento del Sud. Moderati, reazionari e qualunquisti, 1943–1948* (Bologna: Il Mulino, 1996), pp. 15ff. On Giannini's movement, see Sandro Setta, *L'Uomo qualunque, 1944–1948* (Bari: Laterza, 1976).

As the Cold War began and the Communist and Socialist parties were shut out of the government, the new Italy was even less attractive to those on the Left, as well as those who had fought in the Resistance and who now felt bitterly that their hopes for greater equality, justice and liberty had been delayed and "betrayed." Ex-partisans were persecuted by the centrist governments following Pietro Secchia's denunciation speech to the Senate on October 28, 1949.[18] To borrow a famous phrase of Calamandrei, the leftists saw themselves compensated for a "revolution that never happened" with a verbal pledge, from the moderates, for a "promised revolution" on paper (i.e. the Constitution).[19] Even the Christian Democrats, who occupied sectors of the state like little "archipelagos," disliked certain aspects of the new Italy, as did the Church, despite the fact that the latter enjoyed conspicuous spiritual and temporal benefits.[20] Both saw the advancement, alongside American hegemony, of a form of consumerism which, by favoring individualist values and the market economy, threatened to uncouple familial bonds and diminish social solidarity.

This discomfort was due in part to the fact that the apprenticeship of democracy had not been easy or painless for anyone.[21] The introduction of universal male and female suffrage gave all adults the clear personal responsibility to determine the political direction of the country. Although the campaign for democracy was often eclipsed by pressing requests for loyalty to this or that party, and although many who contributed to the extremely high voter turnout rates were nonetheless voting as others instructed them (their husbands, priests or those who promised economic benefits and jobs), more than fifty years of democratic practice in Italy shows the existence of a highly "individualized" education in the "rules of the game."[22]

---

18 See Pietro Secchia, *La Resistenza accusa, 1945–1973* (Milan: Mazzotta, 1973), pp. 66–99.

19 Piero Calamandrei, "Cenni introduttivi sulla Costituente e sui suoi lavori" in Piero Calamandrei and Alessandro Levi, eds., *Commentario sistematico alla Costituzione italiana* (Florence: G. Barbèra, 1950), vol. I, p. xxxv.

20 See Carlo Donolo, "Social Change and Transformation of the State in Italy" in Richard Scase, ed., *The State in Western Europe* (London: Croom Helm, 1980), p. 165.

21 "The return of democracy entails citizens to think and requires a return of morality in public life; it depends on ethical resources that the totalitarian regimes spent instead of building up"; Pietro Scoppola, *La repubblica dei partiti. Profilo storico della democrazia in Italia* (Bologna: Il Mulino, 1991), p. 424.

22 On this period, see Francesco Barbagallo, "La formazione dell'Italia democratica" in *Storia dell'Italia repubblicana* (Turin: Einaudi, 1994), vol. I, pp. 5–128.

CHAPTER 3
Territories of the Imaginary

The Colors of Passion

Mass mobilization today is synchronized according to varying visions of the world and distributed according to the affections and hatreds of "perturbed and passionate souls" rather than the serenity and understanding of "open minds." More than the battles of ideas and programs, there are real and explicit struggles of passion that are publicly displayed and ritualized. One might examine these passions according to a "chromatic" subdivision rooted in the history of Western political symbolism and classify them as "red," "black," "grey" or "white."[1]

The "red passions" typical of Socialist and Communist movements (political parties and unions) have, at least until recently, generally come forth in expectation of sudden and sweeping change. They kept awake those who watched and waited for the first rays of the "sun of the future" which, rising on the horizon, was supposed to emancipate "all of humanity" in accordance with "scientific" plans (and thus with "the force of things" and the logic of history). Oriented toward a future of equality and fraternity among all men, the red passions were the fruit of a difficult struggle and were thus impatient and all-encompassing, but also flexible and coldly aware of changing circumstances and power structures.

---

1 I have discussed this subject at greater length and in a more analytical way (but from another point of view) in my essay "Il rosso, il nero, il grigio. Il colore delle moderne passioni politiche" in Silvia Vegetti Finzi, ed., *Storia delle passioni* (Rome-Bari: Laterza, 1995), pp. 315 55, and in my book *Geometria delle passioni* (Milan: Feltrinelli, 1997). See also Ennio di Nolfo, *Le speranze e le paure degli italiani, 1943–1963* (Milan: Mondadori, 1986).

During phases of acute conflict, these passions can become fanatical, at times even legitimizing class hatred (in Italy, however, this occurred only in specific moments: in the immediate post-war period in some geographic areas and during the period of terrorist activity, from 1962–1985, at the extreme fringes of workers' movement). In any case, the "red passions" reveal an unresolved tension and an internal contradiction in the nature of any self-proclaimed "revolutionary" party. In fact, given that politics and ethics should immediately promote the interests and ideals of "all classes" in order to achieve – at an undetermined time and at the conclusion of a long and bloody process – a universal human ethics, the passions and the morals of one party become those of one part calling itself the representative of a future whole. Within the structure of a "democratic republic," this causes ruptures, internal maneuvering, discrepancies and inevitable ideological inconsistencies, but it also leaves room for opposing movements (compromise or violence; an unreserved allegiance to, or calculated provisional support of, democracy). The resolution of such divergent tendencies is entrusted to the judgment of political elites, for whom the party's membership base and "middle management" often serve – despite constant mobilization – as a mere sounding board. Thus, a single person, like Togliatti, could appear to have a "duplicitous" psychology.[2]

Diametrically opposed to the red are the "black passions" (again, most prevalent during the immediate post-war period, peaking at the end of the 1960s and throughout the 1970s), which were largely inherited from Fascism, but more specifically from its latest "social" incarnation. The black passions encouraged rebellion against the existing state and contempt for democracy as a weak system, devoid of intrinsic values and enslaved by foreigners and Communists. In comparison to the universalistic "reds," the "black passions" seem at once less "abstract" and harder to conceptualize. They are best expressed in the form of myths or systems of images and symbols. Against individualism and wary of the search for personal happiness, the "black passions" aimed instead at a return to the monolithic unity of citizens around the fatherland and the intransigent restoration of its interests and "sacred borders." Those who were imbued with the black passions considered conflict a permanent condition of life, dictated by nature. They

---

2 For another point of view, see Pietro di Loreto, *Togliatti e la "doppiezza". Il PCI tra democrazia e insurrezione 1944–1949* (Bologna: Il Mulino, 1991).

thus applied a model of political Darwinism to the struggle for supremacy among nations, combined, in turn, with the memory of Imperial Rome and the civilizing mission of Italy (only later would some groups of young people look to Nordic myths and symbology or to the fairy-tale-like novels of Tolkien, proclaiming Europe the land of the spirit, as opposed to the materialism of America and the Soviet Union).

Although the neo-fascists existed at the margins of constitutional legality in the democratic Italian Republic ("born out of the Resistance") and were merely tolerated politically (if for no other reason than as a possible reservoir of votes), they were not seen as "extra-terrestrials," even by their adversaries. Many representatives of the Left, some even from personal experience, recognized the fact that "Fascism was born from the bowels of our own society" (as was declared in 1945 in the opening article of the first issue of *Società*, the journal of the Communist intellectuals).[3] Judging the society that had sprung forth from the moral and material rubble of the war to be opportunist and corrupt, the Italian neo-fascists firmly believed that this society did not need to be changed, so much as reconstructed according to a "new order," which, for the most part, was no more than a return to the old. Paradoxically, due to a peculiar "duplicity" of their own, the neo-fascists thought they had a monopoly on the idea of order through the practice of disorder, as well as a claim on the idea of the nation, despite the fact that it was they who had brought it to ruins. The virtues to which neo-fascists ascribe are exemplified, once again, by the courage to go against the mainstream, the preference for "blood" over "gold," pride in defeat for a noble cause and a refusal to follow the rules of a democracy that gave rights

---

3   During the 5th Congress of the MSI in 1956, Giorgio Almirante attempted to clear up a misunderstanding: "the misunderstanding is just one and it is called *being Fascist in a democracy*. We are the only *outsiders*, and this is a title of honor but it is also a frightening difficulty for this democracy, for this Italy of the post-war period. Our courage was forged in 1946 when the MSI became a working party in this democracy"; quoted in Gian Enrico Rusconi, *Resistenza e postfascismo* (Bologna: Il Mulino, 1995), p.193; see also Marco Tarchi, "Esuli in patria. I fascisti nella Repubblica italiana" in Enrico Pozzi, ed., *Lo straniero interno* (Florence: Ponte delle Grazie, 1993) and *idem*, *Cinquant'anni di nostalgia. La destra italiana dopo il fascismo, Intervista con A. Cairoti* (Milano: Rizzoli , 1995). Indeed, they were outsiders, although, as has been observed elsewhere, they were prisoners of the paradoxical "ability to combine anti-social sentiment with a defense of the existing social order"; see Adrian Lyttelton, "Fascismo e violenza: conflitto sociale e azione politica in Italia nel primo dopoguerra," *Storia contemporanea*, vol. XIII (1982), p. 983. It is important to remember that in Southern Italy, a weak clandestine Fascist resistance was organized and enjoyed the support of the Ministry of the Interior and the Vatican, thanks to the Jesuits of *Civiltà Cattolica*.

to those who did not deserve them. In addition to these were the virtues – together and inseparable – of loyalty and honor. A lingering fascination with death and sacrifice had been passed on "genetically" to the younger generations, shaped by the experience of the recently waged "war of movement" and the trench warfare that preceded it. This attraction to sacrificial death was the legacy of Fascism at Salò, whose heirs were guided not by the Fascist "Victory!" slogans, but by the act of losing and landing feet-first.

The soldier of World War I who survived the battlefield, the perils of the unfathomed deep, as well as the dangers of a sky barely conquered by technology was another Fascist prototype. The World War I combatant was marked by the sight and smell of death and by the agony of those who had been his only neighbors and confidants. Separated from his family and origins, from the places, friends and rhythms of peacetime, he lost his former identity. The army – community of all possible *morituri*, bearers of abstract hatred which was nonetheless organized and aimed at potential enemies – predisposed him for entrance into his new, great authoritarian family, the collectivity of the totalitarian state, which reinforced individuality and simultaneously dissolved it. War was an unforgettable experience of the abnormal and the extraordinary: it was a blazing interchange between shock and mental respite, an alternation between exaltation and depression, hope and desperation and a haughty sensation – for the youngest soldiers – of finding themselves unexpectedly in command of companies and battalions, with responsibilities concerning the life and death of other men. In a world in which the horizons of meaning had become confused, war appeared to many to be a concrete means of redemption from the unsatisfying banality of lives devoid of strong civil interests or consistent affective bonds, and it offered a realistic surrogate of the sacred. This world of war created a quasi-religious hatred of internal enemies, even during peacetime, along with a spirit of adventurism, restlessness and encouragement of illegality. It also gave rise to "black courage" and its particular forms of aggressive melancholy, desperate exhibitionism of violence and intentionally crude contempt for "culture" and "intellectuals." The war seemed to bring deep passions to the surface, those raw and "primordial instincts" which peace and the nascent movements of emancipation had negated or covered with a thin layer of optimism and a faith in "progress."

The "black passions" were a return to a negative anthropology founded on the conviction – considered realistic – that man is basically an instinctual being who can be tamed or commanded, but not improved or made responsible for himself. The only men who could rise above this animal state and attain the level of "superman" or hero were those exceptional individuals capable of freeing themselves from the mentality and wretched preoccupations of the "herd," i.e., the citizen-soldier-workers who blindly obey anyone recognized as a superior. All men, however, had to be ready to sacrifice themselves and their own relatives for the cause (the case of Mussolini's son-in-law, Galeazzo Ciano, condemned to death by Il Duce for his betrayal of family, party and fatherland was therefore considered exemplary).

The theories of Julius Evola, particularly those developed after the war, put forth the idea of a "special human type," who "despite being a part of today's world and involved in modern life even at its most problematic and paroxysmal, does not belong internally to this world, nor does he intend to give in to it. He feels, in essence, that he belongs to a different race than that of the greater part of our contemporaries." Such men reject bourgeois values, which have the same roots as socialist values, and link themselves with tradition, a secular transcendence that surpasses simple human and individual dimensions and attains a vision of a natural and eternal order. They are able to "remain standing amid the ruins and the dissolution" of this world by thinking of the other world to which they belong by choice, and thus they are even ready "to fight losing battles."[4] These special individuals are capable of reducing values to "absolute zero" and bringing nihilism to completion, rendering it "active" in order to be and become nothing but themselves. For them, moral duty derives from power, "from the lust for life, the sense of one's own strength, which 'demands exertion' ('I can, therefore I must')."[5] This lesson, interlaced with Nietzschean themes, did not fail to influence rightwing terrorists, who rejected the so-called "Fas-

---

4   Julius Evola, *Cavalcare la tigre* (Milan: Pesce d'Oro, 1981), pp. 9, 10. See also *idem*, *Rivolta contro il mondo moderno* (Rome: Edizioni Mediteranee, 1969) and *Gli uomini e le rovine* (Rome: Edizioni Mediteranee, 1967).

5   Julius Evola, *Cavalcare la tigre*, pp. 44–46. The "special human type" cannot currently swear allegiance to any state because the "hierarchical and organic state" has ceased to exist, nor can he swear allegiance to any party or movement because they are unable to present "any superior ideas" (*ibid.*, p. 172). The only group with which Evola would find an affinity after WWII was Ordine Nuovo. See his *Il cammino del cinabro* (Milan: Scheiwiller, 1972), p. 212.

cism in a double-breasted suit" of Almirante and his basic respect for law and order. We find this lesson restated in the political positions of Giusva Fioravanti, who in a memoir of 1978 expounded the *summa* of his own convictions in a these terms: "I have lost many prejudices, like those of good and evil. Zarathustra himself says that good and evil are subjective... I reject the preconceived notion that stealing is bad or that killing is bad and praying is good. Killing is considered a grave crime, but when we do it during war they give us a medal... For me, death is not forbidden just as violence in general is not forbidden... Mine is a 'new morality' where good and evil are up to me... The superior man is destined to remain isolated, to live in small oases of disciples which he creates for himself... Democracy is nothing but the tyranny of a majority over a minority. In democratic Republican Italy, the majority oppresses and represses the 'Fascist' minority, not for actual crimes that could in fact be committed, but because thinking a certain way is itself considered a crime."[6]

The "grey passions" describe the sentiments of liberalism and democracy (either republican or monarchic, but always morally intransigent). They are typical of liberals like Benedetto Croce, of some members of the Partito d'Azione (at least those "card-carrying members" of the Action Party, if not those who took up arms), and of the so-called "bourgeois heroes," like the lawyer Giorgio Ambrosoli, who, when given the responsibility of liquidating Michele Sindona's Banca Privata Italiana (Private Bank of Italy), wrote to his wife on February 25, 1975 predicting his own tragic end (he was killed at the hands of an Italian-American assassin in 1979): "There is no doubt that, one way or another, I will have to pay a high price for the responsibility I have accepted. I knew this before I accepted it, and therefore I am not complaining. For me, it was a unique opportunity to do something for my country... You will have to raise our children so that they will respect the values we believe in... May they be conscious of their duties toward each other and our family in the transcendent sense which I have toward my country, call it Italy or Europe."[7] The "grey passions," rare in Italy, are connected to individualistic values of ordered liberty, a civic sense and a concern for the public good. They are committed to a

---

6 Valerio [Giusva] Fioravanti, quoted in Giovanni Bianconi, *A mano armata. Vita violenta di Giusva Fioravanti* (Milan: Baldini & Castoldi, 1996), pp. 127–28.

7 Corrado Stajano, *Un eroe borghese. Il caso dell'avvocato Ambrosoli assassinato dalla mafia politica* (Turin: Einaudi, 1991), pp. 102–3.

spontaneous or negotiated resolution of conflicts of interest, and they shun fanaticism and extremism (as well as the search for the extraordinary and the absolute) by favoring efficiency and normalcy. The "grey passions" bring to the forefront questions of duties and rights, rectitude, reasonableness, honesty, industriousness, professionalism and seriousness. These passions appear "grey" and clerical, modest and routine, only to those who consider democracy either to be a regime oriented toward popular tastes and the superficial opinions of the masses or as one buttressed by powerful lobbies that unscrupulously manipulate opinion. In effect, they are "demilitarized" civil passions and can rarely be mobilized on a mass level, especially since they exist far from demagoguery and prosper either in civic commitment and the tussle of public debate among the elite or in the silence and invisibility of the private sector.

The "white passions," finally, are those that were developed and transformed into values by the Catholic Church over the centuries, penetrating all levels of Italian society, along with an "earthly wisdom" which took shape in the shrewd exercise of power. This "earthly wisdom" was the fruit of experience that had been refined over time, the capacity to recognize and exploit (especially in times of political crisis) the vices and weaknesses of man to their utmost. For the Christian Democrats and the organizations that support them (such as the Church, which constitutes a transpolitical resource of immense value), these passions revolve around the ideals of the family, the parish, solidarity and purity, symbolized by the "white flower." Religious faith and its promise of a heavenly reward for earthly militancy were important factors – at least at the beginning – in the involvement of great masses of people in politics and civil activism, within both the party and Catholic associations. Organizations like the ACLI, the FUCI, the Coltivatori Diretti and the Comitati Civici formed a close network of human, religious and political relations that competed against Communist youth groups (like the "Italian Pioneers," accused of being a "school of corruption" that organized promiscuous dances for boys and girls, as well as the notorious "blasphemy contests" in which the person who said the most blasphemous things won). Several of these groups were so strongly rooted that they were able to persevere during the years of Fascist dictatorship. Such was the case of the Unione Femminile Cattolica (the Women's Catholic Union), which during the Fascist period – with its *angiolette* (little angels), *piccolissime* (little ones), *beniamine* (little darlings), *aspiranti* (aspiring ones) and *effettive* (effective ones), ranging from newborns to thirty-five-year-olds – had almost double the number of members as the Fasci Femminili (Fascist women's groups). With some mediation, such commitment to Catholic collaboration brought millions of women closer to politics (even if it was only at election times or during household or neighborhood discussions), especially in the South and Northeast.

Besides promoting neo-Guelf tendencies and attracting the troubled secular bourgeoisie to the "totem of eternity" that is the Church, the Catholic missionary onslaught *in partibus fidelium* ethically revived and renewed the archaic sentiments and virtues of the agricultural world, the family and obedience to ecclesiastical hierarchies. Similar values and passions were solemnly celebrated, in a monumental and spectacular manner, on the occasion of the Holy Year of 1950, and with the various pilgrimages and "marches of faith" that took place all over Italy. Emblematic of this climate was the success of the American film *Bernadette*, about the miracle at Lourdes, and the Spanish film *Marcellino, Pane, e Vino*, about a boy raised by monks. To assess the change in climate that had taken place, one need only compare these films with Rossellini's *Rome, Open City* of 1945, which featured the humble yet upstanding figure of the priest executed by the Germans for having helped the partisans.

"We are the soldiers of faith/ we are the bearers of the cross," sang the young members of the Azione Cattolica (Catholic Action), at a moment when the Christian Democrats were divided on economic policy between a cautious, protectionist solidarity and a timid economic liberalism, between overtures to address the exigencies and needs of the representatives of the "world of labor" and the repeated warnings to respect the inexorable laws of the market – warnings given to Christian Democratic governments not only by Luigi Einaudi, but also by the United States, which was restless over the excessive welfarist and clientelistic use of the assistance offered in the Marshall Plan. Through a vast array of instruments and initiatives, the Christian presence deepened its roots in Italian society. The electorate rewarded the Christian Democrats with a relative majority, and in 1954 three million people were participants in the network of Catholic organizations. While evocations of tradition and antiquity – and sometimes even bigotry – were prevalent, there was no lack of impetus to find new forms of organization, new ways to conquer the conscience and new means of structuring society.

Fantasized Fatherlands: America and the Westernization of Italy

Unhappy, to some extent, with the country in which they were living, Italians dreamed of alternative or complementary lands, without moving away from their own. In mythical terms, they imagined at least two earthly paradises (the United States and the Soviet Union, i.e., "America" and "Russia") and a heavenly one (promised by the Catholic Church). In real terms, they looked to the nations and continents favored by emigrants.

With regard to the former, a double loyalty developed (or in some cases a triple or even multiple allegiance).[8] Among voters of the center-right parties, this implied loyalty either to Italy and the West (which was threatened by the Communist Bloc and by the rebellion of the old Asian and African colonies) or to Italy, the United States and the Vatican. Among the voters of the leftist parties, there was instead loyalty to Italy, the Soviet Union and the "anti-imperialist" countries of the "Socialist camp." In the case of the emigrants, the double loyalty was often a "loyalty of transition," in the sense that, with the passing of generations, it was gradually transferred from the nation of origin to the nation of adoption.

The Italian orientation toward imaginary fatherlands was hardly new, but rather a remnant of ancient universalist tendencies (of the Church and the Empire, from the Middle Ages through the first modern age) combined with an intrinsic fragility of the sense of belonging – or the weak roots of one's own community within the state – which Gentile's "ethical state" had sought to counter. Vicenzo Cuoco, speaking of the Neapolitan Jacobins, remarked on the distance between their ideals, those of the French Revolution and their effective awareness of the conditions of the people and places in which they were acting. It was as if their feet were in Naples and their heads were in Paris.

Upon what did this distance depend? Why were their "heads" elsewhere? Why do one's own state and one's own people seem not to deserve sufficient love and respect, even to the point that an imaginary fatherland was invented recently within the real fatherland and given the name Padania?

---

8 Franco De Felice, "Doppia lealtà e doppio Stato," *Studi storici*, no. 3 (1989).

It is clear that for various historical reasons, once the period of Fascist-proclaimed autarchy was over and the world's horizon widened, the identification of citizens with the state was meager at best. The fact that Italy became "the Western country most influenced by the bipolar split of the world, with Christian Democracy standing as an internal shield protecting the West, and a Communist Party, the strongest in the capitalist world, enlisted in the service of Socialist transformation," created "a domestic political system tied to the international system, with the latter not only profoundly influencing the former but conditioning it structurally as well, so much so that the domestic political system was rendered entirely subordinate." The constant exclusion of a substantial part of the citizenry from both effective power and the recognition of the legitimacy of their claims helped to weaken further their previously affirmed national identity, often creating forms of "solidarity without a nation."[9] A better description, in this age of ideological rigidity, might be "national dis-identity."

One had to look elsewhere, therefore, for models of a better life, which provoked an implicit hybridization of the ethical codes that were effective *in loco*. Above all, Italians looked toward America, a country that already inhabited their imagination (even before the advent of commercial television) through the stories of emigrants, through cinema and through literature. Even those who had never been there "knew" America and something of its citizens, although they had never met them either as soldiers or as tourists. The negative stereotypes of Americans – propagated by Fascism after the principal target of state propaganda was switched from the "treacherous Albion" to the "demo-plutocracy" and racial impurity of American society and the American armed forces – did not last very long during the course of the war. The poster of Boccasile, which depicted a Negro soldier with a wide nose and thick lips staring libidinously at an unprotected Aryan girl, did not impress; nor did the repeated portrayals of Americans as monument-destroying barbarians or ferocious gangsters. The first encounter with "real" Americans immediately reversed these recent stereotypes spread by the regime: "The well-dressed soldier, well-equipped, clean-shaven, with cigarettes and chocolate, is the best form of propaganda" because it not only established a visible connection between prosperity and democracy,

---

9   Massimo L. Salvadori, *Storia d'Italia e crisi di regime. Alle radici della politica italiana* (Bologna: Il Mulino, 1994), pp. 65–66. On the expression, "solidarity without a nation," see Silvio Lanaro, *Storia dell'Italia repubblicana. Dalla fine della guerra agli anni novanta*, pp. 412ff.

but also between a possible rise of the Italian economy and loyalty to the new ally."[10] Most striking about the Americans was their immense wealth of material resources, which afforded them the war-time luxury of risking their men's lives relatively sparingly.

As they discovered powdered milk, dehydrated carrots, candies wrapped in cellophane, chewing-gum and the smell of Camels and Lucky Strikes (very different from that of the Milits and Nazionali they were used to smoking), many Italians began to dream of a land of luxury where they could enjoy pleasures unknown to most of their compatriots, who rarely had meat on the table and continued to turn their overcoats inside out with each new winter. In post-war imagery relating to the United States, however, "there were three central symbols: the atomic bomb, Coca Cola and the dollar. The first was threatening, the second was tempting and the third was the interpretive and connective tissue shared by the first two."[11] Although there was no lack of "autarchic" resistance to their presence (as when some young neo-fascists from the Fronte Universitario di Azione Nazionale [University Front for National Action] began a campaign against Coca Cola in favor of San Pellegrino orangeade)[12] and although the image of the American dream would change (after 1947–1948 and during the

---

10   Pier Paolo D'Attorre, "Sogno americano e miti sovietici nell'Italia contemporanea" in *Nemici per la pelle*, (Milan: Franco Angeli, 1991), p. 27. See also Aurelio Lepre, *Storia della prima Repubblica. L'Italia dal 1942 al 1992* (Bologna: Il Mulino, 1993), p. 108. On the influence of the American model on the mentality and customs of the Italians, see: Victoria De Grazia, "La sfida dello 'star system': l'americanismo nella formazione della cultura di massa in Europa, 1920–1965," *Quaderni storici*, 58 (1985), pp. 95–133; Tiziano Bonazzi, ed., *America-Europa: la circolazione delle idee* (Bologna: Il Mulino, 1976); Stephen Gundle, "L'americanizzazione del quotidiano. Televisione e consumismo nell'Italia degli anni Cinquanta," *Quaderni storici*, 62 (1986); Carlo Chiarenza, ed., *Immaginari a confronto. I rapporti culturali tra Italia e Stati Uniti: la percezione della realtà tra stereotipo e mito* (Venice: Marsilio, 1992); David W. Ellwood and R. Kroes, eds., *Hollywood in Europe. Experiences of a Cultural Hegemony* (Amsterdam: VW University Press, 1994). On the political, diplomatic, and cultural relations between the two states and the benefits of dependence on Washington, see H. Stuart Hughes, *The United States and Italy* (Cambridge, Mass.: Harvard University Press, 1965), in which he observes how Italy was *terra incognita* for the U.S., unknown and falsely familiar. See also F. Romero, "Gli Stati Uniti in Italia" in *Storia dell'Italia repubblicana*, vol. I: *La costruzione della democrazia* (Turin: Einaudi, 1994), pp. 265ff.; and Nico Perrone, *De Gasperi e l'America* (Palermo: Sellerio, 1995). On the triangular relationship between the U.S., the Vatican, and Italy, and the effect on Italian policies see Bruno Marolo, *Made in USA. Le origini americane della Prima Repubblica Italiana* (Milan: Rizzoli, 1993).

11   A. Portelli, "L'orsacchiotto e la tigre di carta. Il Rock and Roll arriva in Italia," *Quaderni storici*, 20 (1985), p. 136. See also Guido Fink and Franco Minganti, "La vita privata italiana sul modello americano," in *La vita privata. Il Novecento* (Bari: Laterza, 1994), pp. 350–89.

12   Boneschi, *Poveri ma belli. I nostri anni cinquanta*, p. 19.

Korean War), the United States – synonymous with modernity – continued at length to represent the "promised land" and "reproducible prosperity." So great was America's influence that it prompted subordinate imitation of its lifestyle and language, even to the point of "pidginization."[13]

The "Workers' Paradise"

For as much as "the Russians, as a last resort, have been perceived for the entire post-war era as 'godless' or 'barbarian',"[14] the historical merit of their having stopped Hitler's advance through the world has been recognized. Millions of Italians – including many non-communists – venerated Stalin, the hero of the epoch, as an "Atheist God," and they sincerely mourned his death.[15]

To these Italians, "Russia" meant peace, work, social justice and health guaranteed to all of its inhabitants. To them it was the infallible bulwark of the weakest classes and peoples, while for others it was synonymous with terror, iniquitous inequalities, a police state and "Siberia"). Less known to Italians through cinema and contemporary literature, less "visible" by foreigners (and therefore largely unknown, as if it were another planet), the Soviet Union became an even more mythical place than the United States. Irrefutable legends were born, hiding the dramatic reality of the "crimes of Stalin" and the gulags: "Unemployment no longer exists in the USSR. Socialism is now a reality. The exploitation of workers by other men has

---

13 See Umberto Eco, "Il modello americano" in Umberto Eco, Gian Paolo Ceserani and Beniamino Placido, *La riscoperta dell'America* (Roma-Bari: Laterza, 1994), p. 28. See also Boneschi, *Poveri ma belli*, p. 19: "Pidgin is a language of colonial areas, which blends in a disarticulated way elements of the hegemonic language (in the tradition of English cultural anthropology) with local languages in order to create a useable language with practical aims, but which is creatively impoverished and incapable of registering the needs of abstract thought; on the whole, it is therefore repressive. Fiat's Topolino represents a creative way of referring to Ford's Model-T, while Sordi's Italian-American is not a creative and autonomous imitation of the Anglo-Saxon model."

14 D'Attorre, *Sogno americano e mito sovietico nell'Italia contemporanea*, p. 49; Donald Sassoon, "Italian Images of Russia, 1945-1956" in Christopher Duggan and Christopher Wagstaff, eds., *Italy in the Cold War: Politics, Culture, and Society, 1948-1958* (Oxford: Berg, 1995), pp. 189-202. See also Marcello Flores, *L'immagine dell'Urss. L'Occidente e la Russia di Stalin, 1927-1956* (Milano: Il Saggiatore, 1990).

15 Benedetto Croce, "La città del Dio Ateo," *Il Mondo*, 8 (October 1949). As the 1948 elections approached, the walls become covered in graffiti spouting opposing slogans like, "Long Live God" and "Long Live Stalin"; see Angelo Ventrone, *La cittadinanza repubblicana. Forma partito e identità nazionale alle origini della democrazia italiana, 1943-1948* (Bologna: Il Mulino, 1996), p. 97.

disappeared. The citizens' quality of life grows along with the increase in production, and each citizen is guaranteed tranquility and work. Culture is free for all and illiteracy has completely disappeared."[16] It was added that, in this immense country, "substantive liberty" was thriving, the only type capable of eradicating the ancient evils of hunger, exploitation, prostitution and ignorance and of restoring a good relationship between man and nature through work and machinery, thus proceeding simultaneously toward the Marxist "humanization of nature" and the "naturalization of man." With the construction of gigantic public works (subways, power plants, levies along the great rivers), science and technology put society in harmony with natural energy. On October 4, 1957, when the first artificial satellite, Sputnik, was launched into space, hopes of Soviet technological-scientific supremacy began to take shape, anticipating the imminent "surpassing" of American consumption and quality of life promised by Khrushchev.

The Militant Church and the Triumphant Church

The other fatherland, the "heavenly" one, from which Pope Pius XII excluded the Communists, was the "true" Paradise for practicing Catholics, and it was represented on earth by its visible promise, i.e., the Church – the Ark of Salvation destined to ferry men from time toward eternity. Despite some resistance by De Gasperi to excessive meddling from "across the Tiber," the Vatican[17] often played a willing supporting role for the government and for Christian Democrats. With its presence throughout the entire country,

---

16 These were some of the claims made by some Italian communists with regard to the 19th Soviet Congress in 1952 – at least as they were reported by the police. See Pietro di Loreto, *La difficile transizione. Dalla fine del centrismo al centro-sinistra, 1953–1960* (Bologna: Il Mulino, 1993), p. 59.

17 Despite having a relatively secular vision of the state, De Gasperi's background was too Catholic not to concede some advantages to religious sentiments and to the Church in matters pertaining to the schools and to society. At the same time, he was well aware of the existence of certain insurmountable limits and this sometimes created friction or put him on a collision course with the ecclesiastical hierarchy. Particularly significant is the letter that De Gasperi received from Benedetto Croce, not long before the latter's death. In it, the aging philosopher wrote: "I think of you often, not politically, but rather humanly, and I remember the life that you are forced to live and I admire you and I feel for you and I defend you against people with limited imaginations who cannot understand the difficulties and bitterness that you must endure as you carry out your office in the hope of doing some good and eliminating some evils"; cited in Silvio Bertoldi, *Dopoguerra* (Milan: Rizzoli, 1993), p. 136. On some of the affinities between Croce's and De Gasperi's ideas, see Agostino Giovagnoli, *La cultura democristiana. Tra Chiesa cattolica e identità italiana. 1918–1948* (Rome-Bari: Laterza, 1991), pp. 106–23.

its penetrating hold on the Italian conscience and its efforts to align itself systematically with civil society, the Church was a key player in this period. While Pope Pius XII, in a crusade-like atmosphere, was warning all the faithful to remember that in politics one must "be with Christ or against Christ," the Church was able to make its voice heard, in a selective and persuasive manner, among representatives of all the professions and modern sciences, from obstetricians to biologists. Pius XII was the first pontiff capable of systematically using meetings with the masses (as he inaugurated the new "oceanic gatherings" in St. Peter's Square) and the mass media (first radio, then television) as functional tools, not only to serve the mysterious designs of Providence, but to re-introduce the sacred into a society that was rapidly becoming "secularized."[18] This change was taking place in part because Italy's agrarian society, which still made up 42% of the population in 1951, was disappearing and with it the coexistence in Southern Italy of Christian faith with the magical practices and beliefs that had so impressed Ernesto De Martino. In 1946, it was to these values that Pope Pius XII appealed on the occasion of the first national congress of farmers. "One must ensure," he said in his address, "that the essential elements of what we might call genuine rural society be protected by our nation: industriousness, simplicity and purity in life; respect for authority, above all for one's parents; love of one's country and loyalty to the traditions that have been the source of so much good in the course of the centuries; readiness to aid others, not only within one's own family, but from family to family, household to household; and lastly, that value without which these other values would be worthless, devoid of substance and dissolved in the unfettered desire for profit – true religious spirit."[19]

Thus, the long "era of the Church" continued to intertwine itself with the briefer era of Italy's political institutions. In the world as it was divided at Yalta, Italy had become the counterpart of Poland, another country where –

---

18   On Pope Pacelli, see Giovanni Miccoli, "La Chiesa di Pio XII nella società italiana del dopoguerra" in *Storia dell'Italia repubblicana*, vol. I, pp. 537–613. The Jesuit priest Riccardo Lombardi – dubbed the "microphone of God" – made good use of the radio during the 1948 elections; see Giancarlo Zizola, *Il microfono di Dio. Pio XII, padre Lombardi e i cattolici italiani* (Milano: Mondadori, 1990). On the crisis of the human conscience when exposed to the overwhelming force of nature and society, see Ernesto De Martino's *Il mondo magico* (Turin: Einaudi, 1948), *Sud e magia* (Milan: Feltrinelli, 1959), *La terra del rimorso* (Milan: Il Saggiatore, 1961), and the never completed *La fine del mondo* (1977).

19   Quoted by G. Guizzardi in "Potere ideologico, organizzazioni e classi sociali" in *La DC dal fascismo al 18 aprile* (Venice: Marsilio, 1978), p. 373.

aside from historical and ideological differences – the state must recognize, in a manner akin to Constantine, the effective and universal power of the Holy See and the local ecclesiastical authorities. The relationship between the Church and the faithful was regulated, in political terms, by the Christian Democrats, although a group of "leftist Catholics" or "Communist Catholics" – ranging from Dossetti to Balbo and even Pedrazzi and some founders, in 1951, of the journal *Il Mulino* – sought to escape this logic. Italy was lacking "that characteristic trait of democratic societies, which is the mediation between religion and politics at the level of individual conscience and customs; [in Italy] such mediation is institutionalized in the party."[20] Hence the expansion of the Christian Democratic electoral base, through religion and the skillful distribution of social advantages which served to quiet protests and attract votes, as in the case of the Cassa per il Mezzogiorno (Southern Italy Development Fund), with which, in 1950, "the Christian Democrats added … the material base to the ideological and cultural hegemony provided by the network of parishes, and upon which they were able to build support for the party."[21]

The Communist Party was more cautious and tried to avoid introducing any divisions other than political ones in their encounters with Catholics. However, even this attitude was not one of simple religious compromise or passive acquiescence to the overwhelming power of the clergy, as is clear in a confidential document of the Italian Communist Party of March 1953, intercepted by the police in Genoa: "We must denounce the reactionary function of the clergy… Churches have become the headquarters of a po-

---

20 Pietro Scoppola, *La repubblica dei partiti*, pp. 113, 115. On this basis, Dossetti argued at the Constituent Assembly (November 21, 1946) that there was a need to regulate the relations between the Church and the Italian Republic in the way that Article 7 of the Constitution later prescribed. The Catholic Church is indeed an institution that possesses an autonomous legal system, "which is to say, legislative, executive, and judicial branches." Consequently, it cannot be compared to "other embryonic forms that have yet to be consolidated." The result is that "the relations between Church and state cannot always be unilaterally regulated by the actions of one of the two parties but rather only through bilateral action, which is based on a reciprocal recognition of the original autonomy of the two systems"; see Giuseppe Dossetti, *La ricerca costituente: 1945–1952*, ed. Alberto Melloni (Bologna: Il Mulino, 1994), pp. 214–15. On Dossetti, his prescient critique of the totalitarian state, and his followers, see Paolo Pombeni, *Il gruppo dossettiano e la fondazione della democrazia italiana, 1938–1948* (Bologna: Il Mulino, 1979).

21 Paul Ginsborg, *Storia dell'Italia dal dopoguerra a oggi*, p. 187. See also Giuseppe Barone, "Stato e Mezzogiorno (1943–1960). Il «primo tempo» dell'intervento straordinario" in *Storia dell'Italia repubblicana*, vol. I, pp. 291–409.

litical party and priests have taken it upon themselves to intervene in political and social issues... Pilgrimages, miracles, exorcism and damnation have all come into the picture." In terms of future action, however, the author of the document added: "We must avoid an anti-religious battle that could divide Italians, but we must also unmask the myth of the Church's moral and cultural monopoly on our country. The right to freedom of thought and secular anti-clerical culture must be vindicated."[22]

Looking back now at all these imagined nations, one might ask what has happened to those voluntary allegiances that weighed so heavily in the attitudes and imaginations of two generations. Today they seem either to have disappeared from the horizon or been integrated into Italian identity (with a shortening of the distance between the "head" and the "feet"), or else re-enforced in a way that is different from in the past. America – after a moment of eclipse due to the strong ideological aversion it garnered for the war in Vietnam and during the period of terrorism – has in part ended up, in everyday perception, seeming not very different from Italy. This has happened through cultural homogenization and the diffusion and hybridization of ethical codes (through cinema and television) that come with American hegemony. The Soviet Union, on the other hand (as well as, in descending order, China, Vietnam and Cuba), gradually stopped being a fatal attraction for the Italian Left. Especially since 1989, it is the "ethical Church," compensating in a surrogate role for certain deficiencies of the state, that has re-gained prestige, perhaps in connection with the unique circumstances of recent years, as well as the figure of Pope John Paul II.

Under Another Sky

Alongside imagined fatherlands, real ones were also sought out, with Italians abandoning Italy and becoming expatriates in faraway lands, uprooted by necessity from their native soil. The problem of finding work or another place to live was already difficult after the blocking of transoceanic emigration during the mid-1920s, but it became urgent after the return of veterans from the "deserts of sand and ice" of World War II (even though many ex-prisoners of war chose to remain in Canada and the United States) and

---

22   Quoted by Di Loreto in *La difficile transizione*, pp. 91–92. On those years, see also Antonio Gambino, *Storia del dopoguerra dalla liberazione al potere DC* (Bari: Laterza, 1975).

with the loss of part of Venezia-Giulia and Istria, as well as the colonies in Eastern Africa, the Dodecanese Islands and most significantly Libya, home to more than 160,000 Italians before the war. Emigration, which began again at the end of the 1940s, reached a first peak in 1950–1951, and did so even through illegal means, as can be seen in Pietro Germi's 1950 film *Il Cammino della Speranza*, which tells the story of "the possibility of finding elsewhere what the fatherland does not offer."[23]

Much greater and with more direct influence on Italian society were the migrations from the countryside to the big cities, which started in the 1950s (with the resultant growth of Naples, Rome, Milan and Turin), and the migration from Southern Italy to the North, equal in magnitude to the emigration to the Americas and Australia from the end of the nineteenth century to the beginning of the "Great War." This internal migration gave rise to one of the most radical changes in the history of the Italian Republic.[24] Internal migration did not, however, begin only after World War II. During Fascism – despite the attack on "urban tabes" and the ideology promoting increased settlement in the colonies – there was notable demographic flux due to factors like the reclaiming of lands, reforestation, an increased birthrate and the creation of new cities, some of which were built to answer the needs of the autarchic economy (Latina, Carbonia and others).[25]

While migratory currents flowed from Southern to Northern Italy, Germany and Switzerland became the preferred destination of emigrants, rath-

---

23 See Di Nolfo, *Le paure e le speranze degli italiani*, p. 276.
24 See Aurelio Lepre, *Storia della prima Repubblica*, p. 174: "From 1951 to 1960, 167,116 Italians emigrated to other European countries and 1,170,290 to other continents. In all, there were 2,937,406. During the same period, 1,323,589 persons returned to Italy, making for a net of 1,613,817." On the transoceanic and European migratory flows see Ugo Ascoli, *Movimenti migratori in Italia* (Bologna: Il Mulino, 1979), pp. 36ff. On internal immigration, see Lepre, *Storia della prima Repubblica*, p. 174: during the 1950s, "2,052,000 persons left the South; some of them went abroad, others to the North." See also Ginsborg, *Storia d'Italia dal dopoguerra a oggi*, pp. ixff. From 1958 to the end of the 1960s, there was a negative balance in the South of 1,637,512 inhabitants. From 1951 to 1974, 4,200,000 Italians left the South. It is often impossible to return from faraway destinations: in Calabria they called South America "the land of oblivion." For a description of the emigrant experience, see Goffredo Fofi, *L'immigrazione meridionale a Torino* (Milan: Feltrinelli, 1964). On the problems of immigration, see: Ercole Sori, *L'emigrazione italiana dall'unità alla seconda guerra mondiale* (Bologna: Il Mulino, 1975); E. Sonnino, "Popolazione italiana: dall'espansione al contenimento" in *Storia dell'Italia repubblicana* (Turin: Einaudi, 1995), vol. II, tome 1, pp. 531–75; and A. Signorelli, "Movimenti di popolazione e trasformazioni culturali," *ibid.*, pp. 589–658.
25 See Anna Treves, *Le migrazioni interne nell'Italia fascista* (Turin: Einaudi, 1976).

er than the transoceanic countries, during the economic boom dubbed the "Italian miracle." Today, amazingly enough, Italian emigrants and their descendants make up a population almost equal to that of Italians who live in their own country – around fifty-seven million. There is, therefore, another Italy outside Italy, where certain ethical codes and forms of behavior that have since disappeared in Italy continue to endure. Elsewhere, these ethical codes tend to crystallize into norms that are quite rigid, often as a means of protection in hostile and indifferent social environments. One notable example of an "archaic" ethos in a zone of hyper-modern innovation like the United States can be found among working class Italian-Americans originally from Southern Italy, who still observe "the order of the family," a set of rules which minutely regulate what is considered honorable or dishonorable both inside and outside the familial institution.[26] Gradually, however, the children, grandchildren and great-grandchildren of emigrants distance themselves from the humble professions of their parents and from the Italian language and customs (encouraged by the memory of their parents' and grandparents' shame at having to abandon their own country). They begin to integrate into the community in which they live, often transforming the memory of their origins into folklore. The Italian-Canadians, for example, who maintain the closest relationship with Italy, steadfastly continue to make wine in their homes, with grape must from California. Most of the stories of the first generation recount hardship, separations and reunions with relatives and compatriots, hard work, suffering, linguistic disorientation, disease and solitude. One emigrant in Brooklyn wrote in 1960: "Beyond all thoughts and worries, money slips away like water. Five children is a problem and I try to make myself useful as much as my strength allows. Next August I'll be sixty-five years old and I'll retire. If I can, I'll work small jobs, as long as the Lord gives me strength. I have definitely worked too hard and the years have accumulated and aged me. Even a steel motor wears out; so do we. There's nothing we can do."[27]

---

26 See Raymond A. Belliotti, *Seeking Identity: Individualism versus Community in an Ethnic Context* (Lawrence: University of Kansas Press, 1995), pp. 1–38.

27 See Giannino Di Stasio, ed., *Ti sono scritto questa lettera. Le lettere che gli emigranti non scriveranno più* (Milan: Mursia, 1991), p. 13. On the toil of living and illnesses that strike family members, see the following testimonials: "This is a land where you could earn your bread ten years ago. Your sister-in-law can tell you what America means and what it means to break up a family" (*ibid.*, p. 27); "Days go by and I can feel my life ending little by little" (*ibid.*, p. 81).

For those who remained behind, the social effects of the migrations were severe: depopulation of the countryside, an aging population, empty houses, a large majority of women (there were many "white widows") and children, as well as "industrialization without development."[28] In Southern Italy, habits and patterns of life changed. Even more remarkable, ethically, was the impact on men from the South of the mentality, traditions and customs of the northern regions where they were trying to plant new roots. The phenomenon of violent friction and the blending, alteration or rejection of the moral codes of each culture gave rise to protracted disagreements that continue today. Those accustomed to integration within the neighborhood community and the more intense social relationships of the southern villages and small cities felt injured and offended by the indifference and latent hostility of the residents of unfamiliar northern metropolitan environments. The reaction of young people was generally one of desperation and rage.[29] In only a few cases were Southern Italians able to become fully and rapidly integrated in their new homes (which were often like giant barracks situated in the squalid city outskirts, similar to those Pasolini described as "sad Bedouin/ boroughs of yellow prairies grazed upon/ by a wind without peace"). These few succeeded because they had dragged along a chain of relatives and countrymen who reproduced a familiar and supportive microclimate, an enclave of the South within the North. Rendering the emigrants' experience even more difficult was the transition from a generally agrarian or white collar culture to that of a factory, as well as the inadequacy of the infrastructures that received them (housing, day-care, schools, recreational facilities) and the perceived indifference of many Northerners. The farmers of the South became the factory workers of the North, while emigrants with minimal higher education entered state administration jobs and professional positions. They went to Rome or, in one way or another, made their way throughout the rest of the country. The "precocious expansion of tertiary industry," a tendency already discernible under Fascism, continued with a marked growth in public service, as well as a boom in the number

---

28   See Eyvind Hytten and Marco Marchioni, *Industrializzazione senza sviluppo. Gela: una storia meridionale* (Milan: Franco Angeli, 1970).

29   In the field of literature, this brings to mind, for example, Pasolini's *Ragazzi di vita* (1955) and *Una vita violenta*, but also of the genre of so-called "industrial literature" in works of those who had worked with Adriano Olivetti – like Ottiero Ottieri's *Donnarumma all'assalto* and Paolo Volponi's *Memoriale* (1962), as well as later novels like *La strada per Roma* and *Le mosche del capitale*.

of commercial enterprises – Italy had, in fact, one of the highest levels of growth among European countries in this sector.[30] The wounds left by this mixing of populations have still not healed in the Italian conscience. On the contrary, they seem, paradoxically, to have reopened decades later: the ideology of the Lega Nord (Northern League) today is for the most part a vociferous repetition of the discourses heard formerly in private among families and in bars and taverns of the North, with the addition of new and confused "Celtic" mythologies.

Both the emigration and the very ethos of certain zones in Italy were markedly affected by the intertwining of natural and human history, the combination of poor soil (due partly to deforestation and lack of attention to irrigation systems), natural disasters and the abandonment of the countryside, as was seen both in the flooding around the Po river in the early 1950s and in Calabria, or later in the earthquakes of Belice, Friuli and Irpinia (events which reawakened national solidarity, with admiration in certain Northern areas for the rapidity and efficiency of recovery, but contempt in the South for the corruption and gigantic waste of resources – once again underlining the effective distance between the two Italies). Droughts in certain zones, limits imposed on private ownership and the difficulty of life in the countryside were vividly imprinted in the testimonial of Carlo Levi in his *Cristo si è fermato a Eboli* (*Christ Stopped at Eboli*), published in 1945 and in Francesco Jovine's novel *Le terre del sacramento* (*The Lands of the Sacrament*) published in 1950. These cataclysms were certainly acts of nature, but they were also the result of negligence and ignorance. Italy is a geologically young country, even though the human settlements there are relatively ancient. With the growth of ecological awareness, the signs of natural degradation, even the most subtle, are beginning to be more carefully watched. Thus, besides the famous disappearance of fireflies denounced by Pasolini, other evidence, once overlooked, is now being collected. Some still "remember an element of the landscape that is now disappearing: the poppy, which had a pleasant visual function in the wheat fields, despite its negative economic impact. Today their numbers have been greatly diminished by pesticides, which eliminate anything but wheat, rice or other commercial

---

30 P. Ciocca, "L'Italia nell'economia mondiale," *Quaderni storici*, nos. 29–30 (1975) and Massimo Paci, *La struttura sociale italiana. Costanti storiche e trasformazioni recenti* (Bologna: Il Mulino, 1982), p. 34.

products with no regard for pretty flowers."[31]

As for people, many were losing the "roots" of their own culture: old communitarian values and respect for former hierarchies and customs were beginning to deteriorate, allowing for forms of behavior largely marked by individualism and aspiration for economic success (resulting also from increased "horizontal" mobility – geographical movement – and "vertical" mobility – abandonment of the paternal line of work). In the euphoria of the boom through the early 1970s, with a new desire for profit and an increased propensity toward risk-taking as opposed to the safety of the secure office job and measly state salary, many tried to establish their own small family-run factories (Lucio Mastronardi's novel *Il maestro di Vigevano* mirrored these changes).[32] When tradition no longer offered enough options, individuals ended up at once liberated and disoriented. The state sought to adapt to these changes by renewing its institutions and laws, while the Church reacted by re-launching the theme of the centrality of the family as a refuge from the inclement world and a sturdy pivot on which one could hinge one's values no matter where one found oneself. But it was already too late.

Italian Dreams

During the years of reconstruction and the "cold civil war," life was not easy: the average salary of 1945 was barely half that of 1939. Italians therefore began to seek out forms of compensation in the more unpleasant corners of reality where politics seemed to count less. The desire to be well-off increased, but in the absence of the possibility of rapid social ascent (comparatively more accessible in the 1960s and 1970s) many believed more in luck than in success. When, in 1946, one could first place bets with SISAL (soon to become Totocalcio), the "hope of winning the Italian soccer match pools" (the "Totocalcio Thirteen" for the thirteen matches in each pool) became "an important instrument of indirect democratization, a tool for the cooling of conflicts and the propagation of pacifist instincts. The weekly

---

31   G. Bellezza, "I mutamenti geo-morfologici" in Giulio Carlo Argan, Ottavio Cecchi and Enrico Ghidetti, eds., *Profili dell'Italia repubblicana* (Rome: Editori Riuniti, 1985), p. 50. On ecological disruption in Italy, see Paolo Gardin and Massimo Pazienti, *L'ambiente in Italia: problemi e prospettive* (Milan: Franco Angeli, 1992).

32   See Lucio Mastronardi, *Il maestro di Vigevano* (Turin: Einaudi, 1962).

appointment with Totocalcio did not bring personal affirmation or social excellence, stimulate any form of competition or classify the players according to their abilities. It openly simulated the electoral process, while losses did not lead to despondency or frustration."[33]

The enthusiasm with which sporting events were followed during those years also represented the need – in a moral climate that had become clouded with savage crimes, robberies and scandals widely publicized in print and on radio – to return to normalcy and everyday life. "The desire to forget was generally underestimated by the Left. For the majority of Italians, as was evidenced by election results, the mere fact that they had made it through the war alive was extraordinarily important. For them, the present was much better than the past, and the past did not mean the two decades of Fascism as much as the five years of the war – five years of hunger and death."[34] Although Italy did not want to erase its past to the same extent that "Germany without mourning" or France did with regard to Vichy, there was undoubtedly a phase in which, even among the working class, the temptation to forget was strong, especially after the resounding victory of the Christian Democrats in the elections of 1948, a traumatic event for the Fronte Popolare (Popular Front).

The same need to turn the page was felt in areas other than sports. One expression of this need was the spread of mass motorization, beginning with tiny scooters like the Vespa and the Lambretta (which took the place of bicycles and – as others have observed – gradually reduced the importance of the sport of road cycling, already weakened by the decision to connect gambling to soccer). The Vespa, which needed only one liter of fuel per fifty kilometers, was the result of a well-conceived policy of industrial

---

33   Lanaro, *Storia dell'Italia repubblicana*, pp. 199–200. On the implications of this situation, see Alan Milward, *The Reconstruction of Western Europe 1945–1952* (London: Methuen, 1984); Giorgio Candeloro, *Storia dell'Italia moderna*, vol. XI: *La fondazione della repubblica e la ricostruzione. Considerazioni finali* (Milan: Feltrinelli, 1986); Pietro Nenni, *Tempo di guerra fredda. Diari. 1943–1956* (Milan: SugarCo, 1987); Filippo Mazzonis, *Storia della società italiana*, vol. XXIII: *La società italiana dalla Resistenza alla guerra fredda*, ed. E. Lepore et al. (Milan: Teti, 1989); and Aris Aceornero, *Gli anni '50 in fabbrica* (Bari: De Donato, 1973). On popular sentiment and ideals, see Angelo Ventrone, "Tra propaganda e passione: Grand'Hotel e l'Italia degli anni '50," *Rivista di storia contemporanea*, vol. 17, no. 4 (1988), pp. 603–31; and Gian Franco Venè, *Vola colomba* (Milan: Mondadori, 1990). On the "cold civil war" see Aurelio Lepre, *Storia degli italiani nel Novecento* (Milan: Mondadori, 2003), pp. 240–55.

34   Lepre, *Storia della prima repubblica*, p. 147. The Wilma Montesi scandal was among the most indicative of this era in the history of the Republic; see Hilton Wayland Young, *The Montesi Scandal* (London: Faber and Faber, 1977).

conversion. It was created in 1946 through the adaptation of an old stock of air-cooled motors with reduced capacity (it had been commissioned by the Ministry of Colonies). By October, 1953, over 500,000 models had been sold. The maker of the Vespa, Piaggio (forced to make kitchen pots after long operating in the aeronautic and naval fields), had found its new calling. The second vehicle, the Lambretta, was introduced to the public in 1948 by Innocenti, a well-known maker of tubular scaffolding. Lifestyles were transformed by the advent of the scooters: "The farmhouse was suddenly close to the village, the school to the theater, the office or factory to the home and ultimately everyone was nearer to each other. Every circuit of ideas, transactions, cultures and associations had more breadth, and the exchange of reality and experiences among individuals multiplied."[35]

During the 1950s, and with a marked acceleration in the period thereafter, the automobile outflanked the scooter in many families and began to replace the train as a means of transportation (one quarter of the railways had been destroyed by the war, but by the time they were rebuilt and even expanded, the transportation of persons and goods by road had taken priority). A few decades later than in the United States (where the family car was a staple of privileged families as early as the 1920s and of working class families from the 1950s),[36] the automobile entered the fabric of Italian daily life, greatly facilitating the mobility of individuals and the family unit alike. In 1952 there were half a million vehicles in Italy (though 88% of them were motorcycles and scooters), a number that would triple merely six years later. Beginning with the Fiat "600," first sold in 1955, the number of vehicles in circulation began to skyrocket, as did the need for a highway network (in 1956, after long discussion of possible routes, construction began on the "Autostrada del Sole" [Highway of the Sun], which crosses Italy from north to south, and in 1962–1986 the highway system grew from 1,341 to 5,901 kilometers). The automobile changed the way of life, forms of socialization and perception of distances and intimacy in Italy: "Entire families could now transport themselves. This was less a conquest of open space, as in the case of the scooter, than the possession of a new space, outside the home, that was mobile yet closed and protected and therefore not subject to the usual norms of social behavior and dependence. It was

---

35   Alberto Caracciolo, "Caratteristiche della vita privata nell'Italia contemporanea" in *La vita privata. Il Novecento*, pp. 17–18.

36   See James J. Flink, *The Automobile Age* (Cambridge, Mass: MIT Press, 1990), pp. 158ff.

an element of democracy, but one that generated new arrogance at the micro-level of social behavior."[37] Young couples, no longer confined to their houses when their parents were absent, now had new intimacy. Only in the early 1960s did the airplane appear on the Italian horizon of transportation possibilities, eventually weakening the widely shared assumption of belonging naturally to one specific place.

---

37 Lepre, *Storia della prima repubblica*, p.186.

CHAPTER 4
Philosophizing a Divided World

A Constant Civil Vocation

It is often said that Italian philosophy was transformed at the end of the war, as it opened up to the outside world and truly developed an "instinct for combination," blending Marxism, neo-positivism, existentialism and phenomenology. This common belief, however, is only partly true, for in reality the traditional nucleus of Italian philosophy was preserved. Against the backdrop of its long history, and taking into due account its internal complexity, Italian philosophy remained a constant civil vocation.

From its Renaissance humanist origins to the present, Italian philosophy's largest audience is made up not of specialists, intellectuals or academics, but a much wider public. For philosophers and men of letters, the inner circle consists of their compatriots. These fallen heirs of a great past are citizens of a community initially defined only by language, politically divided into a multiplicity of fragile regional states and spiritually influenced by an overbearing Catholic Church. The second circle, with an accent on "universalistic" traits, includes everyone else. The most representative philosophers thus did not enclose themselves within narrow fields or dedicate themselves to questions involving particular logical, metaphysical or theological subtleties, as occurred in other nations – England, Germany or Spain – where the weight of scholastic or academic philosophy was felt for a longer time, since for them the caesura of the Renaissance was not as strong as elsewhere. The Italian objects of investigation are rather questions which involve the majority of mankind (the "non-philosophers," as Croce called them) and assume that men are not only rational animals, but animals with desires and plans, whose thoughts, actions and expectations elude previous argumentative schema and rigorous methodologies.

Italian philosophy is at its best when attempting to solve problems in which the universal and the particular, the logical and the empirical, collide. Such problems arise from the intersections of associational life and various social networks, from individual conscience which combines the awareness of the limits imposed by reality with projections of desire, the opacity of historical experience with its transcription into images and concepts, the impotence of morality with the harshness of the world, and thought with experience. There have been thus many (successful) attempts to preserve zones of rationality in territories that appeared to have none and to make sense of forms of knowledge and practices that seemed dominated by the imponderability of arbitrariness, taste and chance. This pertains to political philosophy, the theory and philosophy of history, aesthetics and the history of philosophy (all fields in which subjectivity and individuality are decisive).

The civil vocation of Italian philosophy rarely manifests itself in the form of frontal opposition to ecclesiastic power or the political establishment. The great exceptions to this rule were Giordano Bruno and Giulio Cesare Vanini, burned at the stake in the 17th century and Antonio Gramsci, who died in prison during the 20th century. Only rarely has Italy known philosophers like the attackers of religion in France: Pascal, who wrote against the Jesuits in his *Provincial Letters*, Diderot and his *Encyclopédie*, or Voltaire and his pamphlets. More often than not, the civic mission of Italian philosophers is seen as a noble, paternalistic, benevolent education for both the privileged and the masses.

In contrast to the prevalent point of view, it must be stressed that there was no "weakening" of the demands for intelligibility of the real, but rather an effort to reclaim areas that had been too hurriedly abandoned (and had become unpopular) by a form of reasoning identified with the victorious models of physical-mathematical sciences. Italian philosophy is a philosophy of "impure reason" which takes into account the conditions, imperfections and possibilities of the world, as opposed to pure reason, which is instead concerned with knowledge of the absolute, the immutable and the rigidly normative.

Curiously, despite Italy's fundamental contribution to the world of scientific study – from Leonardo da Vinci to Galileo, Volta to Pacinotti, Marconi to Fermi – in the recent centuries and even until a few decades ago, there has never been a practice of autochthonous reflection on the philosophy of science or on logic (if we exclude Galileo himself and the solitary figures of Peano, Vailati and Enriques, and later, in the field of history of science, Ludovico Geymonat and Paolo Rossi). And despite the importance of the Church and widespread religious practice (or perhaps because of it), there has never been a philosophy of interiority, of the dramatic dialogue with the self (as existed in France from Pascal to Maine de Biran). This absence was not so much the result of the oft-noted tendency toward theatricality in Roman Catholic ritual or the psychological blocks provoked by the fear of the Counter-Reformation's "tribunals of conscience." It was caused instead by the largely hierarchical institutionalization of the relationship between the faithful and the divinity within the juridical culture of the Church of Rome, which, formalized over centuries, meticulously and skillfully regulates the behavior of its faithful.

The Gramsci-Togliatti Line

In the second half of the nineteenth century, an historiographical perspective emerged that would prove to be long-lasting. Advanced by Bertrando Spaventa, and later partially revived by Gentile, it elaborated on the view which held that the remnants of Italian Renaissance philosophy had little effect on Italy itself – due to the religious intolerance of the Counter-Reformation and national decadence – and instead passed on to influence European culture more broadly (in particular German Idealism). On this account, these remnants were to have finally returned – thanks to the European and German mediation – to contemporary Italian thought, which in this way did no more than reconnect with its own roots. While this myth is clearly one of re-legitimization, it is interesting to see how the attempt to link Italian with European philosophy was accomplished: in the form of a *nostos* from which Italian philosophy emerged as both identical to itself and enriched by contributions of others, national and international. With the advent of political unification and the separation of church and state, Italian thought was deemed worthy of resuming its place in the theoretical forum between nations. The prestige garnered by Italian philosophy, due to the dissemination, even on the journalistic level, of Croce's thought and "Gentile's reform" of secondary education (which introduced the history of philosophy to secondary schools and teachers' colleges), led to an inferior, apologetic version of the myth, in which European philosophy in its entirety was seen to flow into Italian Idealism. Between the two wars, there was a sharpening of the conviction that philosophy, as an organizational factor of consensus and a stimulus toward civil action, played a determining role in molding the ruling classes.

Thus, when Italian philosophy seemed to "reopen" itself to foreign thought after World War II, such tasks remained a priority even as the tools changed. Although Italian philosophy maintained "provincial" traces, it had not awaited this moment to become actively involved with its European and American counterparts. Even during fascism there was a striking variety of theoretical positions that were not crushed by the duopoly of Croce and Gentile, positions sensitive to French and Anglo-Saxon themes rather than those of the German Reich, of which Italy was supposed to be a mere "province." However, a wider circulation of ideas should not be confused with a greater autonomy of thought. One can remain "provincial" – as was later sometimes the case – even with increased importation of other ideas. The result was that, in the "pluralistic" post-World War II period, unlike in the first decades of the 20th century, no philosophical doctrine achieved a visible and uncontested hegemony. This was also because, as Luporini has maintained, "in my generation, as in the ones that followed, there were no more – fortunately perhaps – true intellectual protagonists in Italy as there had been in the first thirty years of the century."[1]

Furthermore, rather than a discontinuity with the recent past, one can speak of continuity, a bridge between idealistic historicism and "Italian

---

1 Cesare Luporini, *Dialettica e materialismo* (Rome: Editori Riuniti, 1974), p. xxvi. On developments in Italian philosophy during this period, see Eugenio Garin, *Cronache di filosofia italiana 1900/1943. Quindici anni dopo 1945/1960* (Bari: Laterza, 1966), esp. pp. 491–616; Giuseppe Bedeschi, *La parabola del marxismo in Italia, 1945–1983* (Rome-Bari: Laterza, 1983); Bruno Maiorca, ed., *Filosofi italiani contemporanei. Parlano i protagonisti* (Bari: Dedalo, 1984); *La filosofia italiana dal dopoguerra a oggi* (Rome-Bari: Laterza, 1985); Pietro Rossi and Carlo Augusto Viano, *Filosofia italiana e filosofie straniere nel dopoguerra* (Bologna: Il Mulino, 1992); V. Mathieu, "L'Italie" in Raymond Klibansky and David Pears, eds., *La philosophie en Europe* (Paris: Gallimard, 1993), pp. 223–40; and Franco Restaino, "Il dibattito filosofico in Italia (1925–1990)," in [N. Abbagnano], *Storia della filosofia*, vol. IV, eds., Giovanni Fornero, Franco Restaino and Dario Antiseri (Turin: UTET, 1994), pp. 560–758.

Marxism." It was an extra-philosophical factor that reintroduced Marxism to Italy after its teaching had been suppressed, at least on an official level, for almost twenty years (sheltering an entire generation from its influence), and after the theory of class struggle had been abandoned in favor of the inter-classist solidarity of the "Ethical State." On the level of cultural politics Palmiro Togliatti gradually succeeded, through cautious and able maneuvers, in releasing Italian Communism from its ideological obedience to Moscow and in promoting the massive transfer of many Italian "intellectuals" to the left without significant repercussions. He shifted them from Gentilian and Crocian idealism, which they had generally professed in the past, to a historicist national Marxism oriented along the axis that went from De Sanctis to Labriola and Croce to Gramsci. Spaventa's circular model, without losing its civil imperative, became a national line, existing as an important variant alongside the other parallels of "progress" and the heroic genealogies of foreign theorists' "national pathways" to socialism. The accreditation of this national line happened over a relatively short period of time, due partly to a number of inconspicuous actions, such as the publication of the writings of Labriola and Gramsci, together with those of Marx, Engels, Lenin and Stalin in a series of supplements to the journal *Rinascita* (under the rubric "Guide to the Classics of Marxism").

While Italian philosophy had often been pushed to metaphysical heights, where the air was rarefied and political questions were treated allusively or had to be read between the lines, now politics and the historical influences of current events entered philosophical debate with great force (it was often forgotten that philosophy must come to terms not only "horizontally" with the reality of its own times, but also "vertically," with its multi-millennial tradition).[2] In the charged climate of the Cold War, especially after the exclusion of the communist and socialist left from the government, the inflexibility of the cultural debate permeated all fields. The overtures of the post-war period toward dialogue with Catholics close to the Italian Com-

---

2 On Togliatti and the political and cultural atmosphere he found himself working in, see Giorgio Bocca, *Palmiro Togliatti* (Bari: Laterza, 1973); Giuseppe Vacca, *Saggio su Togliatti e la tradizione comunista* (Bari: De Donato, 1974); Di Loreto, *Togliatti e la doppiezza*; Giuseppe Carlo Marino, *Autoritratto del PCI staliniano, 1946–1953* (Rome: Editori Riuniti, 1991); and Aldo Agosti, *Palmiro Togliatti* (Turin: UTET, 1996). On the recurring theme of the relationship between the PCI and Italian intellectuals, see Nello Ajello, *Intellettuali e PCI. 1944–1958* (Bari: Laterza, 1979); Albertina Vittoria, *Togliatti e gli intellettuali* (Rome: Editori Riuniti, 1992); and Flores and Gallerano, *Sul PCI. Un'interpretazione storica*, pp. 195–213.

munist Party (roughly from 1945 to 1947, with new journals like *Società*, first published in 1945, and *Belfagor*, founded in 1946) were followed by the close-mindedness, of Togliatti and other leftist intellectuals, toward the review *Politecnico* and all other attempts to allow more room for philosophical thought not so closely tied to politics or "history." Somewhat later with respect to politics, even what might playfully be termed the "philosophical Committee for National Liberation" was dissolved. The crushing of intermediary positions and the calculated rejection of any critical views (or the *ad hoc* adjustments of inconvenient theories) were considered a bearable sacrifice in order to philosophize effectively and to be heard in a divided world. In *Crisi dell'Uomo* (*The Crisis of Man*, 1948) and *La Coscienza Inquieta* (*The Restless Conscience*, 1949), Remo Cantoni introduced Italian philosophy to contemporary anthropological thought and the tormented dilemmas of Dostoyevsky and Kierkegaard. As soon as Cantoni tried to resolve doubts about Marxism by attempting to make a notch in its imperturbable orthodoxy, he found in Antonio Banfi an interlocutor who was impervious to criticism. Privately, by letter, Cantoni reacted: "You write that 'not to be a communist is to die'." And yet "the need to consolidate, to form a front or a mass, without borrowing arguments from our adversaries, is with each and every day killing the critical spirit and historical purpose. Marx, Engels, Lenin and Stalin are worshipped as saints, as authors whose thought cannot even be minimally criticized since they have been placed in a sphere of untouchable truth. I have never – I repeat, never – found a communist writer who has had the sincerity to say: 'here it seems that Marx or Lenin or Stalin has fallen into error; or this thought of Lenin's is disproved by the facts'; or anything similar."[3] Even Luporini, reminiscing in 1974, would recall the experience this way: "It seems now that we lived (and thought and worked) in an interstice, the interstice between two orthodoxies and, in the final analysis, two dogmatisms, Stalinist and historicist."[4]

---

3   Remo Cantoni, "Lettera ad Antonio Banfi del 4 settembre 1949" in Carlo Montaleone, *Cultura a Milano nel dopoguerra. Filosofia e engagement in Remo Cantoni* (Turin: Bollati Boringhieri, 1996), pp. 164–65. On Cantoni and the "Milan School," see Fulvio Papi, *Vita e filosofia. La scuola di Milano: Banfi, Cantoni, Paci, Preti* (Milan: Guerini, 1990). On Paci, see Enzo Paci, *Il filosofo e la città*, ed. Salvatore Veca (Milan: Il Saggiatore, 1979); and Amedeo Vigorelli, *L'esistenzialismo positivo di Enzo Paci. Una biografia intellettuale, 1929–1950* (Milan: Franco Angeli, 1987).
4   Luporini, *Dialettica e materialismo*, p. xxxii.

Historicism and the Pathos of the Concrete

But why did historicism become so deeply rooted in post-war Italy? Essentially, because it did not deal with "Jacobin abstractions," but with the concrete specificity of historical situations and the need to focus thought on reality. It examined domestic and international relations of power with sober realism and gave rise – partly through the spread of Gramsci's work, which after the war initiated the great period of Italian experimental political theory – to an often implicit but constant reflection on why the West had seen a series of unsuccessful revolutions with successful reactions. Historicism made use of the lessons of the past in order to avoid the frequent desire to forget – the desire to rid oneself of the past without coming to terms with it. An indictment analogous to the one put forth by historicist philosophy came from Edoardo Cacciatore with heartfelt strains of civil passion in the poem "*Campo dei Fiori*" (the Roman square where a statue of Giordano Bruno commemorates the place where he was burned at the stake), in which he illustrates the programmatic "rinsing" of any efforts toward emancipation:

> Freedom always has an incredibly high price
> If it were cheap, it would be perishable merchandise
> As usual, street-sweepers activate the fire hydrants
> "Blood can be washed away," the conformists are quick to declare.
>
> [La libertà sempre ha un prezzo incredibile
> A buon mercato è merce deperibile
> Gli spazzini al solito azionano gli idranti
> Il sangue si lava affermano i benpensanti.][5]

There was acute awareness that a long "war of position" was necessary, which would pass first through the slow conquest of consensus and acceptance of the obstacles imposed by representative democracy, then make its way, eventually, toward a new society. After two decades of use as a primarily nationalist and rhetorical device, history was now once again regarded as a lesson in realism. It was, however, a divided history, split into two stages: the present, which meant tolerance of the bad conditions of the current

---
5 Edoardo Cacciatore, "Campo dei fiori" in *La restituzione* (Florence: Valecchi, 1955).

political situation, and the future, which was an undetermined destination with an essentially trans-political nature, called "the revolution."

The emergence of a relative hegemony of communists in high culture (not in middle-low culture, still dominated by ecclesiastical organizations, mainstream newspapers and pro-government journals), in place of an impossible political hegemony, unleashed a struggle between intellectuals and the party for political appointments. Not only was the question of who-represented-whom put into play, but also of who would act as a privileged intermediary between different institutions and cultures, especially Catholic culture. Only after the electoral defeat of 1948 and increasing intolerance of some sectors of the Church did Togliatti try to move closer to liberal secular thought by publishing in 1949 an Italian edition of Voltaire's *Traité sur la Tolerance*. When read between the lines (indirect discourse was a prevalent sign of the times), Togliatti's maneuvers were also an attempt to mitigate the "civil cold war" climate within the Italian Communist Party, to smooth over the rough spots created by its sectarianism and perhaps to reflect on the damage done by an overly rigid conception of political loyalty among "organic intellectuals."

The almost "neo-realist" importance of concrete lived experience, as well as the connections between determinate historical and economic situations, had become the center of Italian historicism (dipping into the concepts formulated and tested by Gramsci in his *Prison Notebooks*). The emphasis was on recognizing the rights and hardships of immanence – of one's own time – rather than succumbing to the temptations of transcendence offered by the Church for centuries. One had to avoid taking refuge in the closed, moldy compartment of consciousness, in the reassuring but sterile isolation of private life, or in the glorified but fallacious utopias of immediate regeneration. In contrast to idealism, spiritualism and existentialism, historicism sought to bring philosophy down from the celestial realm of ideas and deliver it to the homes and lives of men: "Contemporary philosophy recognizes that it is *filia temporis*... It knows that it is historically determined and accepts its temporality, its connection to the radical problematic of its time, even posing this to itself as a problem."[6] More than anyone else, Eugenio Garin insisted with vigorous moral and civil overtones on the connection

---

6 Antonio Banfi, *Filosofi contemporanei* (Milano: Parenti, 1961), p. 5. On Banfi, see Guido D. Neri, *Crisi e costituzione della storia. Sviluppi del pensiero di Antonio Banfi* (Naples: Bibliopolis, 1988).

between philosophy and the effective history of man, on the "*real* roots of *ideal* choices," since for him philosophy had to "rediscover the humanity of thought and bring that humanity into focus, for without this *human flesh* thought would not exist."[7] Thus, the ibid. dependence of any philosophy upon the diversity among human beings and their intellectual instruments in the comprehension of reality was a given. Garin, a historian of philosophy, now discovered that "philosophy, rather than an autonomous development of self-sufficient knowledge, was a plurality of fields of investigation, formulations and visions. Unity in philosophy is configured as a certain level of critical awareness, or at the very least as an exigency to unify the fields of research."[8]

In this march toward the concrete – this search for an "Italian pathway toward rationality," this desire to create, as expressed in the inaugural editorial of *Politecnico*, "a culture that no longer provides consolation for suffering, but instead protects from suffering by combating and eliminating it" – Italian philosophers were in effect seeking to merge history and utopia; they wanted history to be strengthened and made dynamic by a utopian end (emancipation) which was a grounded utopia, a utopia that accepts the

---

7 Eugenio Garin, *La filosofia come sapere storico* (Bari: Laterza, 1959), pp. 136–37.

8 *Idem*, *La filosofia dal '45 a oggi*, ed. Valerio Verra (Turin: ERI, 1976), p. 451. Garin himself underscored the legacy of Croce's philosophy when he remembered the impression that one of Croce's 1938 essays made on him: "La filosofia come idea antiquata e l'idea antiquata di filosofia" in *La storia come pensiero e come azione* ("Philosophy as an Antiquated Idea and the Antiquated Idea of Philosophy"). "The concept of a philosophy above and beyond history" is connected with the idea of "'greatest,' 'supreme,' 'universal,' 'eternal' problems of thought," which remain the same and should be distinguished from "other 'minor,' 'inferior,' 'particular,' 'contingent'" problems. But philosophy – serious contemporary philosophy – deals, and *must* deal, with small problems "which is only where the greatest problems lie and only where they can be found and resolved"; cited by Eugenio Garin in *Intervista sull'intellettuale*, ed. Mario Ajello (Rome-Bari: Laterza, 1997), p. 125. In 1938 Croce wrote: "With the anticipated and now fulfilled reduction of philosophy to historiography, we can say – if you will – that philosophy is dead. But since what appears to have died was never really alive, it would be more precise to say that the antiquated idea of philosophy has died and given way to a new idea of philosophy, which springs forth from the deep thought of the modern world. To be sure, it has died in an ideal way since materially its life will drag on just like so many other things that have been surpassed ideally, and the work of the philosopher will continue to be of use to the world as merely one lowly profession among many." Garin adds: "I cannot forget the impression that the thick 1951 Ricciardi volume [of Croce's work] made on me and my almost transparent reading on the tasks and the sense of philosophy as an attempt to give meaning to life, to work, and human vicissitudes: a meaning that is indissolubly linked to a historical moment… I will never forget the sense – so different than the usual discussion of eternity – of a philosophy immersed in historical becoming and linked to a profound connection with moral and political commitment for a better world"; *Ibid.*, p. 126.

lessons of realism. By drawing a sort of historical treasure map, one could simultaneously take into account the obstacles and the possibilities, the bottlenecks and the exit strategies, the attempted and the contemplated. History and utopia would progressively part company, however, leading to their present state of almost complete separation. The process got under way in 1962 when – beginning with the discussion of Nicola Badaloni's book *Marxismo come storicismo* (*Marxism as Historicism*), in which he rejected the notion of Marxism as a "fortress" while hailing it as an instrument to analyze reality – the theory of the "objectivity of contradiction" came into question. This was a crucial change because (besides touching on the more academic and theoretical question of continuity between Hegel and Marx) it raised serious doubts about the existence of an internal logic within history that was supposedly independent of the intentions and volitions of individuals. This very logic, the indispensable foundation of Marxist historicism, had led to so many subsequent justificatory conclusions that it became difficult to distinguish clearly between facts and value judgments.[9]

Anti-historicist Marxists

Historicism's monopoly was not uncontested. There were even Marxist philosophers who aligned themselves against historicism, such as Cesare Luporini, who was initially influenced by Leopardi and then by Althusser's French structuralism, and Galvano della Volpe, who had an even greater influence on the political playing field. Despite Della Volpe's tendency, like that of his antagonists, toward greater concreteness and adherence to reality, he sought – not without an often intolerable preponderance of ideological baggage and certainly not without provoking controversies within the PCI – to shift the course of Italian Marxism from tracks of historicist idealism. With a background in Hume and English empiricism, and building on the critique of the tradition of spiritualistic individualism (which, from Plato to Saint Augustine and Rousseau, would ultimately reach the existentialists), Della Volpe proceeded toward the rediscovery of a different Marx, one whose principal concern was the struggle against all forms of "alienation."

---

9   This is documented in Franco Cassano, *Marxismo e filosofia in Italia, 1958–1971* (Bari: De Donato, 1973). See also Nicola Badaloni, *Il marxismo italiano degli anni sessanta* (Rome: Editori Riuniti, 1971).

Already in 1946, when *La libertà comunista* was released, the pathway to Marx passed through Rousseau and completely cut out Hegel (who, in turn, was dubbed a "romantic and a mystic"). Although Marx's scarce sympathy for Rousseau was well known, and even Della Volpe made reference to Rousseau's "spiritual narcissism," it was still possible for Della Volpe to interweave Rousseau's thought with that of the young Marx, showing how the gap between communism and liberalism was unbridgeable. The Communist *libertas maior* (material and egalitarian) was considered incomparably superior to the bourgeois *libertas minor* (civil and formal).

Della Volpe returned to this theme in 1957 when he published *Rousseau e Marx*. Two years had passed since his polemical debate with Bobbio in *Politica e Cultura* (in which, having noted the lesser freedom of citizens in socialist countries, Bobbio invited his interlocutor to "appreciate the liberal-democratic type of regime as representing a more refined and advanced method" of governance) and a year since both the Twentieth Congress of the Communist Party of the U.S.S.R. and what were modestly referred to as the "events in Hungary." On the one hand, Della Volpe responded by retrieving for Marxism certain so-called "bourgeois" values originating in natural law theory, such as "liberty" (but attributing to them a "substantial" or concrete character, as opposed to a merely juridical-formal or moralistically "abstract" character), and on the other hand, he reworked Rousseau's concepts of popular sovereignty and direct democracy. The scope was that of assaying the possible revitalization of political structures – in both the East and the West – through reinforcing citizen participation in the management of the *res pubblica*.

Such ever-expanding political participation would eliminate "alienation," a notion that Della Volpe found primarily in the writings of the young Marx – writings that were cited for anti-dogmatic purposes and mined for ideas that had not yet been regimented. In polemic with Hegelian idealism, which dissolved the weight of the actual and the "finite" in the diaphanous network of relationships that eclipsed materiality (removing man from the world and cutting his ties to the "social being," thus isolating him in an "alienated" dimension), Marx showed the value of a sensory conscience that was open to the reality of the world. The father of modern communism thus took his place in a genealogy that began with Aristotle, critic of Platonic idealism and champion of the prerogatives of the senses, and passed through Galileo, destroyer of scholasticism and its apriorism. Hence Della Volpe's insistence on the "moral Galileism" of Marx, who was, for Della Volpe, the author of a true revolution in the field of the social sciences, escaping both idealism and positivism and finding liberation from the Hegelian abstraction of the "self-conscience," as well as the fetishism of uninterpreted facts. From this point of view, Della Volpe advanced, in *La Logica come Scienza Positiva* (*Logic as Positive Science*) published in 1950, a model of rationality that could maintain contact simultaneously with the undeniable positivity of the manifold senses and with the determinancy of events and deeds, without, however, sanctifying their unrelated particularity.

The Turin School and other Secular Philosophies

A different but no less important demand for concreteness animated "secular" philosophy, which was anti-speculative and anti-metaphysical in orientation, and thus anti-Hegelian and often anti-Marxist. All of the "new lands that emerged in the philosophical explosion between 1945 and 1950" (existentialism, Marxism and neo-positivism),[10] had in common not only a pathos for the concrete, but also a recourse to the direct testimony of personal experience or to reason, conceived largely as a family of ideas and linguistic practices. An end was sought to that period in which, as Mussolini said to Emil Ludwig, the disposition of modern man to believe was quite unbelievable.

The so-called "Turin School," which gravitated around Nicola Abbagnano (and later his students Carlo Augusto Viano and Pietro Rossi), Ludovico Geymonat and Norberto Bobbio, appealed to an anti-rhetorical "commitment" which sought to introduce into philosophy the scientific criteria of logical rigor and empirical control that had already been adopted by the hard sciences or by those doing "fieldwork." The Turin School tried, as has already been noted, to "take account of history in view of the truth,"[11] or rather to take events and deeds into consideration without transforming what has happened into a criterion of judgment. This was true in particular

---

10 Norberto Bobbio, *Profilo ideologico del Novecento italiano* (Turin: Einaudi, 1986), p. 166.
11 Luca Bagetto, *Il pensiero della possibilità. La filosofia torinese come storia della filosofia* (Turin: Paravia, 1995), p. 9. See also Santucci, "Esistenzialismo e filosofia italiana"; and Mirella Pasini and Daniele Rolando, eds., *Il neo-illuminismo italiano. Cronache di filosofia, 1953–1962* (Milan: Il Saggiatore, 1991).

of Ludovico Geymonat, who symbolically dated the conclusion of his *Studi per un nuovo razionalismo* (*Studies for a New Rationalism*) "April 25, 1945." In his philosophy, while referring to a reality describable by "finite" and "historically situated" man, Geymonat was unwilling to recognize problems that did not fall within the domain of rationality.[12] It is true, however, that as years passed, such positions tended more and more to privilege aspects of the historicity of reason or, in the analyses of philosophy of science, the primacy of praxis and "external history." They insisted on taking account of the conditions of scientific thought, as in the case of the development of artillery leading to the discovery of the mathematics of curves, or the importance of the technological experiments going on within the Arsenale of Venice for the theories of Galileo (the tutelary deity so often referred to in this period).

Nicola Abbagnano proposed instead a "positive existentialism" that was secular and immanentist, bound to the world of effective experience and diametrically opposed to both the Sartrean conscious oriented existentialism of *Being and Nothingness* and transcendent "Christian" existentialism. To this end, Abbagnano purified existentialism of its intimist aspects and, as an antidote, injected it with a massive dose of pragmatism. His was not, however, the pragmatism of William James – imported at the beginning of the century – but rather that of John Dewey, which had spread quickly in the pedagogical world, contributing to the education of elementary and middle-school teachers. The manifestos of this "positive existentialism" and the related "neo-enlightenment" were an essay published in 1948 called "Verso un nuovo illuminismo: John Dewey" (Toward a New Enlightenment: John Dewey) and another published in 1952, "L'Appello alla Ragione e le Tecniche della Ragione" (Appeal to Reason and the Techniques of Reason). For Abbagnano as well, science was the only vehicle of knowledge inasmuch as it must take into consideration the point of view of human subjectivity: "The world is a totality of which man is a part, and man has no other way to know the world but as part of it, and therefore he himself is subject to the conditions which observation brings to light. But this situation implicates the action of man as an observing system over an observed

---

12 See Ludovico Geymonat, *Saggi di filosofia neorazionalista* (Turin: Einaudi, 1953), p. 25. On scientific culture and the philosophy of science after the war, see C. Pogliano, "Le culture scientifiche e tecnologiche" in *Storia dell'Italia repubblicana*, vol. II, tome 2: *La trasformazione dell'Italia. Sviluppo e squilibri* (Turin: Einaudi, 1995), pp. 555–634.

system and hence the principle of indetermination. This principle demonstrates that science has arrived at its root position: the self-insertion of man into the world as part of the world."[13] This conception was shared only in part by Francesco Barone, who – identifying the rhetoric of anti-rhetoric in the exaltation of rationality and empirics – was against neo-positivism because of its "uncontaminated faith in the capability of science to absorb into itself the totality of significant problems." In this way, neo-positivism "cripples the organism of culture and withers the understanding of many cultural manifestations that are not reducible to science. And while it aspires to the advent of a luminous age from which the phantoms of tradition will have disappeared, neo-positivism seems rather a prelude to the advent of a sort of barbaric anti-humanism."[14] Overall, this anti-metaphysical enlightenment even entered the realm of the already disparaged social sciences and led to the foundation – by Abbagnano and Franco Ferrarotti – of the review *Quaderni di Sociologia* (*Review of Sociology*) and to the establishment, in 1953, of the Centro di Studi Metodologici (Center for Methodological Studies) in Turin, which brought together philosophers and scientists alike.

What linked the Turin School to Giulio Preti – who unfortunately remained a marginal and eccentric figure, first teaching at the University of Pavia and then at the Teachers' College of Florence – was "the need to find levels of discourse and more inter-subjective methods in order to make philosophy an honest profession and not just a way of yelling out one's own passions, or worse, releasing a type of personal *libido loquendi*."[15] In *Praxis e Empirismo* (*Praxis and Empiricism*), he saw the "philosophy of praxis" as another soberly anti-rhetorical form of concreteness and a means of effective intervention in the world: "a concept according to which the act of *interpretation* is already one of *modification* and modification itself is the only valid and guaranteed interpretation." With regard to the eleventh of Marx's *Theses on Feuerbach*, Preti essentially stated not only that one cannot be limited to interpreting the world without transforming it, but also

---

13   Nicola Abbagnano, "Sul problema filosofico della scienza" in Nicola Abbagnano, ed. *Fondamenti logici della scienza* (Turin: Silva, 1947), pp. 153–54.
14   Francesco Barone, *Il Neopositivismo logico* (Turin: Edizioni di "Filosofia", 1953), p. 400.
15   Giulio Preti, "Il mio punto di vista empiristico" [1958], in *Saggi filosofici* (Florence: La Nuova Italia,1976), vol. I, p. 476. See Preti's most important work, *Praxis ed empirismo* (Turin: Einaudi, 1957).

– and of equal importance – that the world cannot be transformed without interpreting it adequately. Although not explicit, the political message is relatively clear: one must renounce preconceived ideologies and forms of blind activism and open one's eyes to the complexity of the real. Only by rectifying one's errors over and over, by "trying and trying again," can one hope, in ethics as well as politics, to strengthen the democratic mentality. Preti linked his thought to "the restoration of democracy, i.e., a society in which man finally takes his own destiny in hand and shows a predilection for scientific culture over humanistic culture. The fundamental ethical idea of such a society is the social contract, whereby all values, not just political ones, are based on agreement. Culture must be public to the greatest possible extent and must entrust the victory of its values not to violence but to rational persuasion."[16]

Even before Preti (and, more recently, Jürgen Habermas), analogous concerns – albeit of entirely different provenance – were expressed by Guido Calogero, who made rational persuasion and the dialogic model the hinge of his philosophy: "There is something undebatable at the basis of every one of our discussions and that is – for each of us – our own will to debate."[17] He who participates in dialogue always presupposes something: "which is, of course, his constant will to understand. Everything else can be put in doubt by his interlocutor, and he is obliged to examine the reasons given: but this disposition toward understanding, this *principle of colloquium,* can be put in doubt by no one, unless he renounces it himself." The *logos* – the principle of non-contradiction – is "a specification of the ethical imperative and not the other way around, i.e., the ethical imperative is not a specification of the principle of non-contradiction. Logic does not create morality, but morality logic." Proof of this lies in the fact that "the 'principle of dialogue' appears more cogent than the 'principle of *logos.*' Moreover, if non-contradiction is an imperative that must be obeyed in order to be

---

16 Norberto Bobbio, "L'impegno dell'intellettuale ieri e oggi," *Rivista di filosofia,* LXXXVII (1997), n. 1, p. 18.

17 Guido Calogero, *Logo e dialogo. Saggio sullo spirito critico e la libertà di coscienza* (Milan: Edizioni di Comunità, 1950), pp. 41, 47, 48. Calogero was a leading voice of "Giustizia e libertà" and the Partito d'Azione: the principle of dialogue extends even to the political sphere, in which one need not be ashamed of seeking a "just politics" but rather a "naive politics": "The politician must be (as the Gospel says of an apostle) simple like a dove and shrewd like a snake: simple in his faith in his own ethical finality, and shrewd and well versed in using the means which, on a case-by-case basis, seem most suitable to reach it"; Guido Calogero, *Etica, giuridica, politica* (Turin: Einaudi, 1946), p. 322.

understood by others and not to fool them, does it not also belong to the sphere of dialogue?"[18]

The Anti-Modernists

Although it was less visible than Marxist or secular historiography, philosophy which took Catholicism as its point of reference was by no means inert, nor could it be reduced to the mere propaganda of faith. Alongside the Università Cattolica – where the rigid and cantankerous neo-Thomist Father Gemelli held court – were now new research institutes that spread Christian thought. Foremost among these was the Centro di Studi Filosofici (Center for Philosophical Studies) in Gallarate, founded in 1945, where Jesuits hosted debates and prepared the monumental *Enciclopedia Filosofica*, published in 1957.

In the variegated universe of philosophers associated with spiritualism and "personalism" (from Michele Federico Sciacca to Carmelo Ottaviano and from Luigi Stefanini to Armando Rigobello), the combative figure of Augusto del Noce stands out for his radicalism and diversity. While Marxist and secular thought were marked by a pathos for "progress" and "reason," this militant theoretician and protagonist of the Catholic revival never lacked the energy to fight against the former, considering them to be dangerous idols capable of intimidating and paralyzing a philosophy no longer Christian in nature. By obstinately rejecting "modernity" and "immanentism," Del Noce defended Catholic traditionalism from positions that appeared to be openly obscurantist and apologist. He sought, in fact, to extirpate rationalism by identifying its deepest and most tenacious roots in Descartes and by claiming that Marxism was a mere development of Cartesianism, driven to its ultimate consequences. By attributing to man the autonomous capacity to guide himself and to create his own history without the intervention of Divine Providence or reference to external authority, Cartesian rationalism had involuntarily contributed to the rise of

---

18 See A. Bausola and G. Penati, "Neoscolastica" in Paolo Rossi, ed., *La filosofia*, vol. IV: *Stili e modelli teorici del Novecento* (Turin: UTET, 1995), pp. 281–311.

modern atheism.[19] Marxist revolutionary doctrine – simplified Hegelianism made coherent for the masses – certainly expressed "a faith and a hope" which were apparently detached from immanentistic materialism, but this was only because Marxist doctrine "is not a part of theoretical philosophy, but *coincides with morality.*"[20] A similar immanentistic stance, transformed into a praxis lacking reference points beyond the absolute and transcendent events themselves, marked the triumph of "secularization" which leads to nihilism.[21] In response to this rationalistic and nihilistic trajectory, which denied the presence of sin in man, Del Noce countered with that of Pascal and the Catholic Reformation, declaring a return to the Christian values (absolutely transcendent, reassuring and positive) of truth and moral norms: "One must refer to the presence in the human spirit of the idea of perfection as a principle of the hierarchical order of the real and of that which, in terms that today risk being entirely misunderstood, used to be called eternal, universal, necessary and meta-historical truths. These truths allow man to live out eternity in time and as eternal they can be transmitted (the word "tradition" derives from the Latin *tradere*, to transmit or hand down) from generation to generation (or, better, that which is transmitted is the perceptible sign that serves to recall these truths)."[22]

---

19 The Prometheanism of modern man is exalted above all through the idea of "Revolution [which] is the opposite of the idea of Providence. In Revolution, it is believed that man can redeem himself through a process of liberation"; Augusto Del Noce, preface to Marcello Veneziani, *Processo all'Occidente* (Milan: SugarCo, 1990), p. 12.
20 Augusto Del Noce, *Il problema dell'ateismo* (Bologna: Il Mulino, 1964), pp. cix, cxxiii.
21 See Augusto Del Noce, *Riforma cattolica e filosofia moderna*, vol. I: *Cartesio* (Bologna: Il Mulino, 1966).
22 *Idem*, "Tramonto o eclissi dei valori tradizionali?" in Ugo Spirito and Augusto Del Noce, *Tramonto o eclissi dei valori tradizionali?* (Milan: Rusconi, 1971), p. 149. On Del Noce, see Francesco Barone, ed., *Augusto Del Noce. Il problema della modernità* (Rome: Edizioni Studium, 1995); and Vittorio Possenti, *Cattolicesimo & Modernità. Balbo, Del Noce, Rodano* (Milan: Ares, 1995), pp. 25–116.

CHAPTER 5
Home and Society

From the Ethics of Production to the Ethics of Consumption

At the beginning of the 1950s, Italian society was by no means rich. The average family income was modest: a thirteenth, an eighth and a fifth that of American, English and German families respectively. As is typical of a predominantly agricultural country, consumption was quite modest. The working class earned meager salaries; the middle-class maintained external decorum through hidden sacrifice; and the well off were not ostentatious with their wealth. Wanting too much from life was still considered a flaw, a sin, or hubris for which many people secretly feared divine punishment or a reversal of fortune. Parsimony, saving and an overall modest standard of living – even among the rich – created a system of virtues that were fully integrated with the work ethic. This moral architecture would soon fall to pieces and nearly vanish.

Jobs were precious and few. In 1951, there were 2,500,000 unemployed and approximately 1,000,000 manual laborers who worked only irregularly. The climate was one of economic stagnation, from which the government was nervously trying to extricate itself and for which the "Piano di Lavoro" (Work Plan) launched by Giuseppe Di Vittorio in 1949, proposed remedies modeled on Roosevelt's New Deal. All classes of Italian society unanimously shared the ideal of work as an absolute value. This sentiment was almost instinctual for those who had always been accustomed to "toiling" in the fields. It was recognized by the Church of Pope Pius XII, who added to the *Rerum Novarum* an expression of the Church's hostility toward the first symptoms of consumerism (for the time being only "imaginary," fueled by the "American dream," but already condemnable for revealing that the individual was incapable of controlling his needs and desires on both individual and societal levels, thus wasting resources that could be more usefully distributed among the poor). This ideal of work would strongly affect John Paul II, the first pope who had personally experienced workers' conditions and who, in the encyclical *Laborem Exercens*, would attribute to labor a greater function than to capital.

It was, however, in the traditions of the political left and the organized labor movement that the centrality of labor was upheld, especially during the phase of reconstruction. From being a biblical form of punishment or a Calvinist sign of salvation, labor would come to represent – in the long-term – a vessel of dignity and the "self-sufficiency of man"; it was the means by which a future classless society would emerge. Labor was the basis of legitimization, freedom and pride for the working class, and it was labor that distinguished the working class man from his exploiters, the supervisors and absentee owners. Labor's prestige explained the pathos for reconstruction and productivity, the latter an objective which would become unpopular and all but forgotten in the early 1960s, when the ethics of consumption would surpass that of production and irremediable frontal antagonism would become the norm between workers and "owners" in the factories. Even the first article of the Italian constitution would become unintelligible: in a linguistic compromise, so as not to speak of Italy as a "republic of laborers," Italy was defined as "a republic founded on labor," thereby linking citizenship to labor. In the meantime, there was a constant growth of dependent labor (which, paradoxically, would free people from earlier forms of subordination inherent in the conditions of farmers and women, and which would allow for the creation of new rights), and in the early 1980s the predominance of large factories and their concentration in the northern "industrial triangle" would come to an end.[1] In the golden years of the 1980s, the working class, which had grown markedly after the

---

[1] See Aris Accornero, *Il lavoro come ideologia* (Bologna: Il Mulino, 1980); Carlo Carboni, *Lavoro e culture del lavoro* (Roma-Bari: Laterza, 1991); and Jean-Louis Laville, "La crise de la condition salariale: emploi, activité et nouvelle question sociale" in Pierre Boissard, ed., *Le travail, quel avenir?* (Paris: Gallimard, 1997). On the history of Italian unions and ethical power, see Emilio Lussu, "I sindacati" in Achille Battaglia, ed., *Dieci anni dopo 1945–1955* (Bari: Laterza, 1955), pp. 459–514; Sergio Turone, *Storia del sindacato in Italia 1943–1969* (Bari: Laterza, 1973); and Walter Tobagi, "Il sindacato nella ricostruzione 1949–1950," *Il Mulino*, 236 (1974), pp. 944ff.; and Alberto Preti, ed., *Italia 1943–1950. La ricostruzione* (Bari: Laterza, 1974), pp. 330ff.

war, would begin to diminish both in number and in political clout. In fact, the accelerated technological development of those years eliminated more jobs than it created, producing massive unemployment that – at least according to some interpretations of the phenomenon – risked being not merely cyclical but structural. For every vision of technological utopia there is the opposing hypothesis that in the near future the progressive substitution of human labor with machines will leave only those jobs where human intervention is indispensable, creating a new worldly elite that acts as an "analyst of symbols" in the sectors of information and innovation, leaving behind a growing number of poor and desperate, many of whom will devote themselves to crime.[2] Although work has remained the most binding social relationship, it has become more "fluid" and perhaps more interesting, but also harder to find and less "supervised." In any case, even in Italy, with the extension of the years of education and the parallel earlier retirement age, there was, starting in the 1970s, an enormous increase in the amount of free or "freed up" time.[3] Few, however, were able to manage and use it well: it was considered, for the most part, either a radical alternative to time spent at work or an ephemeral entity known as time "to kill." Moreover, owing to the weakening of social integration that previously took place at work, the mentality of "fun" often prevailed: the decision to forget every worry and think of nothing but the pleasures of the senses, of wasting one's life away. Although students and workers mobilized for two decades, from 1965 to 1985, there was a general decrease – imperceptible yet continuous – in the determination to invest time and energy in the future, especially when it required excessive sacrifice. The interest and pleasure in planning and fulfilling long-term collective projects had weakened. Thus, the hori-

---

2 See Jeremy Rifkin, *The End of Work: the decline of the global labor force and the dawn of the post-market era* (New York: G. P. Puntam's Sons, 1995). See also Claus Offe and Rolf Heinze, *Beyond Employment* (Philadelphia: Temple University Press, 1992); Peter Drucker, *Post-Capitalist Society* (New York: HarperBusiness, 1993); Martin Kenney and Richard Florida, *Beyond Mass Production: The Japanese System and Its Transfer to the US* (New York: Oxford University Press, 1993); Bennett Harrison, *Lean and Mean: The Changing Landscape of Corporate Power in the Age of Flexibility* (New York: Basic Books, 1994). For some contributions by Italian scholars regarding changes in the structure of production, see Marco Revelli's, *Le due destre* (Turin: Bollati Boringhieri, 1996) and *La sinistra sociale. Oltre la civiltà del lavoro* (Turin: Bollati Boringhieri, 1997); and Aldo Bonomi, *Il capitalismo molecolare. La società al lavoro nel Nord Italia* (Turin: Einaudi, 1997).

3 Helga Nowotny, *Tempo privato. Origine e struttura del concetto di tempo* (Bologna: Il Mulino, 1993), pp. 107–8; Accornero, *Era il secolo del Lavoro*, pp. 160–71. On the history of free time from work, see Witold Rybczynski, *Waiting for the Weekend* (New York: Penguin, 1992).

zons of expectation were lowered as the demands of daily life grew, and any sweeping epochal changes now involved fewer numbers of people and were reduced to attenuated echoes of news stories. The ethical party (even in its lesser components) suffered, since it was accustomed to demanding the sacrifice of the present in favor of either a distant future or – for Catholics – eternal life. Politics as a whole will probably suffer even more from this situation in the near future. If and when high levels of permanent unemployment make the free time of those waiting for work seem nothing less than pitiful, politics (understood in the noble sense of the "good life") will become more and more an activity geared toward the self-centered satisfaction of individuals or groups.

With the advent of the so-called "economic miracle" of the 1960s, even Italy saw the birth of a paradoxical "individualism of the masses" among those citizens who belonged to the "Church-party" or "Party-church." Work, which had lost its noble halo of sobering daily heroism, tended to be seen as an unpleasant necessity. This change in perspective took place when for the first time – at the beginning of the 1960s – virtual complete employment was achieved, with unemployment reduced to 3% (causing a sudden rise in salaries and, counterintuitive as it may appear, an intensification of the workers' struggles).

The entry into the world of consumption – aided by an increase in free time or, put differently, time in which to spend money – was inscribed within a process that developed, albeit with notable confusion, on a global scale and is referred to as a "golden age." It is a phase in which humanity, by achieving the maximum affluence known to man (however unequally distributed), turned a decisive corner. The period that spans from 1947 to 1973 (though in Italy the process got underway somewhat later) demarcates "an unprecedented and perhaps anomalous epoch," owing to an event so great in magnitude that it risks passing unobserved: "The third quarter of the century marked the end of seven or eight millennia of human history that began in the Stone Age with the invention of agriculture, if for no other reason than because the end has come of a long age in which the great majority of the human species lived by cultivating the fields and raising animals."[4] Even though half the population of the world continues to be occupied with these activities, technological innovations (from the first

---

4 Eric Hobsbawm, *Il secolo breve. 1914-1991: l'era dei grandi cataclismi*, pp. 20-21.

metal animal-drawn plow in 1837 and the prototypes of gas tractors in 1892 through the robotization and current biotechnologies employed in farming) assure that the number of farmers is destined to fall drastically, with perhaps the consequent effect of engendering unemployment of global proportions.

Comparatively, however, the amelioration of the conditions of existence that has taken place in this "golden age" is astonishing. This change is reflected in the following account, by a man who has led a long life, accustomed from infancy to the most bitter sacrifices: "I have seen three generations grow up with my own eyes: my own, that of my children and that of my grandchildren. And now I am about to see that of my great-grandchildren. As I watch them, I think to myself: the decades of struggle were not in vain. Today we are much better off than in my time. Yes, life is infinitely less hard today. There is no comparison with the world in which my father and grandfather were born."[5]

The Transformation of the Domestic World

With the elections of 1946, women entered the official sphere of politics in Italy for the first time. The war had given them strength by forcing them to leave the home, look for work and make decisions on their own, "without the help or supervision of fathers, husbands, or boyfriends." In the face of "danger and poverty," they had become their own masters, creating "individual paths" in life and expanding the scope of their responsibilities.[6] The progressive feminization of labor gave many women greater access to information and culture outside the home (the number of female high school and college graduates increased rapidly), and family roles and relationships were incessantly "renegotiated" – although not without tension and conflict. With the end of the period of the "nationalization of women," in which "the perfect fascist woman was a hybrid who served all the needs of the family and at the same time bore the weight of the state's interest,"[7] and

---

5   The 1971 interview with Pietro Nenni appears in Orianna Fallaci, *Intervista con la storia* (Milan: Rizzoli, 1975), p. 247.
6   Miriam Mafai, *Pane nero. Donne e vita quotidiana nella seconda guerra mondiale* (Milan: Mondadori, 1987), p. 4. See also her *L'apprendistato della politica. Le donne italiane nel dopoguerra* (Rome: Editori Riuniti, 1979). By the end of the 1950s, "civil society was emancipated decisively from ecclesiastic society"; see Zizola, "Il modello cattolico in Italia" in *La vita privata. Il novecento*, p. 305.
7   Victoria De Grazia, *Le donne nel regime fascista* (Venice: Marsilio, 1993), p. 113.

with the waning of the traditional authority of the husband/father, the political regime and declining patriarchal power left more and more room for consensual behavior. The union model of "articulated" or local bargaining penetrated families to an even greater extent (again not without conflict), and altered the agenda of services and the catalogue of rights and duties of each and every person.

Parallel to the changes in people, there was a change – in both material and affective terms – in domestic space, or in other words, in the "hearth" of intimacy. A process that had been in transition for centuries was intensified: instead of the "home in its entirety" (a place that also existed for the production of garments, storage, processing of foodstuffs and breeding of farm animals),[8] the home was now conceived of as a circumscribed environment of services and consumption. In particular, the quality of domestic life changed. In the immediate post-war period there were few conveniences: "only 76% of homes were outfitted with a stove, 52% with running water, 27% with a toilet, and 7% with a telephone."[9] As late as 1957, only 1% of Italians had a washing machine and 2% a refrigerator.[10] Despite the fact that the overall number of houses built or rebuilt was not very high at first, new housing was being constructed even "in the sprawling tenements of the city outskirts." While the urban landscape became dotted with gas stations full of knick-knacks and bars illuminated by signs of the major franchises like Motta and Alemagna, the countryside was being inundated with roadside rest-stops full of "arrows, signs, colorful underpasses and doors that open only in one direction," leading the unwary customer into a labyrinth of useless gift items like "stuffed animals, many of which are bigger than the 1100cc-engine cars that will have to accommodate them."[11] In the meantime, apartment-dwellers were exchanging their rustic "old tubs and wooden furniture for living/dining room sets made in the Anglo-Saxon style, exemplified by the noble polyurethane armchair; the dinette kitchen was replaced by a functional, compact space…; the bathroom was equipped with a mirror and tiles and the old uncomfortable toilets in the

---

8 *Das ganze Haus*, as understood by Otto Brunner in "Das 'ganze Haus und die alteuropäische 'Oekonomik,'" in *Neue Wege der Verfassungs- und Sozialgeschichte* (Göttingen: Vandenhoeck u. Ruprecht, 1968), pp. 103–27.
9 Lanaro, *Storia dell'Italia repubblicana*, p. 166.
10 See Leslie Caldwell, "The Family in the Fifties" in *Italy in the Cold War*, p. 157.
11 Alberto Arbasino, *Fratelli d'Italia* (Milan: Adelphi, 1993), p. 1031.

external corridor became a curiosity."[12] The advantage of having hot and cold water, a toilet and a bathtub in the home changed the way of life of millions and represented a marked leap in civilization. Using images that would have been incomprehensible just a few decades earlier, Emilio Villa presented a cross-section of daily life that exposed the insides of the new habitations, giving voice to the multiplicity of existences that were enclosed within one confined space yet unaware of each other:

> on the fifth floor the water showers palpitate
> against the tiles the porcelain steering handle
> under the apricot thigh the pipes bud and the board beats
> on the sixth floor the electric light simmers across from Sacred
> Heart in the niches and scrapes the radio crackles "springtime
> in every heart" in the gaudy darkness and the salt cod
> are not left soaking for centuries upon centuries
> *mens optuma quaeque mens optuma*
> [the best mind is whatever the best mind is].[13]

Dinner-table conversation, the last remnant of a rich oral tradition and culture, was for the time being the only remaining privileged and undisturbed zone of communication and mutual exchange of experiences, which took place when the parents returned home from work and the children from school.[14] This exchange has gradually been limited or replaced, first to a lesser extent by the radio and then overwhelmingly by television, whose characters have literally become more "familiar" – by virtue of their celeb-

---

12 Lanaro, *Storia dell'Italia repubblicana*, p. 228. On the transformations of daily life, see Chiara Saraceno, "La famiglia: i paradossi della costruzione del private" in *La vita privata nel Novecento*, p. 39: "In just under twenty years, women over seventy, who once had to look for their children's milk on the black market, now consume meat every day," as they enjoy "their refrigerators, cars and summer vacations." Even the relationship to culture changed, with literature and encyclopedias becoming musts for the upper middle class; see Gabriella Turnaturi, *Gente perbene. Cent'anni di buone maniere* (Milan: SugarCo, 1988), p. 207.

13 Emlio Villa, "Diciassette variazioni su temi proposti per una pura ideologia della fonetica" in *Opere poetiche*, ed. Aldo Tagliaferri (Milan: Coliseum, 1989).

14 On changes in dinner conversation, see Angela Keppler, *Tischgespräche. Über Formen kommunikativer Vergemeinschftung am Beispiel der Konversationen in Familien* (Frankfurt am Main: Suhrkamp, 1994).

rity – than acquaintances or neighbors.[15] At the first signs of such numbing intrusion, Guido Gonella, a Christian preoccupied with the growing number of factors splitting apart the family nucleus, sounded the initial call of alarm in 1946: "An invisible and silent atomic bomb has ruptured the family unit. In fact, the family, if it is not completely broken apart, is only able to gather round the radio – a deafening and overwhelming window onto the world – rather than around the domestic hearth."[16]

Television, by adding image to sound and requiring that attention be directed toward its screen, has taken on an even more important role in the molding of mentality and habits of life. Introduced in Italy in January, 1954, it immediately provoked conflicting reactions. Parishes and Catholic associations saw it as a threat to their role in the formation of young people, since television was an instrument much more powerful than their apparatus of cinema, puppet theaters, dramatic troupes, athletic organizations and newspapers. It was, however, Pope Pius XII who, after an initial reticence toward television, accepted the *fait accompli* and saw in it at least one advantage: compared with the corruption of the outside world and the often reprehensible moral character of the cinema, television did not induce "members of the family to leave home." Indeed, it provided (this being a period of rigid Christian Democratic monopoly) an "honest pastime, far from unhealthy company and places." But doubts remained: "how can one not be horrified by the thought that, through television, the poisonous air of materialism, hedonism and inanity, breathed all too often in cinema halls, is introduced within the very walls of the home?"[17] These fears were amplified in the outskirts of the major cities, with a sorrowful tone in some Catholic associations: "Yes, Mary is crying…at the sight of poor young people…as they precipitate into the frightening vortex of impure sins… Is it possible that hours and hours of time can be found to frequent cinema

---

15 On the use of the radio at home, which had begun to be more common in the 1930s, see A. Caracciolo, "Caratteristiche della vita privata nell'Italia contemporanea" in *La vita privata nel Novecento*, p. 11.

16 Guido Gonella, "La DC per la nuova Costituzione" in *I congressi nazionali della Democrazia Cristiana* (Rome: Tip A. G. I., 1959), p. 43.

17 See "Esortazione di S. S. Pio XII all'Episcopato dell'Italia circa la televisione," *Civiltà cattolica*, January 1, 1954, pp. 129ff. See also Gundle, *L'americanizzazione del quotidiano. Televisione e consumismo nell'Italia degli anni Cinquanta*; Aldo Grasso, *Linea allo studio. Miti e riti della televisione italiana* (Milan: Bompiani, 1989); *idem*, *Storia della televisione italiana* (Milan: Garzanti, 1992); and Franco Monteleone, *Storia della radio e della televisione in Italia. Società, politica, strategie, programmi. 1922–1992* (Venice: Marsilio, 1992).

and watch television, most often contrary...to religion; or to participate in obscene and shameless dances, worthy of Satan or Hell, while it is impossible to find fifteen minutes to recite the Holy Rosary?"[18] In effect, the mass consumption of televised images at home, by showing other ways and lifestyles and culturally connecting Italy's diverse regions and dialects, has encouraged the luxurient growth of desire and illusion. Television has contributed to the erosion of local traditions and created a standard mentality and morality that hovers between the all but abandoned "roots" and an outside world yet to be mastered and understood.

Sexuality and Marriage

With the household increasingly open to the outside world, women's lives, despite a few hitches along the way, have changed a great deal in just a few decades, in terms of both lifestyle and – where contrast with the male universe is even more obvious – sexual emancipation.[19] The use of contraceptives, which separated pleasure from reproduction and reduced the fear of undesired pregnancy to a minimum, made women less vulnerable in the planning and management of their lives. The effects were felt in the realm of women's fidelity to traditional values and their privileged relationship to the Church. The progressive detachment of millions of women from the historical experience of previous generations and from the Catholic tradi-

---

18 "La Madonna, la grande speranza, Appello del Consiglio direttivo della Gioventù di Azione Cattolica di Vaduna, in provincia di Bolzano," in M. Barbanti, "Cultura cattolica, lotta anticomunista e moralità pubblica (1948–60)," *Rivista di storia contemporanea*, vol. 21, no. 1 (1992), p. 143.

19 See Lucetta Scaraffia, ed., *La famiglia italiana dall'Ottocento a oggi* (Bari: Laterza, 1988), pp. 383-416. It is also true that the allure of consumerism had already begun, however tentatively, during the 1930s with the so-called films of the "*telefoni bianchi*"; see Pietro Cavallo and Pasquale Iaccio, "Ceti emergenti e immagini della donna nella letteratura rosa degli anni trenta," *Storia contemporanea*, n. 6 (December 1984); and Giovanni de Luna, *Donne in oggetto. L'antifascismo nella società italiana 1922–1939* (Turin: Bollati Boringhieri, 1995), pp. 236–62. Not only were political films with scant public success broadcast, but films which – like Camerini's *Il Signor Max* – showed not only the aspirations of the petit-bourgeoisie of clerical workers and sales clerks to be socially mobile (and to frequent the Grand Hotel) but also the happy resignation to remain in one's own station in life; see Mino Argentieri, *L'occhio del regime. Informazione e propaganda nel cinema del fascismo* (Florence: Vallecchi, 1979); Jean A. Gili, *Stato fascista e cinematografia, repressione e promozione* (Rome: Bulzoni, 1981); Marcia Landy, *Fascism in Film: The Italian Commercial Cinema, 1931–1943* (Princeton: Princeton University Press, 1986); and James Hay, *Popular Film Culture in Fascist Italy: The Passing of the Rex* (Bloomington: Indiana University Press, 1987). At the same time, this shows the split desire – during the fascist period – both to break and to preserve the social hierarchy, to make overtures to individual happiness and to deny it.

tion (due to the growing disparity between actual behavior and "spoken" values which continued to be professed) has been one of the most visible fracture lines in the first fifty years of the Italian Republic. The ideal of purity, upheld even in the picture stories that were so popular from 1946 to 1960, was becoming less and less attractive.[20] Once the ideal of "romantic" love was exhausted and the Fascist call to propagate the race was no longer heeded, the very texture of emotional relationships was modified. These bonds, now dependent to a greater extent upon the will of individuals, became unstable and were exposed to constant renegotiation.

As the ethic which legitimized sexuality only in the context of matrimony receded, there appeared – in some areas and in some of the more "evolved" social classes – that which has been called "flexible sexuality": "eccentric, liberated from all chains of reproduction" and malleable "like a facet of the personality and therefore intrinsically linked to the ego." There was thus a speedy introduction of "democratization of interpersonal relations on a vast scale" in the sphere of intimacy and the home. Like that which had taken place in the political world,[21] this democratization provoked contentious quandaries among spouses and couples living together, and it increased the expectations (and frustrations) of everyone. The very institution of marriage was plunged into crisis, with an increasing number of "common-law marriages" and marriages "rebuilt" after divorce increasing, along with the number of children born out of wedlock. In the meantime, the extended family, in which grandparents and other relatives lived together with parents and children, began to diminish, and, up to 1965, the number of children per couple rose. The year 1965 – when the term "flexible sexuality" was coined – also marked the end of the baby boom, and starting in 1987 the mortality rate exceeded the birthrate for the first time in centuries. Sur-

---

20   In 1946 and 1947 the publications *Grand Hotel* and *Bolero Film* began to be published and would immediately sell millions of copies. The first weekly comic books for adults, they featured the recurrent theme of married women who triumph over less virtuous ladies who use sex as a weapon of seduction; see Angelo Ventrone, "Tra propaganda e passione: «Grand Hotel» e l'Italia degli anni cinquanta," pp. 615–16. See also Anna Bravo, *Il fotoromanzo* (Bologna: Il Mulino, 2003).

21   Anthony Giddens, *The Transformation of Intimacy: Sexuality, Love and Eroticism in Modern Societies* (Stanford: Stanford University Press, 1995). This "flexible sexuality" seemed to be run up against the rigidity of the rules of married life that had been imposed by the Church in the Middle Ages and which had remained largely effective to this day; see Marie Odile Métral, *Le mariage. Les hésitations de l'Occident* (Paris: Aubier Montaigne, 1977). On the need to re-negotiate the role of women, see Miriam M. Johnson, *Strong Mothers, Weak Wives: the Search for Gender Equality* (Berkeley: University of California Press, 1988).

prisingly, Italy has become one of the least prolific countries in the world, although the birthrate curve has decreased in all of Western Europe, where, for every 100 young people counted in the census of 1988, there will be 63 young people in 2010.[22]

Relatively rapidly in comparison with the past, many women moved from the bigotry and sham respectability of the 1940s and 50s toward the permissiveness of the 1960s; they went from the referenda on divorce and abortion of the 1970s to the growth of the feminist movements of the successive period. They claimed that they did not to want to differ from what was "normal" but rather to discover normality within difference.[23] These movements managed to bring forth acceptance or create tolerance for sexual practices that had been carefully hidden and harshly condemned as perverse and immoral, especially male and female homosexuality. The results of the two referenda (on divorce, May 12, 1975 and on abortion, May 17, 1980), were very surprising. The first had a substantial majority (59.3%) of those in favor of the introduction of this institution in the legal order, while the second was approved with an even higher consensus (67.9%). In the same year, 1975, a reassessment of the rights of the family was introduced, along with the principle of equal rights for married couples and the consequent rejection of the undisputed power of the husband and of disparity in treatment in cases of adultery (Article 29 established that marriage rests "on the moral and legal equality" of both partners). At the same time, patriarchal power was transformed into authority exercised by both parents and the articles regarding abortion, which were leftovers from the fascist legal codes, were abolished.

---

22 For demographic data, see Marzio Barbagli, *Provando e riprovando* (Bologna: Il Mulino, 1990), pp. 9ff; idem, *Sotto lo stesso tetto. Mutamenti della famiglia italiana dal XV al XX secolo* (Bologna: Il Mulino, 1984); Marzio Barbagli and David I. Kertzer, eds., *Storia della famiglia italiana 1750–1950* (Bologna: Il Mulino, 1992); and E. Sonnino, "La popolazione italiana dall'espansione al contenimento," in *Storia dell'Italia repubblicana* (Turin: Einaudi, 1995), vol. II, pp. 532–75.

23 See Anna Rossi-Doria, "Conservazione e rottura nel movimento delle donne," *Ombre rosse*, 25 (1978), pp. 12-16. Feminism began to make inroads in the field of philosophy as early as the 1970s with Carla Lonzi's *Sputiamo su Hegel* and *Sputiamo su Freud*. But it with the works of Luisa Muraro, Adriana Cavarero, and Rosy Braidotti that a contribution was made to the rediscovery of the body and the nomadic character of feminine subjectivity; see Adriana Cavarero, *Nonostante Platone* (Rome: Editori Riuniti, 1990) and eadem. *Corpo in figure. Filosofia e politica della corporeità* (Milan: Feltrinelli, 1995); Rosi Braidotti, *Dissonanze* (Milan: La Tartaruga, 1994) and eadem. *Soggetto nomade. Femminismo e crisi della modernità* (Rome: Donzelli, 1995)

Looking back, it is easy to measure the enormous distance between this phase and the 1950s, when Catholics, predicting the dangers of emancipation, sought by every means possible to bring women back to the sacred sphere of the family and good manners. If women were led astray by the modern theories spread in Italy by the Communists, it was held that "they would then view the home as a place of slavery and deem the sacrifices imposed by family life almost as a restriction on the development of their own personality."[24] Thus, at the same time that women were encouraged to sublimate themselves in the name of "purity" – according to the assumption that "women are elevated by imitating Mary and they return to Eve if they stray from her" – even beauty contests were attacked as expressions of a sort of "paganism that returns to the cult of flesh and the passions."[25] From the 1970s onward, however, women who had long been denied power, history and culture demanded tangible recognition of their role and their rights from the male-dominated world.

Metamorphoses of Life

The legalization of abortion was followed, more recently and with more limited scope, by the introduction of biotechnologies, beginning with assisted procreation. These developments have radically changed convictions, habits and ideas that have been in existence for millennia. Nothing, for example, used to seem more certain than the fact that an individual comes into the world according to the old and well-tested method of natural sexual reproduction, with a body and a mind subject to congenital illness and deformity. Today, this is no longer the case. That which appeared to be linked to inflexible and unfathomable necessity was transformed into an object of choice, and from that moment on, the ethical and legal norms regulating the rights of individuals and families and the variety and intensity of certain passions were compromised. Even the structure of the world of the imaginary, previously conditioned by our biological limits and the

---

24 L. Gatti, "La giovane in famiglia e nel lavoro," *L'Assistente Ecclesiastico*, vol. 23, no. 4 (1953), quoted in Barbanti, *Cultura cattolica, lotta anticomunista e moralità pubblica (1948–60)*, p. 173.

25 See, respectively, R. Manzini, "Le smanie per la Miss," *Famiglia Cristiana*, October 15, 1950, quoted in M. Barbanti, "La «battaglia» per la moralità» tra Oriente, Occidente e italo-centrismo," in *Nemici per la pelle*, p.169; and Gundle, *Cultura di massa e modernizzazione*, p. 248. On the ideals advanced by *Famiglia cristiana*, see M. Marazziti, "Cultura di massa e valori cattolici: il modello di Famiglia cristiana" in *Pio XII* (Rome-Bari: Laterza, 1984), pp. 307–334.

complementary desire to elude them, were affected. Hence, our faith in the power and normative character of so-called divine or natural law begins to dwindle, and as a result, we have become inclined to treat culturally acquired sentiments, such as affective paternity or maternity, as more important than those determined by blood lineage.

When called upon to make decisions previously delegated to the large organisms that promulgate moral norms and orientations (whether church, state, or party), individuals are forced to take on new and weighty responsibilities. Indeed, they must face fundamental problems of "metaphysical" relevance – problems no less than those of life and death, abortion, euthanasia and, potentially, the modification of one's own genetic patrimony. Once these issues come into play, they unleash conflicts and fanaticisms that strike at the individual's conscience and put it on a collision course with other values. The believer, in order to defend his own reasons and dogma, faces the dilemma of either openly opposing the laws of his own country (considering them, in the name of the "sacredness of life," attacks on his creed) or repudiating the supremacy of his own faith.

The current conflicts in bio-ethics represent only one aspect of a much vaster question that secretly traversed the twentieth century in other guises. These conflicts came about at the end of the classical division, originating with Aristotle, between *oikos* and *polis*, the world of the home and the world of politics. In Western thought, the biological existence of the human being – pure "life" or *zoe* – has long been explicitly excluded from the dimension of the *polis*. Only the "good life," when organized within a community of equals (free, male, adult citizens), was capable of transforming the *zoe*, common to the other animals, into *bios*, a recognizable individuated existence. When *oikos* and *polis* were divided, it was forgotten that *zoe* itself (enclosed within the domestic sphere of subordinate relations of wife to husband, children to parents, servants to masters) constituted the tacit and unrevealed presupposition of politics. Without the reproduction of life and without caring for the place in which this reproduction occurs, there is no politics.

The discovery of the political nature of biological life began slowly in Europe at the end of the eighteenth century. It was only in our century (particularly through Nazi death camps and exponential population growth in very poor countries) that "bare life" – in tragic and macroscopic proportions

– became the stakes of politics, whether in the most brutal form of killing or in the less dramatic form of planned "control." In the first case, above all with regard to the concentration camps, "the space of bare life, originally situated at the margins of order, came progressively to coincide with political space, and exclusion and inclusion, external and internal, *bios* and *zoe*, rights and deeds, became irreducibly indistinct." In this context, sovereign power is not exercised by dominion over territory, but by dominion over the population. "Bio-politics" (theorized by Michel Foucault) implies a more efficient government of men through the violent and manipulative regulation of demographic factors, and, consequently, sexual practices, moving from the town square into the boudoir. Even modern democracy with its "mass hedonism" cannot escape the aporia of promoting gigantic processes of individualization and designating greater autonomy to individuals at the very moment of their inexorable subordination and integration within the social totality. Modern democracy wishes, indeed, to "play the game of freedom and happiness" under circumstances that only admit "enslavement." Unlike the era of the great totalitarianisms of the twentieth century, today the progressive reduction of the individual to "bare life" no longer requires blood and death, but only the "perfect senselessness" of the "society of spectacle."[26]

---

26 These subjects have been dealt with at length by Giorgio Agamben in *Homo sacer. Il potere sovrano e la nuda vita* (Turin: Einaudi, 1995) and *Mezzi senza fine* (Turin: Bollati Boringhieri, 1996). The quotes are drawn from *Homo sacer*, pp. 12–13.

CHAPTER 6
Youth and the Unreality Principle

1968

Young people have always been the turbulent link between the home and society, between the sphere they emerge from and the sphere they enter as autonomous persons. In twentieth-century Italy, their mobilization for varied causes, some more noble than others, was frequent. They demonstrated during fascism for colonial expansion and for war and during the first half of the 1950s for the Italian annexation of Trieste. In July 1960 they protested against the Tambroni government and subsequently called for greater internal democracy in the factories of the North. What was unique about the student movements of the second half of the 1960s, however, was that young people found themselves at the center of processes of transformation that involved and unsettled both the private and political spheres, that is, both the home and society.

A variant of a geographically broad phenomenon with a temporal bandwidth of three or four years in either direction depending on the country, "1968" exploded in Italy when students sought to impose anti-authoritarian values on institutions – values of insubordination in the face of all internal or international hierarchy and of renewal in political as well as interpersonal relationships. There was a rejection of both the government and opposition parties on the one hand and, on the other, of the "policemen of the world" – the United States and the Soviet Union – whose conflicts appeared against a background of fundamental complicity. The China of the Cultural Revolution, the Cuba of the Bay of Pigs and the American embargo, and the Vietnam of barefoot guerrillas who withstood deadly

American bombings all became icons and models, examples of innovation and courage to inspire Italy, glaring examples of the fact that revolution is indeed possible on a global scale. The winds of change agitated the stagnant surface of every sphere of existence and broke down the walls between daily and political life. Alongside the implicit renewal of the Sartrean project to keep the masses "in fusion" and at "white heat" for as long as possible, there was also a "private" battle against chains of command of every variety, against conformity, respectability and the "repressive tolerance" of families and institutions. With Marcuse's *Eros and Civilization* and *One Dimensional Man* as theoretical referents, even sexual freedom became a political demand.[1]

The Italian student rebellion, sincere yet confused, filled with humanitarian impulses and improvised rhetoric, and bent on creating an alternative society, emerged not only from the "psychic contagion" of analogous experiences abroad, but from the disappointment which followed the promises of general well-being prompted by the "economic miracle" of the 1960s. The failure of the Center-Left to shift the social relations of power and the unpreparedness and hesitation of the Italian Communist Party, which took the route of reform rather than that of a still unrealized "revolution," also contributed to the emergence of student rebellion. The historical parties of the Left thus provisionally lost their monopoly over mass mobilization and their control of wide-reaching collective action.

Although only three percent of Italians at that time shared the world and the values of 1968, the specific influence of university students on public opinion (parents included) was weighty and, for many, disquieting. Moderates were not the only ones panic-stricken by the student threat to meld their battles with those of the workers. To the students, on the other hand, the entire "capitalistic" social structure seemed responsible – concretely and universally – for oppression, violence and the iniquitous distribution of riches and knowledge. The perspective of the dominant groups in the student movement became global and it altered the previous mental geography, which was dominated, even on the Italian horizon, by the symmetrical confrontation between the two blocs. The movement of 1968 was,

---

1 Herbert Marcuse, *Eros e civiltà* (Turin: Einaudi, 1972); *idem*, *L'uomo a una dimensione* (Turin: Einaudi, 1967). In one year alone, the latter book sold 150,000 copies in Italy. See Robert Lumley, *States of Emergency: Cultures and Revolt in Italy from 1968 to 1978* (London-New York: Verso, 1990), p. 122.

therefore, the first "to treat the entire world as a single integrated system, as a homogenous space within which every place is interconnected in a systemic manner – that is, interdependently and in real time – with every other." The points of reference were the university campus, the factory, or "the mental hospital, prison, or even military barracks – harsh institutions transformed into places of communitarian radicalization."[2]

One of the ways in which insubordination against the existing state of things took expression was the all-out defense of egalitarianism in the form of an unconditional rejection of meritocracy. Theoretically, meritocracy seemed plausible only in the context of the unmentioned or forgotten social inequalities of the past, while it functioned in practice as a perverse and arbitrary instrument of discrimination. The perception of social injustice was thus polarized by social mechanisms of selection, of both integration and exclusion. Education became the central arena, and *Lettere a una professoressa* (Letters to a Professor) was a symptomatic and truly "epochal" expression of the issues for an entire generation. The letters appeared in 1967, written by students at the Barbiana School, and portrayed the influence of the pugnacious figure of Don Lorenzo Milani on the children, with his bitter denunciation of scholastic selection which penalized the socially and culturally underprivileged and resulted in an intolerable waste of intelligence and life. The "Savonarolian" tones in the exaltation of the common people and the idealization of the poor – with the parallel repudiation of modern liberal ideals, in particular that of merit as individual conquest – were a sign of a more general malaise.

Flowering everywhere in this period were fantastic expectations, abstract utopias and adolescent ideologies formed during tumultuous assemblies and "occupations." Thus emerged the affirmation of a type of "unreality principle" (or rather, a disconnection between indefinite aspirations and reality) – of desire programmatically unsatisfied with whatever goal was reached. A bubbling, imaginary history (in a creative sense as well) existed alongside and often surpassed "real history." This marked the end, however unwittingly for these young people, of the hegemony of historicism and of the desire to be anchored to a reality whose limits and possibilities needed to be carefully analyzed. In the profusion of political movements, there

---

2 Marco Revelli, "Movimenti sociali e spazio politico" in *Storia dell'Italia repubblicana*, vol. II, tome 2, pp. 393, 398.

also appeared, equally unwittingly, a sort of renewal, albeit in a different sphere, of the Gentilian political model according to which reality is constantly reformulated in the very "act" of proposing its modification. And while Pasolini maintained polemically that it is "better to be an enemy of the people than to be an enemy of reality,"[3] such animosity did not disturb the protagonists of the "movement," who, though they recognized its legitimate existence, were not interested in supporting a world drenched in injustice, violence and falsehood. The vaguest ideas were extrapolated from the sacred texts of revolutionary thinkers who acted in completely different historical and geographical contexts. Images in "real time," transmitted on television, prompted imitation through the contagion of rebellious behavior, creating a sort of *koinè*, a common world language that appeared preferable to hard meditated confrontation of unpleasant situations. The fact is that for many young people the "reality principle" had been dethroned and the line of demarcation with the "pleasure principle" or with the unending gamut of inviting possibilities had begun to shift. The political dramaturgy of the twentieth century, through its movie sets and the apparatus linking the manipulation of the masses to the discourse of charismatic leaders, had already artificially attenuated the difference between true and false, reason and myth. But in 1968, as in the crucial phases of all great collective movements *in statu nascendi*, myths and manners of interpreting the world arose "from the bottom," although in this case they were unable to crystallize properly or to find institutional outlets. With a certain hint of exaggeration that particular dates acquire under the magnifying glass, 1968 has been seen as the first historical event that could no longer be called "real," since it opened the door to the "collapse of any clear distinction between reality and fiction." Political conscience was no longer formed by collective ideas or representations, but by "simulacra, images and copies with no original."[4] Moreover, in the words of Che Guevara, who had a large following in Italy: "when you dream alone it is just a dream. When your dream is shared by many, it is the beginning of reality." The prevailing buzzwords of 1968 and the years immediately following ("put imagination in power," "contestation," "transgression," "dissident desire," "we want it all") revealed a spontaneous strategic line, which avoided any confrontation with the concrete

---

3 Pier Paolo Pasolini, *Lettere luterane* (Turin: Einaudi, 1976), p. 7.
4 Mario Perniola, *La società dei simulacri* (Bologna: Cappelli, 1983), pp. 8, 52.

or else altered the concrete to fit the prevalent expectations of the moment. The stubborn preservation of an unyielding attitude with regard to any "reasonable" compromise or "reformist" politics was, indeed, integral to the will not to attenuate the drive toward the reversal of the existing social relationships.[5]

Such expectations of imminent upheaval in the world, which brought on serious discussions that treated issues that individuals were totally ignorant about as if the answers were perfectly known to all (such as whether or not the workers in Nanking were "counter-revolutionaries" during the Great Cultural Revolution), were instigated and legitimized by what one might call the "David complex": that is to say, a faith in the possibility of beating the "system" in the same way that the small Vietnamese people were defeating the American Goliath. It was perhaps this hope for the inevitable victory of the small over the great, of the outskirts over the metropolis, which altered the perception of the forces in the field, generating gusts of mobilizing enthusiasm that could stand up to any challenge. Thus, despite the death of Che Guevara in Bolivia, it was still hoped by millions that "we shall overcome someday" and that the unstoppable fire of revolution would spread throughout the world. The dream fatherland of choice was now elsewhere, above all in China, as heard in the words sung by conscripts of those "formidable" years: "And if the fatherland calls/ let it call. / Beyond the Alps and the sea there is another fatherland."

In order to be adequately understood, the ideologies circulating in those years should not only be interpreted on the basis of objective and empirically verifiable historical conditions, but also according to Vico's standard of "poetic logic" – as systems of images, symbols and concepts generated by the creative imagination of myths that follow (or can follow) rules other than those of reason. An example was the impassioned, though inconclusive and exhausting, series of student meetings and debates, which revealed the students' attempts to stand in opposition to the outside world and their search for more ballast to add to the freely flowing speeches. Considering themselves "proletarianized," the students believed they had consolidated their alliance with the working class – mythically conceived of as the bearer of explosive alternative values, who at the moment had unfortunately been

---

5 On this period, see R. Rossanda, *L'anno degli studenti* (Bari: De Donato, 1968); and Peppino Ortoleva, *Saggio sui movimenti del 1968 in Europa e in America. Con una antologia di materiali e documenti* (Rome: Editori Riuniti, 1988).

betrayed by the parties of the Left and by the "classist" unions.

Even the most abstract utopias introduced enduring modifications in people's mentalities, sensibilities and customs, and helped new figures and leaders to emerge.[6] The verbal gymnastics of those who had formerly remained silent and suffered the existing order of things; the increased (albeit often partisan) critical spirit; the pure desire to combat injustice and inequality and deflate all authority; the habit of imagining the best and generously distributing one's energies to the underprivileged; the meeting of different worlds through visits to factories for early-morning distribution of flyers or debates conducted inside the factories – these were all positive experiences that have left their mark. After 1968, Italian society was no longer the same. The ideas of this period have not entirely evaporated, nor have they always been transformed into regret or a veteran's nostalgia for battle. With the state's evasion of responsibilities, and in a moment of danger for democracy, movements like the "Democratic Psychiatric Association" and the "Association of Democratic Magistrates" (the latter founded in 1964 as a wing of the National Association of Magistrates, from which it separated in 1969) sprouted from the soil of 1968 as new ways of connecting professional life and social commitment.

Normalized barbarism?

Since the beginning of time, the younger generations have been decried as being inevitably worse than their predecessors, as well as causing ruinous moral disorder. In Italy, this conviction became even more acute in 1968 and throughout the 1970s, when the barbarism of young people, evident in their very appearance, was forcefully denounced. Pier Paolo Pasolini described them as anthropological mutants: "Their physical look is almost terrorizing, and when it is not terrorizing it is irritatingly unhappy. Horrible facial hair, ridiculous hairstyles, pale skin and lifeless eyes: these are the masks of some type of barbaric – squalidly barbaric – initiation. Or else they are masks of diligent unconscious assimilation, for which one feels no pity." Unbridled consumerism and the blind permissiveness of parents and

---

6   On the rise of these movements, see Luigi Bobbio, *Lotta continua* (Rome: Savelli, 1979). Strangely, when compared with the old university associations in the 1950s and 1960s (such as the Italian Goliardic Union [UGI] and the Catholic group Intesa), the movements of 1968 did not produce any important political elites. Their exponents were mostly journalists and other professionals.

teachers had produced aphasic "monsters" and ferocious criminals: "Two boys from Ladispoli (an organized crime resort town) fatally shot another boy their age because he had refused to give them the sparkplugs from his motorbike, which they needed for their own. The newspaper *Paese Sera* entitled this article 'Absurdity in Ladispoli'. Absurd perhaps in 1965. Today it is the norm. The piece should have been called 'Normality in Ladispoli'."[7]

Further evidence of these changes – thought to be the normal pathology of everyday life – was offered by two acute observers, Piergiorgio Bellocchio and Edmondo Berselli, who wrote respectively on behavior (in 1985) and on language (in 1994). Bellocchio's emblematic episode takes place in an open-air pizzeria: "Close to the tables, there was a group of young thugs sitting on their motorbikes with their engines still running. Every ten or twenty seconds, they would rev the engines and let out a good bit of exhaust. The noise drowned out any conversation and you couldn't hear yourself talk. The air was becoming impossible to breathe. After a good quarter of an hour of this, I yelled, 'Are you leaving?' Two or three of them turned around and looked at me, amazed, as if they hadn't understood. 'Either leave,' I explained, 'or turn off the motors.' After a few minutes they got over their shock and decided to leave. 'What type of person is that?!' I could hear them mumble. 'What manners! What nerve!' But at the other tables, the reaction was of surprise and curiosity. No one had even noticed. No one had been disturbed."[8] Berselli, on the other hand, saw indications of change in the succession of crutch expressions in the speech patterns of young people. "From [the figure of speech] 'the degree to which' [*misura in cui*] – the greatest stylistic element of the late 1960s and the early 1970s, which established complex and binding relationships between different political-social phenomena – to the subsequent triumph of 'that is' [*cioè*]

---

7   Pier Paolo Pasolini, "I giovani infelici" in *Lettere luterane*, pp. 7–8, 94–5. At the beginning of the 1960s, by contrast, there seemed to be an inverse tendency, especially with regard to the students' participation in defending a democracy that had been threatened by Tambroni in July 1960: "The participation of the youth brought with it a release from the intergenerational polemics that had appeared during those years against the new American fashions of jeans, pinball and jukeboxes, which were considered to be agents of corruption and teen rebellion, modeled on "Teddy Boy" style. A cursory glance at the history of 1959–60 shows how there was a great fear of 'moral disorder' that had a strong continuity with previous years: Fellini's *La dolce vita*, Visconti's *Rocco e i suoi fratelli*, Pasolini's *Una vita violenta* – these works depicted the social transformation that Italy was living, which ran the risk of censorship; Rosario Mangiameli, "Gli anni del centrismo" in Piero Bevilacqua, ed., *Lezioni sull'Italia repubblicana* (Rome: Donzelli, 1994), p. 53.

8   P. Bellocchio, "Dalla parte del torto," *Diario*, 1 (1985), p. 15.

which stabilized an axiomatic equivalence between any two concepts (and therefore polarized the great equations of weak ideas: the truth, that is, the falsehood) – we arrive finally in the 1990s to the indiscriminate use of the formula 'in some way' [*in qualche modo*], which alludes to things obscure and indescribable, but nonetheless understandable and relevant – these expressions create friction within the processes of change."[9]

---

9 Edmondo Berselli, "La cultura informale" in Saverio Vertone and Mauro Barberis, eds., *La cultura degli italiani* (Bologna: Il Mulino, 1994), pp. 149–50. At an empirical level, it is not easy to identify the "value systems" of the youth, i.e., the influences on their lives, their principles and the attitudes that shape them. It seems that the family has become a focal point once again, even if in an opportunistic way. The protection afforded by the nuclear family represents a new value in situations characterized by widespread unemployment. As all of the important thresholds of their lives seem to be postponed, young people live longer and longer with their parents (in Italy this phenomenon is much more common that in the rest of Europe); see Alessandro Cavalli and Olivier Galland, eds., *L'allongement de la jeunesse en Europe* (Arles: Actes sud, 1993). The theory regarding Italian "amoral familism" shows its limits, however, when Italian adults are called upon to fulfill new roles; see A. de Lillo, "Orientamenti di valore e immagini della società," *Giovani anni 90*, and Edward Banfield, *The Moral Basis of a Backward Society* (New York: Free Press, 1958). In a poor neighborhood in Rome, the so-called "mothers of Primavalle" have fought criminal activity by organizing neighborhood patrols, while Sicilian shopkeepers in Capo d'Orlando have risked their lives by refusing to pay protection money to the Mafia; see Gabriella Turnaturi and Carlo Donolo, "Familismi morali" in Carlo Donolo and Franco Fichera, eds., *Le vie dell'innovazione* (Milan: Feltrinelli, 1988), pp. 164–85; Gabriella Turnaturi, *Associati per amore* (Milan: Feltrinelli, 1991). According to Pina, the wife of Libero Grassi, a shopkeeper killed in Palermo for refusing to pay protection money, it was no act of uncommon heroism, but simply a given that one would not bow to the racket; see Saverio Lodato, *Poteri. Sicilia, anni Novanta* (Milan: Garzanti, 1996), p. 41. For some modifications to, and criticisms of, the theory amoral familism, see Carlo Tullio-Altan, *La nostra Italia* (Milan: Feltrinelli, 1986), who extends the concept not only to all the regions of Italy, but also to more distant times; G. Gribaudi, "Familismo e famiglia a Napoli e nel Mezzogiorno," *Meridiana*, 17 (1993), pp. 13–41; and Paul Ginsborg, "Familismo" in Paul Ginsborg, ed., *Stato dell'Italia* (Milan: Il Saggiatore, 1994), pp. 78ff, who defines Italian familism as constituted by "family units that are strongly cohesive (centered around the mother, with notable intergenerational solidarities)," which is typical of "a society characterized, particularly in the South, more by vertical relationships than horizontal ones, and a firmly rooted distrust of central state power." But Loredana Sciolla correctly points out fact that the antithesis between Italians' familism and civic values is false: "familism, in fact, turns out to be compatible with modernization and Italians do not display any abnormal attachment to family with respect to the populations of other countries; if anything, they may even be less 'familist' than the Americans or the English, who are generally depicted as peoples with a rooted civic culture." The fact of the matter is that civic spirit in Italy is isolated, that is to say, "it is associated neither with interpersonal trust nor with a trust in institutions." Thus, Italians are not so much "amoral familists" or lacking in "civicness" as they are deluded and distrustful of institutions, at the same time that they are capable of high levels of solidarity (for example, in the voluntary sector or in organizations with a local emphasis); see Loredana Sciolla, *Italiani. Stereotipi di casa nostra* (Bologna: Il Mulino, 1997), pp. 48, 62–64. Finally, it is worth noting that the so-called familism had beneficial effects on the growth of small family businesses; see Arnaldo Bagnasco, *Tre Italie* (Bologna: Il Mulino, 1984) and C. Carboni, "La Terza Italia" in *Lezioni sull'Italia repubblicana*, pp. 161–74.

Terrorism and the Kidnapping of Aldo Moro

The growing expectations of 1968 were quickly followed by the "harsh lessons of history," which tended to be ignored, even by state institutions and the so-called "invisible powers," whose response was often violent. Thus, with Piazza Fontana, the season of carnage began.[10] The need to respond to the "strategy of tension," the lost hopes and the difficulties for young people of finding work suited to their aspirations all turned into bitter disappointment during the 1970s. In a climate poisoned by voices calling for an authoritarian coup d'état, the will to impose abstruse ideals of social justice or superman politics by force was seen as an act of heroism, a repudiation of tepidity, an extreme and courageous choice in favor of consistency and an unyielding decision to refuse to be satisfied with mere slogans in the quest for the most direct way to overturn the existing state of things. The streets and piazzas were transformed into scenes of urban guerrilla warfare and clashes took place not only with the police and Carabinieri, but also between Fascist "blacks" and Communist "reds," with beatings, gun wounds and killings. The idea that "a bourgeois state cannot be changed, but must be knocked down" emerged from a decision to break with the hesitations of "theoreticians" and from the "excessive obsession with discussion and theorizing everything," as Red Brigades member Alberto Franceschini put it (he, together with his comrades, wished to block the "historical compromise" promoted by Berlinguer, which would have meant "the definitive renunciation of revolution and the battle to seize power").[11] It was considered ethical to accept consciously and consistently the legal breach of the state of exception and the declaration of war on existing political structures. From 1970 to 1985 numerous armed formations battled in succession under diverse banners. The one with the greatest longevity was the Red Brigades, founded in 1970 in the name of a "workers' rebellion against owners and the owners' state." Importantly, the transition to the armed phase of struggle was tied – for many groups on the Left – to the progressive decline in social antagonism: the idea was to go against the current, to shock and to sound

---

10 See Nicola Magrone and Giulia Pavese, *Ti ricordi di Piazza fontana?* (Bari: Interno, 1986), 3 vols.; Giorgio Boatti, *Piazza Fontana. 12 dicembre 1969: il giorno dell'innocenza perduta* (Milan: Feltrinelli, 1993).

11 A. Franceschini, Pier Vittorio Buffa, Franco Giustolisi, *Mara, Renato, e io. Storia dei fondatori delle BR* (Milan: Mondadori, 1991), p. 79.

the alarm in order to reverse the decline of the workers' struggles (in the perspective of the terrorists on both Right and Left, little interest is shown for the student movements). As has been said, "the Red Brigades were born from hope. They felt themselves immersed in a workers' movement that was greater and more noble than they were, and they organized in order to express what they felt were inherent needs… They believed firmly that there already was radical class conflict in Italy and that all that was needed was to be a symbol of this conflict – in other words, to be its armed wing."[12] After an initial period in which the factory was considered the fulcrum of a distant social revolution, the members of the Brigades, seeing that they could not increase the number of supporters among the workers, chose instead to attack the "heart" of the "State of Multinationals." Mario Moretti would later observe: "When restructuring changed the factories right under our noses, the myth of the worker masses collapsed. I never believed, to note in passing, that the worker could be the engine of transformation. In any case, the motor of transformation could only be re-launched outside the factory and we have re-launched it."[13] Such "re-launching" was not intended to unleash an immediate civil war, but to prepare for one through "armed propaganda": "Every one of our actions is symbolic, and each works on an imaginary plane of political representation."[14]

Within Leftist terrorism the cries of the Resistance-betrayed, of the deviation of the Italian Communist Party from the "correct" line of reinterpreted Marxism-Leninism, of Latin American guerrilla warfare and of the need to react against the "carnage of the state" were intertwined with a search for the absolute of Catholic variety, or in the case of the Right, with an unyielding defense of Western values through institution of a "new order" created mystically by superior beings who may live in this time of disorder but do

---

12 See Rossana Rossanda's preface to Mario Moretti, *Brigate rosse. Una storia italiana*, ed. Carla Mosca and Rossana Rossanda (Milan: Anabasi, 1994), pp. xix–xx.
13 Moretti, *Brigate rosse. Una storia italiana*, p. 43.
14 *Ibid.*, pp. 47, 101.

not belong to it.[15] Many lives, driven by the thirst for upheaval or reordering of the world and by the decision to carry out justice through violence, took paths of terrorism and clandestine existence, bestowing and receiving death in the hopes of becoming the "detonator of a great revolution." Thousands of young people had "two faces" and immersed themselves in clandestine lives, generally for ideological motives, but also (and sometimes in combination) in order to try new and more significant life experiences, to find roots in "a small community, a small family" and to synchronize themselves with the exciting dimension of accelerated rhythms of frenetic activity: "There was always a sense of urgency in what we did," recounted Moretti.[16] Another member of the Leftist organizations added: "We gave ourselves over to a frightening activism, which means that in the end you slept no more in this zone."[17]

Within these groups, mechanisms of depersonalization functioned to the extent that even killing became a job like any other, to be coldly carried out in the name of the presumed historical necessity of class war, in order to revenge the oppressed and seize power. An ex-militant from Prima Linea (Front Line) said of the assassination of the prison guard Lo Russo in Turin: "I lived out that homicide while still in the logic of the function, because he was an agent of the prison, because he was known – for what it's worth – as a torturer as they used to say back then, and so I had every ideological justification… For me it was like carrying out a work routine…

---

15   I am using the definition of "terrorism" given by Donatella Della Porta in *Il terrorismo di sinistra* (Bologna: Il Mulino, 1990), p. 19: "the activities of those relatively small clandestine organizations who, through the continuous and almost exclusive use of acts of violence, aim to achieve prevalently practical types of objectives." In his novel *Gli invisibili* (Milano, 1987), Nanni Balestrini depicted the life course of one of the terrorists, who passed from being a mediocre university student to a "proletarian expropriator" and finally to jail. On terrorism more generally, see Giorigo Galli, *Storia del partito armato, 1968–1982* (Milan: Rizzoli, 1993); Giorgio Bocca, *Noi terroristi. 12 anni di lotta armata ricostruiti e discussi con i protagonisti* (Milan: Garzanti, 1985); Donatella Della Porta, *I terrorismi in Italia* (Bologna: Il Mulino, 1984); Leonard Weinberg and William Lee Eubank, *The Rise and the Fall of Italian Terrorism* (Boulder: Westview Press, 1987); Giorgio Bocca, *Gli anni del terrorismo. Storia della violenza politica in Italia dal '70 a oggi*, Roma, 1988; Diego Novelli and Nicola Tranfaglia, *Vite sospese. Le generazioni del terrorismo* (Milan: Garzanti, 1988); Lumley, *States of Emergency*; Raimondo Catanzaro, *La politica della violenza* (Bologna: Il Mulino, 1990); and Sergio Zavoli, *La notte della Repubblica* (Milan: Mondadori, 1992). On right-wing terrorist groups, see Franco Ferraresi, *Minacce alla democrazia. La Destra radicale e la strategia della tensione in Italia nel dopoguerra* (Milan: Feltrinelli, 1995), pp. 164ff; and Franklin L. Ford, *Political Murder. From Tyrannicide to Terrorism* (Cambridge: Harvard University Press, 1985).

16   Moretti, *Brigate rosse*, p. 37.

17   Della Porta, *Il terrorismo di sinistra*, p. 101.

This was the actual aberration, the terrifying thing about the ideology... On the one hand you have friends and, on the other hand, enemies, and the enemies are a category, that is, they are functions, they are symbols, but they are not men."[18] Among the photos in the Turin police department's ballistics section there is a particularly impressive image: "The director of Fiat, Ghiglieno, assassinated by terrorists on Via Petrarca, September 21, 1979, is lying in the road. Against the gray of the asphalt, the snare of the trap stands out: it is an overturned fruit crate that had been placed between the wheels of the car to designate the marked man for the assassins. (None of them knew him: they were shooting at a target, Fiat incarnate; and the man – there he is, dead, but he still resembles a man – could not imagine that the wooden box was a shining flare, a kiss of death)."[19]

The traumatic kidnapping of Aldo Moro was an indication of the moral and political climate of the period, both for the kidnappers and the kidnapped. To be really understood, Moro's character should be examined from its origins, beginning with the early years of his career as a professor of the philosophy of law at the University of Bari. Although he came from the neo-Thomist tradition of the Catholic University of Milan, he quickly put himself on the track of "personalism" and "Christian humanism," rep-

---

18   Ibid., pp. 158, 182–83. On the process of "depersonalizing the victim," see also Raimondo Catanzaro, "Il sentito e il vissuto. La violenza nel racconto dei protagonisti" in *La politica della violenza*, pp. 228ff. In an interview with Zavoli, Enrico Fenzi explained political murder in the following way: "It seemed the only way to really act. That's it. This was the great crime – a great error of arrogance. In an entirely materialistic, mechanistic interpretation of reality, the only thing that matters is relationships of power. A person who's convinced that the only thing that matters is force – in the factory, in society, in the streets, in the palace, in the government, among states – is a person not only prepared to use force, but a person who considers the use of violence as the highest form of political intelligence. This deadly combination of presumed intelligence and violence is certainly one of the focal points that can explain the choices made by the Red Brigades"; *La notte della Repubblica*, p. 498. On Fenzi, who "more than a member of the Red Brigades, although a bit vexed by his past, seems like a seventeenth-century Ambassador on a mission to the king of Spain," see Corrado Stajano, *Il disordine* (Turin: Einaudi, 1993), pp. 250–68. Moretti's position was more tied to military and revolutionary traditions: "When we chose armed battle it was because every other path was closed to us and we felt we had no other option. We were forced to do atrocious things... just as in a war, where terrible things are done because they are indeed terrible and necessary; see Moretti, *Brigate rosse. Una storia italiana*, pp. 48. Compare this to Fenzi: "We accept revolutionary violence, the tragedy of death, the suffering of flesh wounds, or the laceration of the soul, but we accept it as an obligatory path to change. The means and the time were not up to us"; *ibid.*, p. 101. When Franceschini decided to break his ties, he recognized that "we were only a sort of drug addict, addicted to one type of drug: ideology. It was a lethal drug – worse than heroin"; see Franceschini et al., *Mara, Renato e io*, p. 204.

19   Guido Ceronetti, *Un viaggio in Italia. 1981–1983* (Turin: Einaudi, 1983), p. 146.

resented in Italy by Giovanni Capograssi and in France by Jacques Maritain and Emanuel Mounier.[20] Moro perceived the change in philosophical climate introduced in the 1930s by the culture of continental Europe, which exercised great influence on the tormented Cardinal Montini, then on Paul VI and on many intellectuals in the Azione Cattolica (Catholic Action) who were close to him. In *Lezioni di filosofia del diritto* (Lectures on Philosophy of Law, delivered in Bari in 1944–45 and 1946–47, and which begin with the significant chapter entitled "The Problem of Life"), the world is governed by love and the Christian principle by which all men are equal before God. As Richard Drake notes:

> Criticizing liberalism and socialism as two incomplete halves of the complete revolution implicit in Christianity, Moro celebrated the Church's basic political teachings. Liberal societies emphasized individual liberty, whereas socialist societies subordinated everything to class terms. Moro argued that individual freedom and social well welfare were entirely dependent upon each other. No enclave of prosperity and stability could survive if conditions of misery and violence prevailed outside of it.[21]

Having become more of a politician than a professor, Moro soon acquired a sense of the fragility of the Italian equilibrium, the frailty of its democracy and the consequent necessity to move toward change with slow circumspection (his worries here are symmetrically analogous to those of Berlinguer), and it was this complexity that the Red Brigades intended to simplify through the shortcut of violence. From the early 1960s, Moro knew that Italy had limited sovereignty under American tutelage and that it was sharply divided and lacking in "democratic maturity." He therefore concluded that in order to strengthen the country it was necessary to en-

---

20   See Jacques Maritain, *L'umanesimo integrale* (Rome: Studium, 1946); idem, *Il contadino della Garonna* (Brescia: Morcelliana, 1969); Giorgio Campanini, *Cristianesimo e democrazia. Studi sul pensiero politico cattolico del '900* (Brescia: Morcelliana, 1980); and idem, *Il pensiero politico di Mounier* (Brescia: Morcelliana, 1983). On Capograssi, see Claudio Vasale, *Società e Stato nel pensiero di Giuseppe Capograssi* (Rome: Edizioni di storia e letteratura, 1972). On Aldo Moro's early years, see R. Moro, "La formazione giovanile di Aldo Moro," *Storia contemporanea*, 14 (1983), pp. 803–968; Italo Pietra, *Moro, fu vera gloria? Sa e non fa. Ha il senso della storia, non quello dello Stato né quello delle cifre. Nella sua vita una chiave del trentennio DC* (Milan: Garzanti, 1983); Antonio Rossano, *L'altro Moro* (Milan: SugarCo, 1985); and Norberto Bobbio, "Il giovane Aldo Moro" in idem, *Dal fascismo alla democrazia. I regimi, le ideologie e le culture politiche* (Milan: Baldini & Castoldi, 1997), pp. 283–307.

21   Richard Drake, *The Aldo Moro Murder Case* (Cambridge: Harvard University Press, 1995), p. 9.

large the area of consensus by including the Socialists and then – following the "double victory" of the Italian Communist Party and the Christian Democrats in the elections of June 20, 1976 – the Communists. But the realization of this project would encounter nearly insurmountable resistance, both internal and external. American hostility, even during the Carter administration, toward any reconciliation with or inclusion of the Communists in the government was well noted. The exasperating slowness of Moro's political maneuvers, his allusive and complicated way of speaking and his theorems from non-Euclidean geometry (he spoke of "parallel convergences") were, however, also an indication – during the period that preceded his kidnapping – of his search for labyrinthine solutions in both life and thought, which resulted from a conflict between a predisposition toward the common good and an unflappable loyalty to the party. All things considered (and with appropriate perspective), Togliatti's "duplicity" would find its counterpart, during the most acute phase of the "cold civil war," in Moro's Hamletic will to reconcile opposites.

But what was the moral temperament of the man? Franco Bonisoli, member of the Red Brigades, attested that during the fifty-five days of imprisonment by his kidnappers, everyone around Moro felt that he was "an extremely dignified man who believed in his role and in his function. His deep religiosity was also very striking and especially his attention to the problems of his family." Family – and similarly the party, but not the state – was one of the principal keys to understanding his behavior. Moro wrote to Zaccagnini about his family from the "people's prison": "My own misfortunate family has been, in a way, suffocated, unable to cry out its desperate pain and need of me. Is it possible that you are all in agreement in wishing my death for some presumed reason of state, which someone has lividly suggested to you as a solution to all the problems of the country?" Even in his last letter to the party, he reaffirmed his positions: "I will die, if my party so desires, in the fullness of my Christian faith and in my immense love for an exemplary family whom I adore and whom I hope to watch over from Heaven." Most tormenting is the letter he wrote to his wife after learning of his death sentence: "Kiss and caress everyone for me, over and over, every eye, every hair. Give everyone immense tenderness from me through your hands. Be strong, my sweetest one, in this absurd and incomprehensible ordeal."²²

Leonardo Sciascia observed, not without severity: "Moro was not a 'great statesman' until March 16. He had been and continued to be, even in the 'people's prison,' a great politician: vigilant, aware and calculating. He appeared flexible but was immovable. He had patience, but the kind of patience that accompanies tenacity. He had a vision of the strengths, or one might say of the weaknesses, that move Italian life – one of the most vast and assured visions that any politician has ever had."²³ He knew the "negativity" of human nature,²⁴ and was endowed with a sensitive intuition and a capacity for the infinite mediations in which the new would slowly be absorbed by the old. He never wanted to give up his legitimate family affections, and he was convinced that everyone had contributed in "digging the catacombs beneath this state, which is now breaking apart under our feet." He did not expect the reactions of firmness and inflexibility of the state and the parties in negotiating with the Red Brigades: "Moro was surprised by the sudden intransigence of the state 'like a solid tower that would not crumble.' How did such an armored and armed monster emerge from this

---

22 *La notte della Repubblica*, pp. 292, 298, 313, 314. On the Socialist Party's contact with the Red Brigades in prison, see Giannino Guiso, *La condanna di Moro* (Milan: SugarCo, 1979), pp. 81–249. See also Franceschini, *Mara, Renato e io*, pp. 156–61.

23 L. Sciascia, *L'affaire Moro* (Palermo: Sellerio, 1978), p. 33.

24 From his intellectual and political beginnings, Moro was clearly well aware of the presence of evil in the world, as well as of the *non praevalebunt*: "we must look reality in the face in order to recognize the weighty baggage of evil that the men of all peoples carry by virtue of weakness or malice. We must look reality in the face in order for all of us together to do the true work aimed at rebirth; and we must to do so in full confidence in the possibility of defeating evil"; Aldo Moro, "I difetti degli italiani," *La Rassegna* 30 November 1944, reprinted in Aldo Moro, *Scritti e discorsi*, vol. I: *1940–1947*, ed. Giuseppe Rossini (Rome: Cinque lune, 1992), p. 8). Later, Moro appeared to be one of those people who Alberto Asor Rosa spoke about, that is, as an incarnation of "one of the great constants of [Italian] national character, which I would call 'Italian pessimism', which spans almost uninterrupted from the first moment of great crisis (Guicciardini and, later, Sarpi) to our own day, running through a series of crises"; Alberto Asor Rosa, *Genus italicum. Saggi sulla identità letteraria italiana nel corso del tempo* (Turin: Einaudi, 1997), p. xxix.

larva?"²⁵ But Moro was unwilling to betray the interests and ideals of the Christian Democrats even in the face of the terrorists – precisely at a moment in which he indicted his own party. Although the party was full of serious defects, which he had nonetheless previously defended tenaciously during the Lockheed scandal (in hopes of redressing them), for Moro it remained an "ethical" party.

---

25 Sciascia, *L'affaire Moro*, p. 64. Mario Moretti was also surprised by the steadfastness of the parties and institutions. He had not expected such resistance and he had mixed feelings for Moro in the end: "I have before me a man who inspires pity, in the Virgilian sense of the word. And sometimes he enrages me, I'll admit. But c'mon, you're the president of the Christian Democrats, and you have governed the country since before I even went to pre-school! You cannot say that 'you have a family' to think about just like anyone other man"; Moretti, *Brigate rosse. Una storia italiana*, p. 142. On Moro, see also the quasi-dramaturgical reconstruction of events in Robert Katz, *Days of Wrath: The Public Agony of Aldo Moro* (London: Granada, 1980) and Sergio Flamigni, *La tela del ragno. Il delitto Moro* (Rome: Edizioni associate, 1988). For Italian intellectuals reaction to the Moro kidnapping at that moment, see Gilberto Polloni and Daniele Romano, eds., *Le cicale e il caso Moro* (Rome: Edizioni delle autonomie, 1978).

CHAPTER 7
Krisis

Democracy without Illusions

The death of Aldo Moro, the end-game rally of terrorism, the murders orchestrated by the secret service and the discovery of collaboration between certain high-ranking politicians and the Masonic Lodge P2 all revealed a widespread moral unravelling and attested to the tenuous roots of Italian democracy, both at the top levels of its institutions and the fringes of society.

In virtue of the dichotomous clarity of his thought and the acumen of his probing questions, Norberto Bobbio became one of the most important and respected interlocutors in public debates. He has been the critical conscience of the Italian Republic's élite for decades and his writings have been characterized – at least since the mid-1950s – by a rejection of preconceived ideologies, an absence of partisan and propagandistic tones and the capacity to continually reformulate political problems by balancing different points of view and incorporating objections. "Beyond the duty to be part of the struggle, the man of culture is further obliged not to accept the terms of the struggle as they have been posed; he has the duty to discuss them and submit them to the critique of reason." In this response to Togliatti was the renewed vindication of freedom against any inflexibility of ideas in the form of dogma: "The only thing that can give life to the stiffened body of society is a breath of freedom, by which I mean the restlessness of the spirit, intolerance of the established order and abhorrence of any conformism, all of which require open-mindedness and energetic character."[1]

---

1 Norberto Bobbio, *Politica e cultura* (Turin: Einaudi, 1955), pp. 17, 280.

By combining the traditions of moral intransigence inspired by actionism and Piero Gobetti with the political perspectives of reformist socialism, Bobbio encouraged the unconditional acceptance of democracy and gradually pushed the Italian Communist Party to abandon its distrust with respect to democracy's supposed "formalism," even as he consistently appreciating the Left's thirst for justice.[2] Bobbio offered a sobering, realistic image of democracy that includes not only noble ideals but good administration and the laborious engineering of social institutions – the prose of democracy rather than the poetry. However, looking back over a quarter of a century, he confessed that he had abandoned the expectations of an earlier era, expectations that now appear excessive to him: "We confronted real democracy as though we were its fathers and were offended and surprised that the creature that we had created had grown up so badly and would probably not last long... We have learned to accept democratic society without any illusions. We have not become more satisfied, but less demanding. This is the difference between our anxieties of an earlier era and our worries today. On the whole, the quality of our common life together has not improved; indeed, in some ways it has worsened. We ourselves have changed: we have become more realistic and less naive."[3] In Italy, democracy unfortunately requires unyielding patience, as even the most modest proposals for effective change rarely turn out to be feasible: "reformers have always had a difficult time in a country like ours, which is too old and too behind the times to have much patience to wait. The result is that, instead of timely reforms, we have always had brief revolutions and long counter-reformations."[4]

Bobbio has identified the many obstacles that stand in the way of change: the passivity of its citizens, the oligarchic politics of political party secretaries, moral indifference, a muddled morass of laws, elephantine bureaucracy, "invisible powers" and the interweaving of politics and business. Faced with so many and such great obstacles, one cannot help but be dismayed. Often

---

[2] See his letter to Carl Schmitt, December 10, 1950: "I am not a Marxist, much less a Communist. My admiration for writers of the Enlightenment has taught me to protect myself from the temptation of fanaticism. Yet while I see in Marx evidence of peoples who are 'thirsty for justice', in ideologues like Donoso I see only the powerful who thirst for more and more power"; Norberto Bobbio, *Autobiografia*, ed. Alberto Papuzzi (Rome-Bari: Laterza, 1997), p. 151.

[3] See Bobbio's preface to the second edition of *Italia civile. Ritratti e testimonianze* (Florence: Passigli, 1986), p. 6. See Bobbio's *Autobiografia* for an account of his intellectual and moral journey.

[4] Idem, *Profilo ideologico del Novecento italiano*, pp. 180–81.

the remedies have been worse than the ills they were meant to redress, like the impractical shortcut of direct democracy, the provisional and qualified loyalty to representative democracy (conceived of as a mere precursor to socialism, a running start before the definitive "elbowing" out of the capitalist system), or, most recently, the manipulation of consensus through the media's echoing of political leaders' opinions. The simple and bitter truth is not easy to accept: that the task of building a democracy is interminable inasmuch as the regime is imperfect and un-heroic; yet it is the only one which we have to perfect. The commitment to change the world without ever refraining from interpreting it is a continuous, thankless and prosaic task. To borrow an expression from Adriano Sofri, which Bobbio might approve of, democracy is based more on the idea of a "knot," that is, the conscientious and patient weaving together of multiple social relationships, and less on the idea of a "nail" or wedge that makes holes or topples the existing equilibrium by applying the greatest possible pressure on the smallest possible surface. All that is left for us is to continue down this chosen path in order to advance the tenacious expansion of the sphere of rights, from political and economic rights to the social rights of the latest "generation," which today are more important than ever. "We are dealing with new rights that have appeared in the constitutions from the end of the war until the present and were consecrated by the Universal Declaration of Human Rights and subsequent international documents. The *raison d'être* of social rights, such as the right to education, the right to work and the right to health, is egalitarian in nature. All three of these rights are aimed at diminishing inequality between the haves and the have-nots, or at least at allowing a greater number of individuals to be less unequal to individuals more fortunate by birth and social condition."[5]

The Decline of Historicism

The greater willingness of politicians and many citizens to accept Bobbio's guidance on rights and the prescriptive "rules of the game" of democracy – independent of the factual context – is an indication that profound changes have taken place, even on the theoretical level. This development

---

5   *Idem, Destra e sinistra. Ragioni e significato di una distinzione politica* (Rome: Donzelli, 1994), p. 79; but more importantly, see Norberto Bobbio, *L'età dei diritti* (Turin: Einaudi, 1990).

is one of the many signs of the decline of historicism or, more precisely, of faith in a logic of history completely internal to events as the guiding light for moral and political action. Since no scale can weigh itself, the criteria of judgment began to be sought outside of history in norms of universal character, or publicly debated on the basis of an intense confrontation of different points of view.

It would be ungenerous, however, to speak today only of the limits and "wrinkles" of historicism, passing over its notable merits. It allowed the carving out of an ample autonomous space for Italian Marxism distinct from the suffocating Stalinism of the majority of Communist parties during the same era; and it sobered (with vigilant attention to the concrete, the far from insignificant details of the overall picture, and the real relationships of power) the perennially unsatisfied Italian tendency toward a sanctified rhetorical enthusiasm that haughtily raises itself above lowly empirics, imposing its abstract models on reality and covering the world with impotent invectives or moralistic potshots. At least in the intentions of the major communist "intellectuals" and laymen, historicism did not represent an astute tactic but rather a testing ground for the "force of things," a visible terrain of transition, a place delegated for the union, in Italy, of theory and practice, democracy and socialism, liberalism and democracy.

Because of its link to politics, Marxist historicism found itself enjoying a double dividend on the positions it took. On the one hand, Marxist historicism was not theoretically aligned with the Zhdanov-Stalin vulgate of "historical materialism" and "dialectic materialism" that was prevalent in the East. On the other hand, it had opened itself at the beginning of the 1960s to the "heretical" variants combated by official Soviet doctrine, from the young Lukács to the Frankfurt School, from psychoanalytical Marxism to the utopian Marxism of Ernst Bloch. The second position originated in the left-over political link to the Communist Party in the Soviet Union, a reference point for a "base" group that, for a long time, continued to see the Soviet Union as the fatherland of socialism and the avant-garde of emancipated humanity.

Once this double dividend was exhausted and the role of historicism had weakened in general (Marxist as well as Liberal-Crocean historicism), the axes of orientation of Italian philosophy began suddenly to turn. Following a brief wave of Structuralism, dominated by the figures of Lévi-Strauss and Althusser, the next wave consisted in circulating the very philosophers who had previously been considered *vitandi*, branded as "irrationalists" and "reactionaries": Schopenhauer, Nietzsche, Schmitt, Wittgenstein and especially Heidegger. This new philosophical culture was helped along by the publication of Heidegger's *Nietzsche* in 1961 and the critical edition of Nietzsche's collected works, edited by Giorgio Colli and Mazzino Montinari beginning in 1964, as well as a renewed Italian interest in Vienna and *Mitteleuropa,* prompted by the studies of Claudio Magris.[6] Thus began a new phase of cultural acquisition, a modification of common sense and an adjustment of ethical perspectives. "Combinatory" artifice – used in the first two post-war decades to make Italian philosophy less "provincial" and temper Marxist and Catholic orthodoxy – no longer seemed necessary. There was also less preoccupation with the safeguarding or defense of the "Piave line" separating rationalism from irrationalism. In working through the philosophical repressed, there was an unconscious tendency to push politics outside the realm of consciousness and theory – which had been usurped or colonized in the age of antagonistic totalitarianism – or (in an apparent paradox) to allow politics to penetrate philosophy, the social sciences and even physics, but without leaving any conscious or unconscious residues. Greater attention was given to the exigencies and rights of the individual when unleashed from his obligations to the collectivity and relieved of the heavy burden of history for which he would otherwise be fully responsible. While the link between philosophical thought and civil commitment remained intact and in some cases became rooted to the point of transforming theoretical reflection into mere militancy, in others it changed appearance or even disappeared. The former "flexible partisanship" and the disposition toward tactical accords were replaced either by revolutionary rigor that rejected mediation and oversimplified "reality" (this explains the

---

6 See Martin Heidegger, *Nietzsche* (Pfullingen: Neske, 1961), vol. II. Beyond Nietzsche, Giorgio Colli restored philosophical dignity to Schopenhauer in Italy. Accepting some presuppositions which run "against the current," such as the "representation" of the individual, that is to say, his Being as an expression of an indecipherable "will to live": "What is the individual? Certainly, nothing absolute or autonomous or fundamental; at most, the individual reflects something that, translated in to a category of abstraction, is a multiplicity. The individual is an ensemble of representations interconnected in time and space that appear to be unified by an internal principle. But no representation has an internal principle, and thus neither will an ensemble of representations... Today, more than ever, the individual is a basic fact, and to go beyond this is impossible or futile"; Giorgio Colli, *Dopo Nietzsche* (Milan: Adelphi, 1974), pp. 101–2.

success of Carl Schmitt and his irreconcilable opposition of friend/enemy) or by "hospitable" or even eclectic thought, which multiplied the facets of reality and dissolved its consistency.

Independent of the will of the two editors of his works, Nietzsche quickly began to be thought of as wearing "an ill-fitting Phrygian cap," a departure from his former image as a philosopher "who had invoked warrior aristocracies and sung hymns to the will to power."[7] Through Nietzsche the charm of the "world of appearances" was discovered, a world which was more vast, variegated and heterogeneous than a reality whose structure and laws are consideredly metaphysically immutable. A side-effect of this multiplication of points of view was the gradual shift of philosophy's center of gravity from politics toward the means of mass communication. Along the way, loyalty to the "ethical party" became less important than the relationship to "non-philosophers" – or to public opinion – and philosophy began to take on problems related to the foundations of knowledge, individual conscience, and even the very metaphysics of "being." In this way, the explicitly ideological component of philosophy diminished, but simplification did not always disappear, due to the style and deadlines of newspapers, radio, television and scholastic textbooks. In short, Italian philosophy now considered the freedom of thought and the autonomy of culture from politics to be obvious, and it drastically reduced the activism and "praxism" which, according to an interpretation at once keen and tendentious, had constituted the common philosophical basis of both fascism and communism.[8]

Nonetheless, it was remarkable that the recovery of "irrationalist" thinkers or even those politically compromised by National Socialism was in part promoted and welcomed as a positive event, especially by the Left.[9] In fact,

---

7 Bobbio, *Profilo ideologico del Novecento italiano*, p. 183.

8 Agusto del Noce, *L'epoca della secolarizzazione* (Milano: Giuffrè, 1970), pp. 111ff.

9 This does not signify an end to the clear ideological distinction between "Right" and "Left" as many argued during the 1980s and 1990s. Norberto Bobbio would contest this claim in the early 1990s, arguing that the idea of equality is what separates "Right" and "Left," and that according to this criterion Nietzsche remains a right-wing thinker: "Rousseau began with the notion that men are born equal, but that civil society – that is to say, the society that gradually supplants the state of nature through the development of the arts – is what made them unequal. Nietzsche, by contrast, began with the assumption that men are by nature unequal (and that it is all the better that they are, for a society based on slavery like Ancient Greece was an evolved society, owing precisely to the existence of slaves), and that society alone – with its herd-like morality, its religion of compassion and its resignation – is what made men equal. The same type of corruption which for Rousseau created inequality, for Nietzsche created equality"; Bobbio, *Destra e sinistra. Ragioni e significati di una distinzione politica*, p. 76.

it was in the sphere of Marxist heretics – in the groups of "workerists" tied to the *Quaderni Rossi* (Red Notebooks) of Raniero Panzieri, *Classe Operaia* (Working Class) of Mario Tronti and Alberto Asor Rosa, or *Angelus Novus* of Massimo Cacciari – that Nietzsche, Heidegger, Wittgenstein, Schmitt and the exponents of Viennese "decadence" found a home (next to Marx, bristling with the technical difficulties of the *Grundrisse* and *Capital* and the sparse traces of the teachings of Della Volpe).[10] The appeal for direct democracy against the position of the historical parties of the Left (or their leaders) and for the "moral Galileism" of Marx can now be read in a twofold manner. On the one hand, it can be seen as an appeal for class antagonism, a rejection of the dialectic culture of mediation and compromise and the advocacy of "wildcat" strikes. On the other hand, in accordance with the passionate and, in his own way, rigorous teachings of Panzieri – the heir of a socialism that rejected both "churches," Catholic and communist alike – it was an appeal to direct scientific study of conflictual capitalistic relationships within the factory or the places of production from which authentic democracy emerges.[11] The militant avant-garde, whose conscience reflected an awareness of the schisms of social conflict, accepted from a theoretical point of view – together with the "unilaterality" of knowledge, seen in the guise of class, and egalitarianism, understood as the one of the highest political and ethical commandments – the sad necessity of violence in the ultimate phase of the old order's destruction: "At the height of development, once power has been ripped away from the capitalists, a hard period of political dictatorship of the workers over all of society will come – this we cannot avoid. It is all we can see of the future, all we wish to see."[12] Later, when the "autonomy of the political" was theorized (together with the glorification of the worker in a way that combined Lenin's *Imperialism, the Highest Stage of Capitalism* and Ernst Jünger's *The Worker [Der Arbeiter]*), the "light" party first proposed to the working class ended up becoming a weighty, robust contender that once again coincided with the Italian Communist Party.

---

10   Mario Alcaro, *Dellavolpismo e nuova sinistra* (Bari: Dedalo, 1976).
11   Massimo Teodori, *Storia delle nuove sinistre in Europa, 1956–1976* (Bologna: Il Mulino, 1976); Mino Monicelli, *L'ultrasinistra in Italia, 1968–1978* (Bari: Laterza, 1978); Mario Maffi, *Le origini della sinistra extraparlamentare* (Milan: Mondadori, 1987).
12   Mario Tronti, *Operai e capitale* (Turin: Einaudi, 1966), p.19 cited in Lanaro, *Storia dell'Italia repubblicana*, p. 278.

Once the winds of history no longer filled the sails of politics and the belief that the dialectics of Hegel and Marx allowed for the advancement of history waned, however painful it may be, the culture of mediation declined and "crisis" itself was welcomed more as an element of opportunity than of decadence. The pathos for *kairos* – for the opportune moment of decisive resolution – and the effort to organize into political and strongly cohesive intellectual groups took the place of the long, anonymous travail of history. It was widely believed that if the struggle was not actively prepared and planned, the stagnation and defeat of the workers' movement could be definitive. Thus, philosophically, the historicist combination of history and utopia broke apart, while politically, the dialectical suture – that Togliatti had so patiently sewn in the torn fabric of Italian history, re-attaching bonds and opportunities, the harshness of the relationships of power and the project of emancipation, democracy and socialism – came undone. At the same time, the decline of historicism (which, in its attention to the concrete and the specific, had implicitly discredited the "great philosophical questions") repaved the way for radical, "metaphysical" questions concerning individual "destiny."

Negative Thought

By way of Nietzsche and the thinkers of *finis Austirae* (Rilke, Trakl, Hoffmannstahl, Roth, Schönberg, Freud, Wittgenstein), Massimo Cacciari left "workerism" for "negative thought." The theme of insurmountable contradictions and the implausibility of "surpassing" them now took the philosophical form of an attack on both the dialectic (for its continuistic and conciliatory nature) and on the Lukács of *The Destruction of Reason* (for his accusations of "irrationalism" and decadence aimed *en masse* at philosophy after Hegel, literature after Goethe and political economics after Ricardo). Reversing this position, Cacciari vindicated the fecundity of "decadence" in the figures of Nietzsche, Wittgenstein (his Austrian rather than English period) and Heidegger, especially the Heidegger of *Being and Time*, which he judged to be "a fundamentally *tragic* work of contemporary thought."[13]

To the glittering images of history and dialectics – reversed at times to look like the rosy harmony of the reign of liberty or the Pentecostal ad-

---

13 Massimo Cacciari, *Pensiero negativo e razionalizzazione* (Venice: Marsilio, 1977), p. 73.

vent of a classless society – Cacciari opposes the idea of *krisis*: a permanent state of emergency in existence and in thought, without any assurance of salvation. The most penetrating elaboration of this concept was located, philosophically, in both the corroborating and disconcerting thought of the "posthumous people." These Viennese masters (who had an obsession for language that reached the margins of the unspeakable and who had a "lucidity of analysis" capable of "stopping at the confines of the 'mystical,' between anguish and irony, but with the discovery of the now fulfilled impossibility of the tragic") taught one how to live by renouncing the dogma of the singularity of truth: "Posthumous people have *too many* reasons and cannot content themselves with a simple truth ('all truth is simple, but is this not a double lie?'). Posthumous people pass through an infinite number of masks without adopting any of them."[14]

In *Icone della Legge* (*Icons of Law*), Cacciari continued to explore the theme of boundaries, this time in the form of the "crises of Nomos" – the lawfulness of crossing the seemingly insuperable limits of laws. In Kafka and Rosenzweig, the image of the "door" now appears as a symbol of enigmatic ambiguity: it is either a barrier which we might break through if we so desire, or a spiral opening onto life at the end of every seemingly completed path. How should we act before this door? Should we wait futilely for the guardian to let us by, like the character in Kafka's celebrated story, "Before the Law"? Or should we forego hesitation and pass through, making a choice that is unjustifiable in terms of pure logic? Contemporary man, Cacciari argues, is continually forced to make decisions in the name of a law or in sight of an end whose meaning has been obscured or lost. His experience is thus that of wandering and nomadism, typified by the children of Israel. Today, however, this condition is generalized and we all live out "the universal absolutization of rootlessness. That which is revealed here is the idealistic autonomy of the subject, although the subject has been irreversibly uprooted."[15] For those who recognize their nature as displaced persons or wanderers, the law remains concealed in the unfathomability of their own foundation, devoid of any guarantee deriving from a divine source or from science. One cannot attempt to measure or to exhaust this

---

14   Massimo Cacciari, *Dallo Steinhof. Prospettive viennesi del primo Novecento* (Milan: Adelphi, 1980), p. 16.

15   Massimo Cacciari, *Icone della Legge* (Milan: Adelphi, 1985), p. 5. See also Massimo Cacciari, *Geo-filosofia dell'Europa* (Milan: Adelphi, 1994), and *idem*, *L'arcipelago* (Milan: Adelphi, 1997).

abyss of meaning by enclosing it completely in thought. Instead, one must tend to this hidden zone by maintaining an infinite tension between the limited capacity for representation and the unrepresentable, the allegory of which is the Angel. This "presents the mystery as mystery, transmits the invisible as invisible, without betraying it through the senses." We are pushed, according to Rilke's metaphor, "to gather desperately the honey of the visible, to care for it in the great golden beehive of the invisible."[16]

Through close confrontation with not only classical metaphysics but theology, Cacciari – who learned to distinguish clearly between philosophy and politics, thus breaking with Italian tradition – has purposely made himself "outdated" in recent years. In *Dell'Inizio* (*From the Beginning*), a work of complex conceptual and expositional scope, he seeks the origins of our problems in the depths of the great European philosophical traditions (from the Neoplatonists Proclus and Damascius through Hegel and late Schelling), thus proffering debatable results (in the sense that they merit debate), which require of the reader a tenacious but remunerative "laboring of the concept."[17]

The Crisis of Reason

Drawing on Wittgenstein and Austrian culture, Aldo G. Gargani began to question the solidity of the foundations of scientific knowledge and to identify a clear "crisis of reason" with which philosophy finally had to come to terms.[18] The image of reason as a solemn matron, a monolithic entity, or a mirror of the world that reflects the laws and very forms of reality was declared illusory. The task of reason, hypostatized according to Gargani, was exclusively practical: to reassure men in the face of the inevitable uncertainties of experience and knowledge. "The 'foundation', the 'essence', and the 'basic principles', do not satisfy cognitive functions, but accomplish different functions regarding the social and cultural institutions that discipline our lives. Rather than cognitive needs, these conceptual constructs represented and still represent *epistemological rituals* which aim to preserve the irrevocability accorded to certain values and limit the unbiased use of

---

16   Massimo Cacciari, *L'angelo necessario* (Milan: Adelphi, 1986).
17   Massimo Cacciari, *Dell'inizio* (Milan: Adelphi, 1990).
18   Aldo G. Gargani, *Linguaggio ed esperienza in Ludwig Wittgenstein* (Florence: Le Monnier, 1966).

communication. In this sense, the terms 'objective', 'empirical', 'universal', 'particular', 'essential', and similar adjectives do not express inexorably real states but reflect the models for decision to which men have historically given themselves over in their life plans."[19]

Philosophy changed vocation, abandoning foundationalist expectations and the lofty ambition to compete on equal footing with the sciences and instead, with Gargani, developed a new "style of analysis" called "narrated thought." "Narrated thought" is the interweaving of reflection with narration, idea development with personal events and philosophy with the cognitive contributions of literature. It is only in a position to explore – with values that are "not yet secure" – the places, trodden paths and enigmatic "surroundings" of shared existence.[20] Once deprived of ever-suspect preliminary guarantees, our thoughts seem perilously unstable, moving across unreal bridges suspended over the void like the "imaginary numbers" of mathematics, which function without anyone's knowing why. We are therefore forced to make a "leap into the unverifiable," or rather a "leap through the unverifiable." Since we – in both our collective and private lives – are assured of nothing from the outset and have no faith to sustain us in the current of necessity, we must learn the art of transforming the accidental event into an advantageous situation, for chance is "the fortuitous occasion which opens within an already predisposed conception of the world."[21]

Truth, however, does not mean the possession of a fixed good or the arrival at a pre-established and anonymous destination. Instead, there is an eradicable personal sense of truth: "What we call truth has to do with the influential images that direct our lives, commit us to paths of exploration and expose our lives in the face of needs our lives give rise to, generating a transition to a new state, a state of urgency within which one must think from now on. Truth is discovered by following the same route along which it incites us to search." Truth, therefore, is not a photostatic copy of the world, as it is for those who "believe that their minds are the mirror of the universe, while in reality their minds are a *dwelling* constructed by thoughts and words in order to confront existence without *reflecting* that existence, unsustainable and unsupportable without the very dwelling that is their

---

19　Idem, *Il sapere senza fondamenti* (Turin: Einaudi, 1975), p. ix.
20　Idem, *Lo stupore e il caso* (Rome-Bari: Laterza, 1985), p. 18.
21　The expression is Musil's (*Sprung durchs Unbeweisbare*); see Gargani, *Lo stupore e il caso*, pp. 109, 19.

minds."²²

The intolerability of living induces us to enclose ourselves within a defensive stronghold of ideas and phrases and to invent an eternity beneath the opaque surface of the transient. Thus, because we desire a life that is different from our own, we lose the only life in our secure possession, and we sacrifice the density of meaning of our singular discourses (always enclosed in precise relational contexts) for an atemporal truth against which such discourses would be justified. It is difficult, therefore, for us to understand that *"we and our entire language are the inspiration of the place and time in which we find ourselves."* We wish to "get to the bottom" of things, to explain them in a definitive manner and deny their right to evade our identifying embrace. In this way, we suffocate them and destroy their radical autonomy: "Thought and propositions that refer to a phenomenon by simply indicating it and showing it – stopping for an instant before explaining it, then indicating and showing it as if it were an opaque fact – leave intact the essence of the phenomenon, which is otherwise lost whenever it is translated into the language of explanation."²³ Philosophical thought, by renouncing its ambition to discover the orientation of events toward a single end, becomes a sort of occasionalism of life and thought, in which the individual puts himself at risk as he creates, over and over, a path conforming to his own destiny.²⁴

Therefore, when chance and our own needs meet, the protective cocoon of consolatory ideas and feelings in which we have wrapped ourselves is broken. We are then faced with the impossible presence of ourselves. A "second history" flashes before us and in an intense instant summons the result of all of our actions and energies. It is this "friction" that reveals to us the meeting with our *daimon*, marking the "incursion of events" in our broken and altered biography and causing us to leave the circle of pure possibilities to reach a liberating decision: "The threat encountered every so often in our existence is history, which derails us from the geometric line traced by our ideal history. We invented that ideal history in order to protect the geometric space around our existence, and we now learn that

---

22 Aldo G. Gargani, "La verità come immagine influente" in Aldo G. Gargani, ed., *Il destino dell'uomo nella società post-industriale* (Rome-Bari: Laterza, 1987), p. 10.
23 *Idem, Sguardo e destino* (Rome-Bari: Laterza, 1988), pp. 30, 41, 96.
24 See Aldo G. Gargani, *Il coraggio di essere* (Rome-Bari: Laterza, 1992).

it was based on an error."²⁵ An unexpected consistency and inner solidity reaches us, however, with the abandonment of the "theater of the self-centered subject" and the recognition of its character as a "great exorcism in the face of reality."²⁶ Rather than creators of our own history, we discover ourselves to be "creatures of an unwritten history that is stronger than us because it shows that we are different from ourselves,"²⁷ and subject to further metamorphoses. Having the "courage to be" – thus carrying forward the challenge of Wittgenstein and early-twentieth-century Viennese culture – means accepting a sort of existential freedom, opening ourselves to unforeseeable and irrepresentable encounters with what makes us different from ourselves and thus allows us to understand ourselves better.

Insisting on the absence of preliminary guarantees in action and thought, more recent philosophers (from Cacciari to Gargani and Vattimo) shifted the weight of responsibility from the individual in collective history and politics to the personal search for the meaning of one's own "destiny" as it intersects with other destinies. Everyone is sent back to rediscover himself and tackle the always improvised profession of living, gladly communicating to whomever he may meet the essence of his own fragile but precious truth.

---

25 Idem, "L'altra storia" in Gianni Vattimo, ed., *Filosofia '88* (Rome-Bari: Laterza, 1989), p. 70.
26 Idem, "L'attrito del pensiero" in Gianni Vattimo, ed., *Filosofia '86* (Rome-Bari: Laterza, 1987), pp. 10–11, 22.
27 Idem, *L'altra storia*, p. 71.

CHAPTER 8
How the "Ethical Party" Grew Corrupt and Died

The State and Residual Ethics

From an ethical standpoint, the period following the killing of Aldo Moro marked the beginning of a new cycle. In their most dramatic aspects, these years witnessed, together with the spread of hard drugs and the first cases of AIDS, both a further loosening of the bonds between citizens and the state and the first indications (well documented but immediately suppressed) of an indisputable network of corruption and politics.

An entire series of factors, accumulated over time, set the stage for a crisis that, fifteen years later, would explode. These factors included the difficulty in replacing the ruling class and the government (now accustomed to impunity), which resulted in paralysis and moral distress[1]; the political exploitation of the apparatus of the social state[2]; the occupation of jobs and public service posts by "greedy clients" who staked their claims to these positions under the aegis of *consociativismo* or "government by compromise," a phenomenon that has a long history in Italy and is the source of many problems, but which at least can be credited in the immediate post-war period with having helped to avoid the "Greek road to civil war" and, later, with having served as a remedy, albeit a questionable one, for the lack of

---

[1] In addition to Scoppola, *La repubblica dei partiti*, see Francesco Barbagallo, *L'azione parallela. Storia e politica nell'Italia contemporanea* (Naples: Liguori, 1990) and Simona Colarizi, *Storia dei partiti nell'Italia repubblicana* (Rome-Bari: Laterza, 1994).

[2] See Luciano Cafagna, *La grande slavina. L'Italia verso la crisi della democrazia* (Venice: Marsilio, 1992), pp. 32ff.

alternation in government[3]; the confusion between a "crisis of ideology" and the liquidation of ideals; the lack of distinction, in the framework of a mixed economy, between the public and private sector and the parallel systematic exchange of favors between political and economic powers in order to finance the growing "costs of politics." These costs arose from the necessity to resort to television, frequent political conventions and massive propaganda in the form of posters. The "voracity" of politics altered the laws of the market and the equity of taxation (by increasing the impact of the parties on the economy and on society, while their political platforms became more and more inconsistent).[4] Modernity and backwardness intersected, and corruption was transformed into "a functional substitute for state reform, which no one had been able to achieve."[5] The state itself came to be perceived by many as an extraneous entity, and during the most virulent periods of terrorism there were those who proclaimed their allegiance was with "neither the state nor the Red Brigades," invoking instead their right to extra-territoriality – to a niche carved out between the realm of the current unloved political order and that of its most implacable adversaries.

This attack on the state became violent, especially from the beginning of the 1980s through 1993. Taking opportunistic advantage of the state's weakness, the mafia and other important criminal organizations grew sronger. They fulfilled their aspirations of expanding their existing radius of sovereignty, of infiltrating politics more and more directly and of trafficking contraband and carrying out even more frequent kidnappings. The mafia had become an anti-state insofar as it ostentatiously broke apart the state's monopoly on the use of force, established the rights of life and death for its citizens, exacted tributes, counted tens of thousands of affiliates and managed business deals worth roughly 69 billion lira (second in Italy only to IRI, the agency responsible for industrial reconstruction).

As in the past, the mafia presented itself to its members as the bearer of a

---

3   See Alessandro Pizzorno, *Le radici della politica assoluta* (Milan: Feltrinelli, 1994), p. 290. On professional politicians who hold positions both the private and state sectors, see Giovanni Berlinguer, *I duplicanti. Politici in Italia* (Rome-Bari: Laterza, 1991).

4   See Lorenzo Ornaghi and Vittorio Emanuele Parsi, *Le virtù dei migliori. Le élites, la democrazia, l'Italia* (Bologna: Il Mulino, 1994), p. 79.

5   See Mauro Magatti, *Corruzione politica e società italiana* (Bologna: Il Mulino, 1996), p. 24. See also *ibid.*, p. 15: "Therefore, the elements that are usually suggested as factors of Italy's slow development are the very same ones considered to be essential for its success. Italy's backwardness is also its modernity: this contradiction is no small matter and it needs resolution."

certain kind of ethics, comprised of values such as courage, loyalty, friendship, the ability to endure incarceration and imprisonment and the will to sacrifice one's own life, as well as the lives of others. The Mafia had always been able to adorn itself with this positive image by infiltrating people's minds to the point of completely conflating the Sicilian way of life with its own behavior. Leonardo Sciascia, aware of this risk, wrote that "when I denounce the mafia it causes me to suffer since, like in any Sicilian, the remnants of the *mafioso* mentality are present and continue to thrive in me. As I struggle against the mafia, I am also struggling against myself. It is like a scission, an affliction."[6] Even among its *capi* or gang leaders (evoked by Sciascia with great acumen in *Il Giorno della Civetta* [*The Day of the Owl*] through his slightly stereotypical character of Don Mariano), there was every so often a note of savage nobility in the struggle to make sense of a world darkly imbued with violence, where justice and personal will were inextricably connected:

> 'But you, even if you nail me to these documents like Christ to His Cross, you're a man...' 'So are you,' said the captain, not without emotion. Then, with a twinge of discomfort at having exchanged a 'Present Arms' with a head of the mafia, he tried to justify this by remembering that he had once shaken hands with Minister Mancuso and the Honourable Member Livigni as representatives of the people, surrounded by fanfares and flags amid the din of a National Holiday. Unlike them, Don Mariano, at least, was a man. Beyond the pale of morality and law, incapable of pity, an unredeemed mass of human energy and of loneliness, of instinctive, tragic will. As a blind man pictures in his mind, dark and formless, the world outside, so Don Mariano pictured the world of sentiment, legality and normal human relations. What other notion could he have of the world, if, around him, the word 'right' had always been suffocated by violence, and the wind of the world had merely changed the word into a stagnant and putrid reality?[7]

The values of courage, loyalty and friendship for which the *mafiosi* pride themselves have always been and remain today the stakes of a lethal game involving the individual transfer of loyalty from one *cosca* (gang) to another. Death is the price for betrayal, suspicion, calculation, or even the cruel

---

6   Leonardo Sciascia, *La Sicilia come metafora*, ed. Marcelle Padovani (Milan: Mondadori, 1979).
7   *Idem*, *Il giorno della civetta* (Turin: Einaudi, 1961), pp. 101–2.

impulsiveness of the *capi* (as in the case of Luciano Liggio, who killed his own men for pure enjoyment). Anthropologically, the *mafioso* lives his life on alert and in constant uncertainty: "If you don't know when the hit will come or from where, anxiety and mistrust are intensified. Fear becomes indistinct and generalized. This creates an acute, almost paranoid sensitivity to signals, which can transform a raised eyebrow into the most tremendous of threats."[8] Moreover, in the *mafioso* mindset, it is death itself that establishes a rigid hierarchy of values according to which real men can be distinguished from the "*ominicchi, mezzi uomini, e quaquaraquà*" (terms which indicate human nullity and animal stupidity, equating them to geese or chickens). As Pino Arlacchi notes, "the acceptance of death among *mafiosi* seems to be the consequence of a qualitative distinction among human beings. In many ways, the mafia mentality is elitist and deeply anti-egalitarian. Not all men are on the same level, and consequently, not all lives... have the same value. The lives of some are worth less than others."[9] A spontaneous super-heroism and a delirium of omnipotence with regard to the disposable nature of one's own life and the lives of others pervade the mafia mentality.

The new urban "mafia business," which lies at the heart of powerful international financial empires that traffic in drugs but also make legal investments and play the stock market, no longer resembles the rural mafia embodied by Don Mariano. It continues, of course, to sell protection, and even its most recent *capi*, like Totò Riina, are not lacking in feudal archaism and the "combination of coarseness and subtlety."[10] Yet the Mafia has changed profoundly. After the murder of General Dalla Chiesa and an attack of unprecedented intensity on the state (culminating in the killings of the judges Falcone and Borsellino and the bombing of monuments in

---

8   Diego Gambetta, *La mafia siciliana* (Turin: Einaudi, 1994), p. 170.
9   Pino Arlacchi, *La mafia imprenditrice* (Bologna: Il Mulino, 1983), pp. 152–53. To place this attitude in context, see John Davis, *Antropologia della società mediterranea* (Turin: Einaudi, 1980); and Luigi Lombardi Satriani and Mariano Meligrana, *Il ponte di San Giacomo. L'ideologia della morte nella società contadina del Sud* (Palermo: Sellerio, 1982). On the reactions of mafiosi women (wives, sisters, mothers) with respect to turncoat family members and the deaths of relatives in murder sprees that include babies, see Renate Siebert, *Le donne, la mafia* (Milan: Il Saggiatore, 1994). In Euripides' *Trojan Women*, Astyanax is killed by the Greeks so that he will not avenge the death of his father, Hector, in the future. The same holds – albeit in a less heroic form – for *mafiosi* because, like Nitto Santapaola, they know they must exterminate "the sons of those whom we have killed."
10 Corrado Stajano, ed., *Mafia. L'atto di accusa dei giudici di Palermo* (Rome: Editori Riuniti, 1992), p. ix.

Rome and Florence),[11] the mafia now seems to have changed its strategy again, with flexible opportunism, by counting on the wide discredit of the *pentiti* or turncoats and on the further diversification of its investments.

The problem of the mafia is part of a much larger question, which pertains to the consolidation of violence in the hands of the Italian military and the way in which the state subsequently gained a monopoly on the legitimate use of violence. One must look at the ways in which the modern state has asserted its authority, especially after unification,[12] and at the logic and the forms of conduct that the modern state has not been able to incorporate. From a philosophical standpoint, one must also take into account the difficulties faced by systems of ethics tied to universal values (like equality, respect for all men and reciprocity of treatment) when they have tried to plant roots in a society dominated for so long by local traditions of particularism. Such traditions have made the effective implementation of the rule of law difficult, with the exception perhaps of some limited cross sections of the population. And yet, at least as the inheritor of Roman law (which, unlike Anglo-Saxon common law, is not bound by customs or "precedents"), Italy is a country where in certain areas, especially those in which communal civilization flourished, different "communitarian" ethical systems have taken shape around a body of codes promulgated and maintained through written public laws.

Beginning with the banditry of the post-Risorgimento era, "ethical remnants" (even if they be retrograde) have found some emotional legitimacy – a product of a past that refuses to submit to new laws and political condi-

---

11 Among the many studies on the pre-history and history of the mafia, see Paolo Pezzino, *Una certa reciprocità di favori. Mafia e modernizzazione violenta nella Sicilia postunitaria* (Milan: Franco Angeli, 1990); idem, *Mafia: industria della violenza* (Florence: La Nuova Italia, 1995); Nicola Tranfaglia, *Mafia, politica e affari nell'Italia repubblicana. 1945–1991* (Rome-Bari: Laterza, 1992). On recent developments, see Pino Arlacchi, *Gli uomini del disonore* (Milan: Mondadori, 1992); Salvatore Lupo, *Storia della mafia. Dalle origini ai giorni nostri* (Rome: Donzelli, 1993). On other criminal powers, see Isaia Sales, *Storia della camorra* (Rome: Editori Riuniti, 1988); Enzo Ciconte, *'Ndrangheta dall'Unità a oggi* (Rome-Bari: Laterza, 1992), esp. pp. 306–10 for an important discussion of the phenomenon involving a progressive shift from an "*omertà* from below" to an "*omertà* from above" that guarantees the crime cells a degree of protection from politicians, the ruling class and the banks. For a more general account, see Romano Canosa, *Storia della criminalità in Italia* (Turin: Einaudi, 1991).

12 The persistence of a "noble" depiction of the mafia has been connected to the suffering created by modernity, the monopoly on legitimate use of violence held by the modern state and the consequent stern disciplining of society; see Paolo Pezzino, "La mafia" in Mario Isnenghi, ed., *I luoghi della memoria* (Rome-Bari: Laterza, 1977), pp. 113–34, esp. pp. 130–32.

tions, and has been forced to camouflage itself. Thus the relative autonomy of these ethical remnants results from the rejection of, or an unstable compromise with, modernity. The heroes of this compromise have enjoyed privileges assured by the state while exploiting their image as rebels against it.

In Sardinia, what remains of the Codice d'Onore Barbaricino (Honor Code of Barbagia) has more to do with a rejection than a compromise. In the "contemporary prehistory" of the Barbagia Hills of Sardinia, there existed – and continue to exist, though now in ruins – customs and norms of another historical era, of an "archaic" society that had always victoriously opposed any phenomena of colonization and "modernization." They successfully opposed the Carthaginians and the Romans, the penetration of Christianity, the feudal domination of Pisa, Genoa and Spain, as well as that of the Piedmontese government and the unified Italian state. The *su connotu* ("the noted" or "known," i.e., the customary norms passed on by tradition) regulated – and in part still regulate today – the life of the Barbagia community, made up of roughly 65,000 people in scattered villages, surrounded by wild mountainous zones in pristine solitude with thick woods, lentisk and myrtle shrubs, immense granite and dolomite rock face and numerous caverns and hiding places. "Beautiful colors for tourists and artists... but only for them," said Emilio Lussu in his speech to the Senate on December 16, 1953.

Abandoning their homes for months at a time, the men lead their herds from their folds through the sheep tracks toward the pastures of the plains. As a result, women have acquired responsibility and authority unheard of elsewhere. In this ethical microclimate, norms of conduct have taken shape over centuries in order to preserve an isolated society. These norms are based, above all, on a sense of honor and on taking the administration of justice into one's own hands in open opposition to the state, which has always been considered extraneous and hostile. It is impossible to suffer an offense without reacting, and it is precisely this ability to avenge oneself that distinguishes the *su balenti* (the valiant and courageous) from the *su rimitanu* (the lesser man). In the late 1950s, the Sardinian jurist Antonino Pigliaru tried to articulate the Code of Barbagia in legal terms by extrapolating juridical maxims from expressed convictions and from actual behavior. The first article, from which the others derive, is as follows: "An offense must be avenged. No man of honor can fail to exact revenge, except in the case when he forgoes his revenge for a higher moral purpose after having demonstrated his virility throughout his life." Article 23, the last, functions as the beginning of a vicious cycle: "An offense which has been carried out as an act of revenge itself constitutes a new motive for revenge on behalf of the person to whom it was directed, especially if it was carried out in a disproportionate, inappropriate, or unfair manner. Blood revenge constitutes a grave offense, even when its purpose was that of avenging a previous blood offense."[13] The material basis of this ethic rests on the primary factor for the survival and prosperity of the people of Barbagia: the flock. The ancient custom of the *bardana* – raiding the plains, a practice that ensured the survival of this mountain civilization – endures by virtue of the fact that stealing livestock is considered acceptable, especially when the animals are taken from a wealthy owner. But a poor shepherd who has been robbed and those who return from jail may benefit from a form of social solidarity that enables them to reconstitute their flock – the custom of *sa ponidura*, which consists in requesting a sheep from each shepherd of the town. In any case, the conviction that "offense is more serious than robbery" remains intact (even though the hocking of animals is prescribed for revenge in this case). "If one member of the family has been offended, the entire family must support that member and each one is authorized to kill and, in fact, each will."[14] Now that all of these "little worlds" are disappearing, having lost their fortified isolation, their ethos has been transformed: through the integration of the inhabitants of Barbagia into the larger national or inter-

---

13   See Antonio Pigliaru, "La vendetta barbaricina come ordinamento giuridico" (1959), in *idem, Il banditismo in Sardegna* (Milan: Giuffrè, 1975). See also Marvin E. Wolfgang and Franco Ferracuti, *The Subculture of Violence* (London: Tavistock, 1967); Alberto Ledda, *La civiltà fuorilegge* (Milan: Mursia, 1971); and Pietro Marongiu, *Teoria e storia del banditismo sociale in Sardegna* (Cagliari: Edizioni Della Torre, 1981). For a more general account, see also Susan Jacoby, *Wild Justice: The Evolution of Revenge* (New York: Harper & Row, 1983).

14   Maria Pitzalis Acciaro, *In nome della madre. Ipotesi sul matriarcato barbaricino* (Milan: Feltrinelli, 1978), p. 121. As she writes (pp. 128–29): "The morality lies in the fact that there is a will to see justice done, even at the cost of one's own life... This ethic resides in the individual: it is just to die... because there is a fusion of two moral obligations in each individual – desperate survival (either life or death) and survival of the family. In this fusion, if the individual dies, it is an act of valor; his conscience is clean, whether he is firing or being fired upon. Mothers are the purveyors of this moral law when they say: my son or my husband is as innocent as the Virgin Mary... It is clear that these people have never been subjugated and that they only depend on themselves, not so much as individuals, but rather as a family clan, inasmuch as there is no philosophy of individualism at work here."

national community (through emigration), or through the transformation of Barbagian customs into instruments of ferocious lawlessness for the sake of profit, particularly in the kidnapping "industry."

In general terms, it seems almost tautological to say that criminal powers prevail where the state has not been able to install itself with respect and authority, and where no transparent public arena has been offered to special interest or lobbying groups (such as in state contracting). In this way, criminality finds an excuse for upholding the self-legitimatizing ethics it has inherited. Take, for example, the justifications offered in defense of kidnapping: criminal powers seek to renew the myth of the bandit as a hero who acts out of necessity and who knows better than the treasury how well-off the rich are. Hence we hear the boasting of those who see themselves as Robin Hood, like Raffaele Cutolo who declared with utmost seriousness: "I bring well-being where there is poverty." These forms of self-legitimization, however, are not immune from compromise or collusion with corrupt representatives of state institutions (as in the intricate relationships between politics and the Neapolitan Camorra after the earthquake of 1980).[15] Whatever the founding ethos of the criminal powers may have been, its ethos is now the product of mimetic processes of continuous adaptation to changing circumstances which are characterized by the paradox of economic globalization, about which the following generalization might be made: "the bigger the world economy, the more powerful its smallest players."[16]

Emergencies and the "Moral Question"

In an oppressive climate characterized by the unravelling of the state and imperiled institutions, the alarm sounded by Enrico Berlinguer at the end of the 1970s, urgently calling for a discussion of the "moral question," went unheeded. His choice of "austerity" as a remedy against the economic troubles induced by the first oil crisis and rampant corruption (he identified

---

15 For Cutolo's statment, see Adriano Baglivo, *Camorra S. p. a.* (Milan: Rizzoli, 1983), p. 132. On the degradation of Naples, the collusion among judges and heads of organized crime, the exchange of votes, and the war between the various "families" during the period that spans from the Irpinia earthquake to the decline of Gava, Pomicino, De Lorenzo, and De Donato, see Francesco Barbagallo, *Napoli fine Novecento. Politici cammorristi imprenditori* (Turin: Einaudi, 1997).

16 John Naisbitt, *Global Paradox: The Bigger the World Economy, the More Powerful Its Smallest Players* (New York: W. Morrow, 1994).

the causes as "uncontrolled individualism" and "crazed consumerism")[17] was interpreted as the unfashionable fear of a sad-faced knight, a noble hidalgo who was fighting windmills without realizing that "modernity" required "grit," that is, a bold, aggressive lifestyle without – whether it was openly stated or merely implied – "moralistic" scruples. Paradoxical situations arose, like that of the mayor of Turin, Diego Novelli, who, having denounced corrupt colleagues, was himself forced to resign. Even the ostentation of wealth, however accumulated, was no longer considered by the Left to be a condemnable aspiration that should be repressed. Thus, the last traces of a traditional ethos founded on the inhibition of consumerist desires disappeared.

With an increase in consumption (including luxury consumption), an improved job market, massive hiring in the schools and state sector, greater freedom of movement and vacations and cruises abroad, "hedonistic" and individualistic attitudes began to develop, especially among the emerging middle classes. This was particularly true during the period of socialist-led government coalitions. An observable discrepancy began to emerge between the professed criteria of judgment and the codes of real behavior.[18] At the same time, an ethics based more on unrestrained individual preferences took precedence over an ethics based on norms which were imposed by tradition, religion, or the search for the "common good." This change was not only a sign that individuals had grown accustomed to bearing the weight of choices imposed on them by the state, but also that the ethical party and the political world in general no longer pervaded individual conscience on a massive scale. Such changes resulted undoubtedly in greater freedom and more widespread wealth, which was easily adapted to and enjoyed by the so-called "*popolo del BOT*" or "Treasury Bond People" (in particular, the urban middle class, which at 22.4% of Italy's population was twice that of other European nations).[19]

---

17 Enrico Berlinguer, *Austerità, occasione per trasformare l'Italia* (Rome: Editori Riuniti, 1977), p. 13.

18 See the reports made by CENSIS: *Gli anni del cambiamento. Il rapporto sulla situazione sociale del paese dal 1967 al 1982* (Milan: Franco Angeli, 1982); *I valori guida degli italiani. Immagini opinioni e rappresentazioni a quarant'anni dalla nascita della Repubblica* (Rome: Presidenza del Consiglio dei Ministri, 1989). See also Gabriele Calvi, *Valori e stili di vita degli italiani* (Milan: ISEDI, 1977).

19 Cfr. Antonio Cobalti and Antonio Schizzerotto, *La mobilità sociale in Italia* (Bologna: Il Mulino, 1994), p. 216.

Justice and the Social State

Meanwhile, the public debt was increasing and the miracle of "clearing entries" was no longer able to hide the abysmal state of government ledgers. The fiscal crisis had been discovered: drastic medicine was needed to cure the ills of the state. But who was going to pay for it? Public perception of injustices and real inequalities began to mount with regard to matters that the revolutionary militants—who were further discredited by their spiraling descent into terrorism—considered insignificant concerns of a tepid reformist politics: the healthcare and pension systems, taxes, employment prospects for the young and the competitiveness of Italian products abroad. At the beginning of the 1990s in Italy, people began to notice a problem that few had hitherto seen, although elsewhere it had long been the subject of discussion and disagreement: the inability of states to redistribute wealth adequately among their citizens, as they had done in the past. Among the various factors, one cause was identified in the criteria employed for the determining eligibility for welfare. There was clearly a need to reformulate the social pact through the elimination of waste and a more equitable distribution of ever-increasing costs and ever-decreasing collective benefits. However, in so doing there was a heightened risk of stripping away the "safety net" from the weakest and of skimping on assistance to those who truly needed essential goods and services. Italy too was entering a phase of diminished expectations. The decline of the Fordist model for mass production and the large-scale renewal of the processes of "globalization" that have redefined world markets generated the virtual disappearance of full employment and simultaneously opened the borders to vast migrations of the earth's dispossessed.

Once it became clear that the social state could not continue to unload the same sacrifices on the usual categories of persons or to distribute indiscriminately the benefits to which its citizens were accustomed, its very ethos was slowly induced to change. This was particularly true now that the "philosophy of guaranteed jobs and salaries" for "state workers" was coming into question, an ideology that had been a stabilizing factor throughout the history of the monarchy and republican Italy alike down to the present day. But as Guido Melis notes, "today, even this social function, which is linked to the unwritten pact between development and underdevelopment, seems clearly to be on the wane."[20] In this way, the "dogmas" regarding the security of employment in the state sector began to crumble. Ethics once again entered politics, coming to the rescue by simplifying the choices and reducing matters to a cut-and-dry alternative: either privilege a notion of justice that protects the weakest classes and individuals or give free reign to competition between individuals and groups with the market as arbiter. Should resources be set aside for the use of future generations, thereby limiting the expectations of those alive today, or should posterity have to fend for itself?

How are we to decide? By this time, the aim was to devise a system of ethics in politics that would not need to refer constantly to the incessant (and largely misunderstood) flux of concrete situations, but would instead be able to justify itself through universal values that were subject to public discussion and hence modifiable. For over twenty years there was a growing interest in normative philosophies, like those of Jürgen Habermas and John Rawls, whose theories of "communicative action" and "political liberalism," respectively, were called upon in Italy to solidify moral intuitions which had sprung from the soil of the oldest democracies: autonomy and self-determination for individuals, the formation of consensus through non-violent and unbiased means, the primacy of freedom over equality, "constitutional patriotism" and "civic religion."

Political philosopher Salvatore Veca translated into the language of "public ethics" the demands for social justice that had previously been championed by Marxism. Together with Bobbio, he kept alive, if in a different way, the traditional civic vocation of Italian philosophy. Beginning with Kant and the phenomenology of Enzo Paci, Veca became increasingly close to Anglo-Saxon political thought in its "contractualistic" form. In particular, he drew upon and developed John Rawls' program that focused on the idea of justice, but he gave it an original twist when it came to the question of how to reach the greatest common good in societies that are characterized by the principles of pluralism and individualism (in which "liberal neutrality" does not allow for any pre-established, absolute, or unquestionable hierarchy of values). His answer lies in the need, on the one hand, to find a shared core of beliefs and deducible moral intuitions and, on the other hand, to develop a model for political justice capable of stabilizing

---

20   Melis, *Storia dell'amministrazione italiana, 1861–1993*, pp. 534–35.

the Rawlsian "overlapping consensus" necessary for the survival and growth of democratic societies.[21] Here, one of the still unresolved issues in modern reflection on ethics is raised once again: in order to obtain specific universal rules and to justify equality and justice among all citizens, one risks eliminating differences between them, along with their right to pursue the good as they see it – in their individual decisions and in specific situations – and of forgetting either Aristotle's "good life" or Foucault's "cultivation of the self."

Dirty Hands, Clean Hands

The theme of justice was suddenly brought to broader public attention in February 1992 – but not exactly by philosophical means. It was at this time that deep-rooted and flagrant corruption was discovered in Milan, polluting the relations between politics (parties, local and national administrations and the state military corps) and the productive world. The latent need for change was suddenly accelerated by the wave of popular disdain that was unleashed by this discovery and led to the removal from power of a good part of the political nomenclature, together with a small but significant number of entrepreneurs. What disturbed and amazed public opinion was not so much the discovery of individual instances of corruption, however visible they may have been – indeed, individual corruption had always been assumed and was easily imagined – but rather the fact that the corruption had been so systematically codified and widespread. The astonishment would have been even greater had the "people" been immediately made aware of the supreme trick that had been played, that is to say the fact that even the systems intended to combat corruption had profited from it, proving that "the authorized personnel know the fool's secret."[22]

---

21   Among Salvatore Veca's many works, see in particular *La società giusta* (Milan: Il Saggiatore, 1982); *Una filosofia pubblica* (Milan: Feltrinelli, 1986); *Etica e politica* (Milan: Garzanti, 1989); and *Dell'incertezza. Tre meditazioni filosofiche* (Milan: Feltrinelli, 1997), esp., pp. 87–251.

22   Agatino Licandro and Aldo Varano, *La città dolente. Confessioni di un sindaco corrotto* (Turin: Einaudi, 1993), p. 62. See also Franco Cazzola, *Della corruzione. Fisiologia e patologia di un sistema politico* (Bologna: Il Mulino, 1988); Sergio Turone, *Politica ladra. Storia della corruzione in Italia, 1861–1992* (Rome-Bari: Laterza, 1992); Giulio Sapelli, *Cleptocrazia. Il "meccanismo unico" della corruzione tra economia e politica* (Milan: Feltrinelli, 1994); and Alessandro Silj, *Malpaese. Criminalità e corruzione politica nell'Italia della Prima Repubblica* (Rome: Donzelli, 1994). On corruption before "Mani pulite," see Giorgio Galli, *Affari di Stato L'Italia sotterranea, 1943–1990: storia politica, partiti, corruzione, misteri, scandali* (Milan: Kaos, 1991).

The Italian magistracy "woke up" and became the leader of the changes that would shake up and renew the image of recent Italian history. Why did it take the magistracy so long to leave the "Foggy Port" and the "Poison Palace" – to overcome the inertia and, in some cases, the subordination to, or perverse collusion with, political and economic power? Perhaps because it was "often unwittingly obsequious with regard to other powers" and "isolated in the ivory tower it had built for itself."[23] But perhaps also because it lacked, as Antonio Di Pietro has maintained, "the access keys to the system" of the highly sophisticated machine of financial corruption that used bank accounts and deposits like "Chinese boxes," hidden in fiscal paradises all over the world. Certainly, the magistracy functioned as a substitute at a moment when a good part of the ruling order had been delegitimized and morally decapitated – that is, when the other powers had been submitted to scrutiny and a siege of public opinion and the existing political order bore visible marks of its fragility.

The causes of this situation were, however, remote. Almost all the judges appointed during Fascism retained their positions after the war, and for decades – with a few rare exceptions – they would remain completely integrated with the ruling powers and would continue, at best, to "pursue a 'paternal' function" for the magistracy. Moreover, the dependence of the magistracy on the government has a long history in Italy. As far back as 1848, Article 68 of the Albertine Statute required the supervision of the judicial branch of government by the executive branch: "Justice emanates from the King and is administered in his name by judges whom he has appointed." When, in 1945, the National Association of Italian Magistrates (ANMI) was founded, there was an attempt to sever this connection and guarantee the apolitical nature of the magistracy. Judges were prohibited from being affiliated with political parties, a ruling which "forgot, or pretended to forget, that one can engage in political activity without being registered in a political party or movement."[24] But while the struggle for liberation from external control and political "structures of influence" was difficult, in the end the magistracy's search for independence from the power of its own internal hierarchies was even more arduous.

Some of the tensions in the relationship between the magistracy and Ital-

---

23 Gherardo Colombo, *Il vizio della memoria* (Milan: Feltrinelli, 1996), p. 26.
24 Romano Canosa and Pietro Federico, *La magistratura in Italia dal 1945 a oggi* (Bologna: Il Mulino, 1974), pp. 91, 95.

ian society became clear over time and in newspaper reporting; but the tensions were also evident in the change in the image of judges held by the Italian people. We can see this shift in three important films produced over the course of a decade in which many films of this nature were made. The first was *In nome della legge* (*In the Name of the Law*) by Pietro Germi, released in 1949. In this film, the "magistrate hero," a simple lower court judge in a small city, confronts the mafia. In his attempt to defeat the *pax mafiosa* and the city inhabitants' unyielding distrust in institutions, he is forced to show – in a perspective one might call "Hegelian" – that the state is effectively capable of resolving social conflict by providing order and safety on a greater and more dignified level than its adversaries. The other two films were both made by Luigi Zampa: *Processo alla città* (*The City Stands Trial*), released in 1952, dealt with the Neapolitan *Camorra*, and generated controversy with its criticism of the police (preventative censorship of cinema and theater was in fact abolished only in 1961); and *Il magistrato* (*The Magistrate*), released in 1959, in which we move from the "figure of the judge as someone who resolves" problems to the image of the "problematic judge who refuses to carry out his role because he is convinced of his own functional ineptitude."[25] The crisis of justice thus manifested itself in the awareness – even on behalf of the judges themselves – of the "mistrust in the law as a body of common rules" that the majority of Zampa's compatriots felt, and which would later be clearly expressed, albeit in a completely different political and civic climate, in Elio Petri's 1969 film *Indagine su un cittadino al di sopra di ogni sospetto* (*Investigation of a Citizen above Suspicion*). The popular belief was thus reinforced that laws are like spider webs: spun by the strong and used to trap the weak.

Beginning in 1992, the simmering indignation of the "people" concerning the arrests of the corrupt, and the live broadcasts of their trials on television, transformed the magistracy's program, dubbed "Mani Pulite" or "Clean Hands," into a ritualistic cleansing and mass self-purification. The "dirty hands" (of the politicians and businessmen) were replaced by the

---

25 See Vincenzo Tomeo, *Il giudice sullo schermo. Magistratura e polizia nel cinema italiano* (Bari: Laterza, 1973), pp. 47–56, 64. On the evolution of the magistrature in Italy, see Ezio Moriondo, *L'ideologia della magistratura italiana* (Bari: Laterza, 1967); Canosa and Federico, *La magistratura in Italia dal 1945 a oggi*; and Edmondo Bruti Liberati, Adolfo Ceretti, and Alberto Giasanti, eds., *Governo dei giudici: la magistratura tra diritto e politica* (Milan: Feltrinelli, 1966).

"clean hands" (of the magistrates and the pool of investigators in Milan).[26] Furthermore, in the collective imagination, the opposition of political parties was often overshadowed by that of single individuals, either honest or dishonest (although there was later a tendency to demonize the parties exclusively and lay the blame for the rottenness of the "First Republic" entirely on them). This "Italian revolution" assigned a spectacular role to the magistracy in light of the shortcomings of the other state powers. Nonetheless, there never was a truly sufficient "expiation," in the sense that many quickly forgot that for years they had accepted all of the benefits which had "rained" upon them, amply disbursed by a ruling order that sought to fulfill each and every request. Because many were distracted by the main judicial battles of Mani Pulite, they lost sight of the fact that the problem of justice in Italy also included trials of intolerable and uncivilized duration, the near impossibility of identifying and prosecuting criminals in adequate numbers and a widespread disdain for the law.

Yet a renewal did take place and, at least for a while, the impunity of many of those in power ceased to be automatically guaranteed (today the challenge has been renewed, as the "party of the unpunished" seek to regain their terrain by naming accomplices and requesting new laws). But not all *tangentocrati* or "career political bribe-takers" are alike. If one compares the unabashed arrogance of Mario Chiesa to the conduct of the socialist member of parliament Sergio Moroni, or to that of Gabriele Cagliari or Raul Gardini, one must recognize in these latter – despite their belief that they have been unjustly persecuted – a "nobility in defeat" and a human grandeur when faced with the end. Moroni expressed this sentiment eloquently in the letter he wrote to Giorgio Napolitano, then-president of the Italian Parliament's Chamber of Deputies, before committing suicide:

> A great veil of hypocrisy (shared by all) has concealed the lifestyles of the parties and their methods of fundraising. There is a uniquely Italian culture of defining rules and laws that everyone knows will never be respected, beginning with the tacit understanding that there will be solidarity in devising the

---

26 For a discussion of the moral dilemmas implicit in the distinction between dirty hands and clean hands, see in addition to Sartre's play *Les mains sales*: Michael Walzer, "Political Action: The Problem of Dirty Hands," *Philosophy and Public Affairs*, II (1973), pp. 160–80; and Philip Bobbitt and Guido Calabresi, *Tragic Choices* (New York: Norton, 1978). On the recent changes in values in Italy and elsewhere, see the comparative study by P. Ester, Loek Halman and R. A. De Moor, *The Individualizing Society: Value Change in Europe and North America* (Tilburg: Tilburg University Press, 1994).

procedures and protocols that will violate the very same rules... I do not believe that our country will build the future it deserves by cultivating a climate of pogroms on politicians, whose limits are well-known but who have also made Italy into one of the freest countries in the world.[27]

Politics Enters the Home

Historically speaking, the most significant precondition of the Clean Hands phenomenon may be located in the end of Italy's "blocked democracy" and the consequent stagnation of the country's ethos. The unexpected end of the Cold War, between 1989 and 1991, loosened seemingly inextricable bonds in a convulsive manner and erased, albeit much more slowly, the classic "cold civil war" equation of the internal enemy with the international enemy. The end of the "red threat," which had justified illegality and corruption in the name of the legitimate defense against communism, eliminated the need to employ certain tools. The armed peacetime that had lasted over half a century under the credible threat of a nuclear holocaust seemed at first to leave space for a better world, more livable for all. The waning of the great value-conflicts and dominant ideologies contributed to the further loss of prestige by the ethical parties and to the actual disappearance of two of the largest of them: the century-old Italian Socialist Party (PSI) and the fifty-year old Christian Democrats (DC). Even some of the "minor" parties which had shaped Italian history in recent years, like the Liberal Party and the Social Democratic Party (though they had been substantially reduced to satellites of the DC) left the scene as well. The strongest Communist party in the Western world (the second anomaly of the Italian situation after that of the Vatican, for it meant the simultaneous presence in Italy of both the "devil" and "holy water"), which had transformed itself over time, but which also held less power at the national level, was barely grazed by this storm and even managed to strengthen itself. No party, however, dared to renew the pursuit of global objectives in the name

---

27 Cited in Enrico Nascimbeni and Andrea Pamparana, *Le mani pulite. L'inchiesta di Milano sulle tangenti* (Milan: Mondadori, 1992), pp. 139, 140. This corruption was undoubtedly rooted in the choice on behalf of the elite to "*evade the challenge of international competition, thereby delaying the modernization of the political system* (democratic alternation), *the economic system* (going beyond the mixed economy), *and the administrative model* (decentralization and reform of welfare and public administration according to the criteria of effectiveness and efficiency)"; Giuseppe Vacca, *Vent'anni dopo* (Turin: Einaudi, 1997), p. 213.

of a specific protagonist or "historical macro-subject" (e.g., the proletariat or the "free world"), as had occurred in the early years of bipolarity.

Often, all that remains after the evaporation of grand ideals is the residue of stale ideological aromas and something like the *caput mortuum* of alchemic reactions – the sediment of a pragmatism which has encountered objective difficulties in distinguishing coherent principles and must therefore adopt the technique of "navigation by sight." During the Cold War, the distance between the "feet" and the "head" pushed Italians to dream of fatherlands other than the one in which they lived, but now that distance seemed to have been foreshortened to such a degree that the "feet" were too close to the "head" (in other words, Italians lost sight of the new international context of which their country was now a part and they concentrated, almost exclusively, on "local realities").

The problem of alternation in government, which had blocked turnover in Italian politics by excluding some parties from power, appeared suddenly to be overcome. Once this obstacle was removed, however, renewal proved to be extremely difficult. Politicians – some more sensitive to the necessity of re-establishing the parties on a new foundation, some more attuned to the moods of public opinion – sought to find a remedy by linking politics to new ideals of stability or to consolidated popular passions of an extra-political nature. Politics became more personalized and different "packages" were offered to different recipients. These appeals were no longer immediately definable in terms of class (as in the case of proposed changes in welfare, initiatives to combat inflation and unemployment and strategies for Italy's "entry into Europe"). This was the result of a sort of "political Toyotaism," in the sense that it reproduced a phenomenon analogous to the one witnessed with the end of Taylorism/Fordism. Since standardized production with a guaranteed market eventually gets bogged down (legend has it that Henry Ford brashly invited consumers to purchase the Model T, saying "buy it in any color, as long as it's black"), political parties are now forced not only to maintain a "lean and mean" apparatus, but also to act according to the system initiated by Toyota in which production is diversified and updated based on specific consumer requests, with the promise of "just in time" delivery. The buyer is thus guaranteed the choice of hundreds of car colors, but the system itself is no longer able to impose its own choices on the buyer, nor can it plan long-term strategies or allow itself a consistent warehouse inventory with the idea that the product will eventually find buyers.[28] In other words, the parties no longer started out with a relatively stable pool of voters or members, or, at the very least, the level of loyalty and the relative predictability of voter behavior were no longer guaranteed as in the past. But, above all, the dictate of "whichever X, provided that it is Y" was no longer valid. This is not to say that there existed a mythical sovereignty of the voter, along the same lines as the equally mythical "sovereignty of the consumer." But voting citizens were more attuned to their own immediate interests, and the "political market" increasingly had to be won over one day at a time by analyzing the expectations and demands, both tacit and explicit, of particular sectors of society and then offering packages that combined these different elements.

With the end of credible ideological alliances abroad and the gradual reduction of class-based politics, the political landscape was transformed (the virtual disappearance of farmers and the gradual decline in number of workers beginning in the 1970s, just when the Left was proclaiming its "centrality," meant the fall of the "sickle" and loss of visibility for the "hammer," while the end of Soviet-style communism destroyed the most powerful *raison d'être* of both the Christian Democrats and the Italian Social Movement). Thus, new and renewed parties and groupings began to appear, hoping to collect the inheritance of the old dissolved parties or reorganize their fragments. They sought, moreover, to replace the idea of the necessary fragility of the new with an image of deep-rooted robust trees that can live for centuries and are traditionally considered difficult to extirpate: the Quercia (oak tree) and the Ulivo (olive tree). On the Left as well as the Right, with the birth of the Democratic Party of the Left (PDS) and the National Alliance (AN), the idea of continuity prevailed over that of rupture. Both the PDS and AN came to terms with the present without

---

28 With the end of Fordism, "the virtuous circle between industrial growth and growth in employment, which had characterized much of the 1900s, was broken. Now, industry no longer grows 'together' with employment – as had happened during the Golden Age of Fordism, when high productivity rates were, by definition, compensated by higher rates of economic development, and thus of production – but in some sense *against* employment. Employment is being devoured. And thus so too are old productive units fragmenting, personnel rolls becoming lighter, internal bureaucracies being dismantled, the mass of skilled workers being replaced by mechanical contraptions and robots, with the hiss of computer processors, and the occasional white-smocked 'operators' and maintenance personnel. The post-Fordist industrial machine thus 'grows as it grows leaner'. It amasses wealth as it unloads itself of workers. It aggregates working power at the same time as it dissolves the social fabric"; Revelli, *La sinistra sociale*, p. 51.

completely repudiating the past, offering a solid bridge to cross the void that had developed and providing for a softer "landing" on the side of the new. Other political groups, like Forza Italia (which means "Go Italy!") have no need for roots in the past because they are completely new. Instead, they have associated their name with soccer jargon, thus ideologically associating politics with rooting for a soccer team and symbolically assigning their followers the same color blue of the National team's jerseys. By doing so, they have synchronized politics with the wave of popular passion for sports, particularly by using the models of public gatherings and social divisions which, since the end of World War II, have created, for many, both the will to take sides and the desire to forget the fractiousness of the parties. All the new parties, and Forza Italia in particular, have ambitiously tried to "drug" a volatile public opinion, not by polarizing it with the platforms and images of a traditional political party, but by anchoring it to a symbolic and iconic figure or "triumphant" leader. All the better if he is a successful man who has forged his career from "the trenches of the working world" and is accustomed to emphasizing his outsider status and his disdain for "political puppet theater" – a man who knows how to make use of marketing techniques and the commercial and production networks of his private companies, the "club" system and door-to-door proselytizing in order to organize elections and the selection of political appointees from the top. With the complicity of television and other media, the quest for "forced" (*forzato*) consensus has prevailed – not forced through violence, but in the sense of accelerated growth in a greenhouse, as certain agricultural products are cultivated out of season.[29]

Politics everywhere has become ever more firmly fastened to imagery conveyed by television, and the effects are irreversible. Television has crystallized or favored – at least up until now – the persistence of, or even an increase in, the number of "socially isolated" persons, which has led many people to replace direct and more interpersonal relationships with solitary afternoons and evenings in front of the small screen. Although its light is

---

29 I am using the expression "forced consensus" in a way analogous with Georges Sorel's use of the verb *forcer*, which he borrowed from the jargon of gardeners. In the introduction to the third edition of *Reflections on Violence* (1919), this term suggests a breaking open of history – a political intervention in phases which are considered still immature in the evolution of society – in order to catapult society forward, as Peter the Great did when he introduced western modernity in Russia and Lenin did when he imposed a Marxist framework.

like that of a semi-hypnotic fishbowl, in recompense television has opened windows on realities that enormously widen the cultural horizons of individuals and classes who in the past had scarcely been provided political information and alternative visions of the world other than those they had inherited. Since the amount of time spent in "*cellule*" (small party organizations or cells), in "*case del popolo*" (community centers run by the Communist and Socialist parties), in parishes, or even with relatives and friends has gradually diminished, television has taken the place of personal relationships for many (out of laziness for some), while also rendering the walls of domestic life much more "porous." Television brings politics and the outside world into the home, virtually abolishing any separation between public and private, between the positive freedom of participation in society and politics and the negative freedom of non-interference from the outside. Thus, television oversteps the boundary between the domestic and political spheres, represented by the threshold of the home, which not even Hobbes' absolute sovereign dared to cross. Now, with the talk-show format, even "mothers, grandmothers and aunts" can take part in political debate from the living room or the kitchen. Unlike the leaders of totalitarian states, who sought to create a condition of subjection and make the individual feel small and subordinate in the piazza or in open spaces, the modern political personality has been turned by television into a "familiar" friend or enemy, hero or victim, who is seen every day in the closed and protected space of one's own apartment. The politician's triumphant weapon, more than his platforms or projects, is now seduction. Thus, politics has become a much more familiar part of everyday life and has lost its extraneousness with respect to the private world of the individual. Without much effort and without any need to attend tiresome meetings or conferences, anyone who lives on the margins of political life can now, without further mediation, bring his personal opinion to bear on elections (opinions have now become sovereign and exempt from the burden of proof now that politics, in its "external use," has transformed the rational weighing of options into a powerful narrative). The home has come to represent the privileged "green house" in which the growth of political consensus is "forced" at reduced prices. This turning point is a given fact, yet one would be mistaken to reduce all of politics to "spectacle." That aspect is its most obvious facet, which furthermore has always existed, from the parades of the Pharaohs to the radio speeches of Hitler and Roosevelt. The means may vary, but politics remains (if not always visibly) an enterprise that effectively changes given situations.

The changed situation has pushed Italian political parties to revise their organizational models, adjust the scope of their objectives and constantly update their methods for obtaining agreement among party members and the support of potential voters. Voter participation through mass media certainly does not substitute for direct participation, especially during crucial moments involving the consolidation and confrontation of political forces, but it does take on an unequivocal strategic role, underlining the difficulty in politics of proposing ideals that require the constant commitment and direct involvement of individuals. Significantly, such ethical exigencies, which were formerly invested in politics, have shifted to the voluntary sector and to religion, taking on a financial dimension with "non-profit" and "Third Sector" initiatives that are rife with implications for the future. Consequently, politics has assumed a more secular and disenchanted character, in line with the requirements of a "normal country." But, in calling for sacrifices regarding goals that were necessary to meet but which did not appear sufficiently lofty or appetizing, politics now demands extra moral stamina at the same time that it has lost some of the important ingredients that made it appealing in the past. As a result, it has dulled the most powerful reasons that made it worth the trouble of direct participation in the first place.

The Splendor of Truth

From the tumultuous transition between the "First" and "Second Republics," the Catholic Church emerged, once again, substantially reinforced. Despite the far-reaching renewal of the Second Vatican Council, the Church was considered to be in decline only a few decades later, implicated as an accomplice, by way of the Institute for Religious Works (IOR), in the Banco Ambrosiano scandal involving Roberto Calvi in the 1980s. But now, the Church seemed to have left its dark side behind. By loosening its previous hold over individual conscience, Italian politics relinquished to the Church, through implicit proxy, the representation of the most important ethical values. For this reason, during the "crisis of the parties" and the chronic inefficiency of certain government sectors, the Church was able to mobilize a great number of volunteers and successfully confront day-to-day emergencies, such as the massive influx of immigrants to Italy from countries to the South and the East. The Church was thus able to maintain its religious monopoly and increase its own prestige, despite the growing presence of Islam and different North American "sects." In more general terms, the transitional crisis of politics allowed the Church to take on a more visible role in overseeing those values that give meaning to life. It was able to reclaim these values not only by taking them away from the last of the great totalitarian regimes of the twentieth century, but also from democracy. Furthermore, when considered from the point of view of visible consensus and its effects in the realm of the "society of spectacle," the Church, with John Paul II, has managed to attract hundreds of thousands – many of them young people – in gigantic assemblies. They are all seeking an antidote within the Christian message for feelings of individual disorientation and solitude, and are testament to the permanence of hope which cannot be falsified by history – unlike the hope held out by the earthly "god that failed."

The Catholic Church has also enjoyed the sympathy of the Left ever since the "Polish pope" began to question the ethical legitimacy of Western democracy, after the attack on the fundamental values of communism had reached its zenith:

> Today, when many countries have seen the fall of ideologies which bound politics to a totalitarian conception of the world – Marxism being foremost among these – there is still a grave danger that the fundamental rights of the human being will be denied and that the religious yearnings which arise in the heart of every person will once again be absorbed into politics. This is the risk of an alliance between democracy and ethical relativism, which would remove any secure moral reference point from political and social life and on a deeper level make the acknowledgement of truth impossible.[30]

This is the new specter that John Paul II saw looming over Europe and the rest of the industrialized world, ready to destroy the residual fabric of solidarity of an opulent and consumerist West, where the reigning "free market economy" rewards the strong and crushes the weak. From April 1989, the

---

30   Pope John Paul II, Encyclical letter *Veritatis splendor* (1993), paragraph 101.

date of a memorable speech in Prague, this ghost fluttered through all John Paul II's writings and speeches, and returned almost hauntingly in his book *Crossing the Threshold of Hope* and in his later reflections on ethics, in addition to the encyclical *Veritatis Splendor*.

The fact of the matter is that democracy cannot – without contradicting itself – do without the very same "ethical relativism" that it is accused of ushering in (the mutual compatibility of all values is itself an absolute value). On a par with the idea of "reason," elaborated by Western culture over 2,500 years, ethical relativism is, so to speak, an evolutionary acquisition of the Western genetic code. Democratic regimes spring up and spread their roots as a concrete alternative to mutual slaughter, relying on that fickle specimen of relativism, the "sovereign people," which is divided into factions and interest groups. In order to co-exist without reopening both ancient and recent wounds, such factions must submit to a taboo, often accepted tacitly: to forego public disputes over ultimate values and to concentrate instead on "penultimate" questions. In private, every person can choose his own ethical, political and religious values, but thereafter can never expect to impose them on others. Modern democracy banishes the absolutism of religious faith from the public sphere, dampening or silencing the supreme values which might be worthy of self-sacrifice by granting priority to the experience of private life.

It is not difficult to understand the grave danger that the intersection of democracy and "ethical relativism" poses for the Catholic Church and any other organization or ideology based on certainties deemed inherently sturdy and untouchable: the Ethical State, the Ethical Party, churches or religious sects. Today, however, the position of the Catholic Church has become, if anything, even more uncomfortable. While it was fiercely combating communist doctrines – a self-proclaimed atheistic and deeply dogmatic ideology that had adopted an alternative catechism – its task was paradoxically less arduous. A clearly defined enemy and a harsh but measurable battlefield allowed for open collision between faiths and values that were visibly irreconcilable. The current, reluctant adversary – yesterday's precious and faithful ally – is more insidious, "underhanded" and faceless. It is an involuntary enemy, who presents a benign and tolerant image and does not react indignantly to provocation. It behaves more like a rubber wall or a reed in the water, bending and waiting for this impetuous papal tide to pass. To eradicate militant ideologies was already difficult, but to reverse the anthropological transformations introduced by civil liberties and the sense of well-being that comes along with them will be presumably much more difficult. The partial autonomy won by individuals after centuries of authoritarianism and suppression of their instincts, needs and desires has created in some privileged zones of the planet a sense of jealous freedom that rejects any imposition coming from on high. In the face of the Church's defense of the poor and the Third World, the growth of consumerism and the improvements in standards of living are now seen as non-negotiable by both the individual and his political representatives. Yet the Church has touched a nerve and a point of weakness in secular ethics: a strong and consistent justification of its norms, which risk being subjected to the interpretation of individuals who act in a purely "strategic" manner, with only their own narrow interests in mind.

CHAPTER 9
Searching for Roots

The Invocation of the Fatherland

The autonomy that the individual won from political and religious institutions (with the growth of his rights and freedoms) came generally at the price of weakened communal ties and the loss of a sense of shared history. With variations according to different local situations, an attempt was made to resist these centrifugal tendencies through the reinforcement–often intentional or instrumental–of collective identity by infusing the civic body with a supplement of love or loyalty to the "fatherland."

In Italy, the need for identity, which has been analyzed in recent studies,[1] was also motivated by other factors. These include the end of the Cold War, which reduced the need for cohesion on an international level and instead favored centrifugal forces on a national level. This took place just as disputes over events of the recent past were being reappraised, finally allowing the historical heirs of fascism and communism to enter into government coalitions. Another factor was the decline in authority of the parties, or rather of distinct factions which, unable to stake a claim to the whole, in-

---

1 The discussion was triggered by Maurizio Viroli, *Per amore della patria. Patriottismo e nazionalismo nella storia* (Rome-Bari: Laterza, 1995), as well as by the volumes by Renzo De Felice, *Rosso e nero*, and by Ernesto Galli della Loggia, *La morte della patria. La crisi dell'idea di nazione tra Resistenza, antifascismo e Repubblica*. These works were followed by those of Silvio Lanaro, *Patria* (Venice: Marsilio, 1996) and Gian Enrico Rusconi, *Patria e repubblica* (Bologna: Il Mulino, 1997). Tommaseo's distinction between *patria* and *paese* is still relevant and worth recalling: "you can love your country without loving your fatherland; you can love the borders within which you were born and not love those laws and obligations that make up the fatherland; you can love out of interest and not out of affection. More or less everyone loves his country; few love the fatherland"; quoted in Piero Melograni, *Dieci perché sulla repubblica* (Milan: Rizzoli, 1994), p. 178.

stead constructed groupings or "poles" that attempted with some difficulty to obtain recognition of their own legitimacy. Cracks were thus revealed in the political and ethical edifice, which nonetheless had withstood time and allowed Italians to overcome severe difficulties. In addition, there was the recent enlargement of the European Community, expanded in 1996 to fifteen member states with the Maastricht treaty, which gave rise to a dual and conflictual tendency: on the one hand, there was a centripetal force brought about through integration, while on the other hand, a centrifugal force obtained in the form of regional separatism. Then there was the economic crisis, which fomented a climate of potential hostility between rich and poor regions over the entire continent. Finally, there were the proclaimed secessionist desires of the Lega Nord (Northern League) with its eccentric invention of a country within the country ("Padania") and its unmitigated use of violence, which hitherto has been only verbal (the calls for secession were symptoms of widespread unease in certain northern regions and of the need felt to break with the centralism of the post-unification state, which had been hardly affected by the institution of regional governments).[2] Thus, the idea of the "*patria*" or "fatherland," with its explicit call to overcome divisions (especially in light of Italy's entry into the European Union), replaced the ethical state or "ethical party."

The newfound spirit of togetherness and national reconciliation thus changed—sometimes opportunistically—the nature of how one viewed the past. Attempts were often made to reconstruct or to forget traumatic divisions by wrapping them up in the tri-colored Italian flag. These past events spanned from the rupture between fascists and anti-fascists on September 8, 1943, which would lead to the "death of the fatherland," to the fall of the Social Italian Republic on April 25, 1945, which immersed Italians in democracy but on a "path of 'separate memberships' rather than a shared path of national belonging."[3] These events included the rupture caused by "discrimination" in the Republican Constitution with regard to the male heirs of the Savoy dynasty and those who did not fit easily within the "constitutional arc," as well as the division created by the conflicts during the "leaden years" of political terrorism in the 1970s. In the view of many, the

---

[2] As early as 1944, the Americans had criticized Italian centralism and had discussed among themselves the need to make Italy an "almost federal" state. See David W. Ellwood, *L'alleato nemico. La politica dell'occupazione americana in Italia 1943–1946* (Milan: Feltrinelli, 1977), p. 264.

[3] Pietro Scoppola, *25 aprile. La liberazione* (Turin: Einaudi, 1995), p. 40.

appeals to the Resistance, to anti-fascism, to the Constitution and the call for a "united front" against terrorism (such as in the solemn declarations of the "founding fathers" of Republican Italy, like Bobbio and Valiani) were elements of "traditionalist" rhetoric that were no longer capable of uniting Italians in solidarity. If anything, these terms brought to mind old wounds in need of healing or factors that undermined the very perception of national unity, thus artificially prolonging tensions and divisions that were believed to have been long overcome in the collective consciousness.

Various remedies were proposed to heal these old fractures, from that of the "revisionist" historians, who sought to limit the political and moral influence of the founding events of Italian democracy (especially the Resistance and the Constitution), to the efforts of those who were worried about the separatist league phenomenon and who sought a "glue" with which to bind the ideas of "fatherland" and "republic." In the case of the latter, it was a matter of reconstructing and interweaving stories and shared memories, even if—and especially when—they were painful, since they were elements that could bring together the winners and losers of the last Italian "civil war." The resulting "expiatory patriotism," therefore, was more than mere "constitutional patriotism." In other words, it argued that the longevity of democratic institutions depended on a common spirit grounded not merely in the individual's respect for the law but in the collective suffering of the people. This "dark sentiment of participation in the grief of the nation" reconciled the "irreconcilable memories" shared by a people (like the massacres in the Ardeatine caves and the Istrian "trenches," the Resistance battles and the retreat of the Russians) in the desire to belong to a single and shared destiny. The resulting advantage was two-fold: one could get people to love democracy without reducing it to a mere technique for collective decision-making and the memories of suffering could be used as an antidote to secessionism. In order to function, it was argued that democracy "needs political loyalty and civic solidarity. These virtues do not descend abstractly into the hearts and minds of common citizens ('the people') from universal principles, but are acquired over the course of history and within a community which one belongs to and in which one can recognize oneself."[4] If secessionism is blocked for the time being, "this is due to the spontaneous

---

[4] Gian Enrico Rusconi, "Scendere da Cosmopoli" in Martha Nussbaum, Gian Enrico Rusconi and Maurizio Viroli, *Piccole patrie, grande mondo* (Milan: Reset, 1995), p. 44.

reaction of the populist (sub)culture which has acted as a shield against the inconsistency of the ruling political culture, in particular of the Left."[5]

There are, however, limits to this acute and impassioned position, since the foundational story of collective experience by which peoples forge and maintain their identity–or etymologically their *mythos*–never manages to reinforce the democratic conscience sufficiently, especially when the epic of collective suffering took place over half a century ago and no longer has much meaning for the younger generations. Moreover, the same weapons employing myth can be used to divide one part of the nation from another: the North from the South. The commitment and critical rigor of historians and journalists in representing events to inspire a sentiment of belonging can undoubtedly contribute to the more solid rooting of the ideals and praxis of democracy. In order to get people to "love" democracy and, more specifically, to defuse the potential subversion of the Northern League, the tools of social and economic justice, education, good government and healthy administration as well as the awareness of the new economic and political context of Europe and the world remain much more useful. It is therefore necessary to realize that today's "nations" are no longer like those which faded away in World War I, along with their expectations of absolute autonomy, but rather are living in a wider context of advanced economic globalization and state sovereignty that has been significantly reformulated both conceptually and in terms of its spheres of influence. In addition, the need for the unanimity of memory in democratic regimes is not clear. As long as divisive memories do not represent possible hotbeds of subversion and civil war, the coexistence of many distinct, un-reconciled memories can actually be an advantage. In this sense, the "we" that is "divided" is not in itself something bad. The desire to be monolithic, in the manner of Gentile and Fascism, or fragmented, by means of secession or myopic and exclusively specific interests, yield results that are equally ruinous.

---

5   Rusconi, *Patria e repubblica*, p. 7. On the divergences between civic traditions in Italy and the phenomenon of the Lega, see Robert Putnam, *Making Democracy Work: Civic Traditions in Modern Italy* (Princeton: Princeton University Press, 1993); Ilvo Diamanti, *La Lega. Geografia, storia e sociologia di un nuovo soggetto politico* (Roma: Donzelli, 1993); Roberto Biorcio, *La Padania promessa. La storia, le idee e la logica d'azione della Lega Nord* (Milan: Il Saggiatore, 1997). For an analysis of the concept of identity in relation to the particularistic tendencies in Italy, see Oliver Schmidtke, *Politics of Identity. Ethnicity, Territories, and the Political Opportunity Structure in Modern Italian Society* (Sinzheim: Pro Universitate Verlag, 1996), esp. pp. 137–272. On the positive aspects of Italy's multi-centered culture, see Aldo Schiavone, *Italiani senza Italia. Storia e identità* (Turin: Einaudi, 1998).

In any case, it is now difficult to fabricate foundational myths or stories endowed with any enduring credibility. With the disappearance of comprehensive criteria for bestowing meaning on history in accordance with a final end, and with the fall of the presupposition that there is an intrinsic logic to history, events seem more resistant to being arranged in ordered sequences or into any vast, coherent picture. In this way, since every interpretation becomes even more fleeting and controversial, today long-cultivated utopias and philosophies of history are experiencing–on a philosophical level–a hemorrhage of meaning and a net loss of credibility. When history ceases to advance the exorbitant claim of being able to provide exhaustive explanations of events and corrective prescriptions for the future, neither the final end (emancipation, progress or a classless society), which had been worth the sacrifice of oneself and others, nor the excruciating path toward that end, seem sufficiently convincing.[6]

Between Being and Becoming

In Italian philosophy during the last quarter century, interest has diminished in conceptions that look toward a future to be domesticated or collectively subjugated; instead, there is growing interest in a present that can offer individuals meaningful fulfillment. The idea of an inexorable necessity dictating human events, pushing agents forward and orienting their actions toward a predetermined target has given way to awareness of the presence within us of something enduring that does not wither with the passage of time. Or, alternatively, it gives rise to awareness of possibilities that often diminish the harshness of the dreaded "reality principle." A "new" vision, "more encompassing and less metaphysically anguished," now calls for us to take into consideration "the world of appearances, discursive procedures and 'symbolic forms', viewing them as the place for a possible experience of Being."[7]

On the whole, the main feature of this period boils down to a dual abandonment, by a good number of thinkers, of the formerly omnipresent historical-political dimension, as well as of the accompanying proclivity to be concerned with what "ought to be." This came about via two divergent

---

6 See Remo Bodei, *Se la storia ha un senso* (Bergamo: Moretti & Vitali, 1997).
7 Pier Aldo Rovatti, preface to *Il pensiero debole* (Milan: Feltrinelli, 1983), p. 9.

trajectories. The first trajectory led to a greater appreciation of the need for coherence and for stable points of reference independent of Becoming—that is, located beyond any historicist logic internal to the events—in an effort to capture a truth of "Being" that no longer coincided either with the old metaphysics (which proposed an immovable Being independent of Becoming) or with the modern view of Becoming as the sole possible realm of philosophy and experience. The most extreme expression of this trajectory is represented by the complete negation of history and Becoming as such.

The second trajectory led to a renunciation of truth-claims guaranteed by a determinate historical *telos*. Rather than a belief in the presumed force of things—thought to act through history itself—there is a surrender to unpredictability, variety, surprise and the "innocence" of Becoming. Thus, a taste was discovered for the accidental and the ephemeral, for multiplicity that does not resolve in unity. The solid, univocal concepts which previously had been preferred—following in the footsteps of the hard sciences—are now allowed to vacillate and take on a variety of shifting meanings, remaining always open to new interpretation. The "foundations" of knowledge and the "bases" of morality, once deemed unshakable, are now considered mere amulets, useful solely in the exorcism of uncertainty, while the various projects for the emancipation of humanity put forth by contemporary philosophy have turned out to be fairy tales for adult consolation. Thus, the following expressions and concepts, which can easily be reduced to slogans, have entered into common parlance: "difference," "crisis of reason," "post-modern," "nihilism," "deconstructionism," "simulacra" and "weak thought."

In these perspectives, the structure of history—understood dialectically as becoming real through contradictions—is divided. On one side there are those, like Emanuele Severino, who deny the very existence of Becoming and consider the oscillation between Being and nothingness an absurdity. On the other side, there are those, like Gianni Vattimo, who accentuate Becoming and welcome within it the element of frailty inherent in all beings. Yet in both cases the "big questions" of philosophy—such as the destiny of beings in the world and the consciousness of existence—regain the position of preeminence that militant politics and public ethics had formerly occupied.

The difficult philosophy of Severino stands out by virtue of its isolation:

from the publication of his essay "Ritornare a Parmenide" (Returning to Parmenides) in 1964, through the present, he has completed a long and coherent journey founded on a persistent call to awaken to the truth of "Being" and abandon the "folly of Becoming" that has struck the West. By renouncing the hibernation of thought and declaring an end to the "long winter of reason" that dominated philosophy from its origins in Greek thought, or more precisely, from the fifth century B.C., one can once again recognize the incontrovertible truth according to which "if Being (of each and every being) cannot be thought of as not being, then consequently it cannot be thought that Being (of each and every Being) becomes—for if it were becoming, then it would not be: that is, it would not be, before its own birth and corruption. Therefore, *all* being is immutable. It does not come from nothingness, nor does it return to nothingness. It is eternal."[8]

The history of the West is thus certainly—in Heideggerian terms—the oblivion of Being, but such clouding, according to Severino, comes from having forgotten its indestructible eternity. Therefore, Becoming—essentially unthinkable in and of itself—does not exist. Entities do not change, nor are they born, nor do they die. They simply leave the visible field of appearances in a cyclical fashion, while remaining on the horizon of Being. They take leave temporarily, only to return (appearance, therefore, is not in time, but rather time is in appearance). Indeed, this "*appearance of Becoming*—the appearance or disappearance of the eternal—*does not become.*"[9] Yet our destiny as beings "living in time" induces us to halt this very Becoming, which we ourselves have invented but which we fear, since the thought of our presumed but never determined demise agonizes us. Thus, we imagine or

---

8   Emanuele Severino, postscript to "Ritornare a Parmenide" in *Essenza del nichilismo*, revised edition (Milan: Adelphi, 1995), p. 63. Severino published "Ritornare a Parmenide" in *Rivista di filosofia neo-scolastica* in 1964 as a direct reply to Gustavo Bontadini, his mentor at the Università Cattolica of Milan. His research in this area was developed further in *L'essenza del nichilismo* (Brescia: Paideia, 1972), *Gli abitatori del tempo* (Rome: A. Armando, 1978), *Techne. Le radici della violenza* (Milan: Rusconi, 1979), *Il destino della necessità* (Milan: Adelphi, 1980), *Il nulla e la poesia. Alla fine dell'età della tecnica: Leopardi* (Milan: Rizzoli, 1990), *Oltre il linguaggio* (Milan: Adelphi, 1992), and *Heidegger e la metafisica* (Milan: Adelphi, 1994). Giorgio Colli also proposed a return to the roots of western thought and the "Greek sages" who preceded Socrates and Plato; see *La sapienza greca*, 3 vols. (Milan: Adelphi, 1977-1980) and *La nascita della filosofia* (Milan: Adelphi, 1975), in which the speculative model of the enigma constitutes a tragic challenge to the intellect, a negation of the desire to find the ultimate meaning of the universe, and a perception of the presence of the unfathomable, inexhaustible, and the abyss in the world and in the human soul.

9   Emanuele Severino, *Tautótes* (Milan: Adelphi, 1995), p. 191.

construct "immutable entities" (fabricated by science or religion, such as the laws of physics, Zeus, or the Christian God) as remedies and anchors of salvation in the face of impermanence and death. But these immutable entities come into contradiction with the proclaimed evidence of Becoming, and they are continuously–especially after Nietzsche–eroded and annihilated. But with the destruction of God and the immutable entities, the idea of truth also topples and everything becomes relative. Therefore, what prevails in modern philosophy is skepticism, since there is no truth that can be held above Becoming. In this abandonment of absolute truth, one adapts, for the most part unconsciously, to the nature of technology, the greatest expression of the "will to power" of man and the supreme recognition of Becoming itself. With its overwhelming force and its "innovations," technology assumes control of the processes–at the price, however, of the "destruction and negation of the immutable entities."

The outcome of these two complementary and contradictory attitudes (the elevation and demolition of the simulacra of eternity) is none other than nihilism–an error and an errantry that is eternal in and of itself. One cannot escape from nihilism by way of some dialectical "overcoming" of the actual situation, but only by decisively turning one's back on one's faith in Becoming and by recognizing with almost Spinozian *laetitia* that beneath the banality of everyday life as interpreted by the light of Becoming, *sentimus experimurque nos aeternos esse*:

> In the depth of his being, every man knows that he is eternal. Like every thing else... Even pain and death are eternal like every thing, but they are eternally *overcome* by *Joy* (they are preserved and together they are overcome) ... The simple knowledge that we are eternal does not take us beyond pain and death, but makes us suffer and die differently from those who are ignorant of it ... But beyond Western anthropology and theology, the 'Joy' to which my writings refer is the removal of the totality of contradictions. It is not waiting for the future in order to fulfill itself. It has always existed. It is eternal... Equally eternal are every pain and every anguish. If one stops here, the eternity of every thing can be agonizing. But if one considers that the anguish essential to the West is the anguish of demise, then, when the eternity of all things appears, this anguish is overcome.[10]

---

10 Emanuele Severino, *La Follia dell'Angelo. Conversazioni intorno alla filosofia* (Milan: Rizzoli, 1977), pp. 34, 33, 50.

In order to comprehend how one can reach contemporary nihilism and find an alternative to it in the rediscovery of Being in all its perennial differences, we must go back to the origin. This means returning to the moment preceding the bifurcation of the choices of Becoming and that of "an uncharted path where truth is not power over Becoming"[11]; in other words, turning our focus to those who first clearly posed the problem for posterity, such as Parmenides (against whom Plato did not commit actual "patricide" but only posed the nihilistic principle already present in Parmenides in a different manner) and Aeschylus, who took, in a grandiose manner, an analogously erroneous path. They established the irrevocability and the decisiveness of death, against which even Zeus is unarmed. Once a human being is gone he does not return to life again, and thus—in such awareness—the existence of every person becomes an agonizing expectation of one's own death. In the face of the "immortal gods," the true nature of man manifests itself as well as that of other entities, which come forth from nothingness only to return to it definitively. Unlike the beliefs of many peoples who imagine a permanence of the soul in some form of afterlife, Aeschylus interpreted death for the first time in an "ontological" sense, as the complete annihilation of the individual in juxtaposition to the permanence of being even in its irreversible transformations. But what he saw as absolute empirical evidence was in fact not so:

> In Greek thought, the observation that the dead do not return (the non-observation of their return) is transformed into the conviction that the dead *never return*, and this conviction becomes, in turn, the foundation of the idea that death is annihilation and that annihilation (and the coming forth from nothingness) is visible, that is, it is something which appears and which is observable. The observation of absence (that is, the non-appearance of that which is absent in certain specific ways) interprets itself as an observation of the annihilation of absence.[12]

Only the thought of Zeus, i.e., "that which is identical within difference," can, according to Aeschylus, save itself from terror and folly in the face of the destruction of all things.

It is symptomatic of the times that these ideas of Severino, expounded

---

11 *Ibid.*, p. 82.
12 Emanuele Severino, *Il giogo. Alle origini della ragione: Eschilo* (Milan: Adelphi, 1989), p. 61.

on a similar level of abstraction with respect to the normal interpretation of everyday experience, could find an audience even among the readers of one of the major national daily newspapers. With respect to historicism and the previous dominance of the political dimension over the theoretical, this phenomenon is perhaps a further sign of anxiety for those who look beyond the agonizing spectacle of incessant change to the immobile lighthouse of a truth which stands apart from the will to power of technology in order to escape from nihilism through the redemption of that which exists: "the most humble of beings is 'greater' and more true than the nothingness which, in nihilism, is considered as if it were God." Thus, "destiny" is rediscovered as the totality of what we must recognize as incontrovertible truth: "Destiny is the gaze through which one sees the impossibility of things coming forth and returning to nothingness; therefore, destiny does not require, as in Western history, the destruction of absolute and incontrovertible truth: destiny is instead its real meaning."[13]

Hermeneutics and the Ephemeral

Through Nietzsche and Heidegger, Vattimo arrives at conclusions diametrically opposed to those of Severino, but equally distant from historicism. From his teacher, Luigi Pareyson (who argued that we must cast our gaze into the abysses of freedom and evil thrown wide open by modern nihilism, and who, as a partisan, had directly experienced the unspeakable horror of knowing that some of his young high-school students had been hanged by the Nazi-Fascists and displayed dangling from barbed wire), Vattimo developed an early interest in hermeneutics and the language of myth as a

---

13 Severino, *La Follia* dell'Angelo, pp. 58, 85.

tool for expression of the ineffable.[14] His style and sensibility, however, were marked early on by an extra-philosophical experience: together with Umberto Eco and Furio Colombo (the other *ragazzi della via Po* or "guys from Po Street"), he came into direct and precocious contact with the modern means of mass communication, which explains his Calvinoesque "lightness" and the apparent accessibility of his written or spoken words. He actually worked for a time in Italian television in its early days and was thus sensitive to the problems of the media and, in general, to what would later be called the culture of the "postmodern." After returning, for the most part, to academia, he developed his thought autonomously in dialogue with several foreign philosophers, who he had done so much to promote in Italy. These authors (like Hans-Georg Gadamer, Jacques Derrida and Richard Rorty) represented heterodox branches of the Heideggerian tree.

After having initially sought to obtain through Nietzsche the "dis-alienation" that had also been the objective of humanist Marxism, Vattimo recognized—ever more clearly from the end of the 1970s—the failure of every project aimed at the re-appropriation of history by an "authentic" subject. The desperate attempts of Benjamin, Adorno and Bloch to reform dialectics, whether by deeming conciliation uncertain or by questioning whether or not contradictions can be overcome, confirmed Vattimo's conviction that they were not "thinkers of the dialectic but rather of its dis-

---

14 For Luigi Pareyson's tragic outlook, according to which philosophy is connected—in the manner of Fichte—to the individual "that one is", see "Lo stupore della ragione in Schelling" in *Romanticismo, esistenzialismo, ontologia della libertà* (Milan: Mursia, 1979); *Esistenza e persona*, (Genoa: Melangolo, 1985); *Ontologia della libertà. Il male e la sofferenza* (Turin: Einaudi, 1995); For an elaboratin on Pareyson's themes, see Sergio Givone, *Storia del nulla* (Rome-Bari: Laterza, 1995). But it is in is Pareyson's, *Ontologia della libertà*, which is the *summa* of his thought, where he delves into the abysses of freedom and evil. Even in God, he finds "the possibility for evil, evil as a possibility, indeed, a possibility that is overcome." But here, Pareyson admits—acknowledging the peculiar nature of his hermeneutics—that we are "in the kingdom of the unobjectifiable, a locus where thought or, better still, thinking, objectively has no right to be, either to tackle or deal with the questions that one meets in such a place, or to comprehend or evaluate the theories that surface. These theories are dictated by indirect, existential and hermeneutical thought—which is like saying mythical, symbolic and dialectical—and only as such they can be said to be fully and totally valid." Only religion not philosophic ethics, only mythic thought not abstract, rational thought, can explain what lies deepest in our hearts and troubles us: "the inaccessible and mysterious connection between guilt and pain, sin and suffering, and for this reason, one must resort to [religion] to address the problem of evil." In Christianity he saw a glimmer of meaning in these mysteries, in particular in pain: "without pain, evil remains unredeemed and joy inaccessible"; Pareyson, *Ontologia della libertà*, pp. 244, 248, 249.

solution."[15] Heideggerian *Verwindung*[16] was thus contrasted with Hegelian *Aufhebung*, as the ascertainment of the inexistence in the course of history of any cumulative processes of inevitable advancement and as a formula for departure from the strong ideas and values of modernity: "The 'post' in postmodern indicates a farewell to modernity," inasmuch as it is the will to "remove oneself from its logic of development, above all from the idea of a critical 'overcoming' in the direction of a new foundation." If, therefore, the foundation (*Grund*), or the "being" as a *fundamentum inconcussum* of metaphysics, turns out to be implausible, then every entity collapses into the abyss (*Abgrund*), for in the end it lacks a foundation. The gain achieved by this theoretical strategy consists in the fact that the solid concepts and absolute values of metaphysics, now weakened and diminished, no longer impose themselves on the conscience in an automatic and tyrannical manner, but at the price of blurring the difference between truth and fiction.

At the same rate, the "shifting" of the categories of metaphysics toward nihilism produces an increase in the emancipatory potential of this philosophical position, inasmuch as the renunciation of the absolute worth of powerful values allows for a wide range of freedom for both individuals and groups. With its most anxiety-inducing characteristics tempered, nihilism even becomes a resource. Discussing recent Italian history, Vattimo maintains that there is no use in opposing the irreversible process of de-valuing absolute values out of fear or desperation: "I would even say that the entire period of terrorism can be explained as a neurotic reaction in the face of the horizons of nihilism. In other words, at a certain moment it seemed that it was all too much; and thus a return to power structures, paternity and discipline becomes understandable."[17]

---

15   Gianni Vattimo, "Dialettica, differenza, pensiero debole" in *Il pensiero debole*, p. 17. On Italian philosophy more generally during this period, see Giovanna Borradori, ed., *Recoding Metaphysics: The New Italian Philosophy* (Evanston: Northwestern University Press, 1988). For a polemical interpretation, see Carlo Augusto Viano, *Va' pensiero. Il carattere della filosofia italiana contemporanea* (Turin: Einaudi, 1985) and Paolo Rossi, *Paragone degli ingegni moderni e postmoderni* (Bologna: Il Mulino, 1989). In addition, see C. Sini and M. Mocchi, "Problemi teorici della ricerca filosofica in Italia" in Ludovico Geymonat, ed., *Storia del pensiero filosofico e scientifico*, vol. IX: *Il Novecento* (Milan: Garzanti, 1996), vol. 4, pp. 159–213.

16   This term defines "the resigned, convalescent acceptance (but also re-signed, that is to say, given a new sign) marked by the wanderings of metaphysics"; see Gianni Vattimo, *La fine della modernità. Nichilismo ed ermeneutica nella cultura post-moderna* (Milan: Garzanti, 1985), p. 186.

17   *Ibid.*, pp. 10–11, 153.

In the volume of essays entitled *Il pensiero debole* (*Weak Thought*), edited by Vattimo and Pier Aldo Rovatti, there was a rejection of the objective of saving the power of synthesis and the strong "radiant" authority of reason: "Within itself, rationality must become less powerful and give up some ground; it must no longer be afraid to tread backward toward the supposedly shadowy zone and it must not be paralyzed by the loss of its luminous, unique and stable Cartesian reference."[18] The Nietzschean "death of God" implies the decline of every permanent value and every absolute truth, which man can now control by means of grounded knowledge. In a sort of hasty selling-off, truth thus becomes a "rhetorical capacity for persuasion" which demands respect and love from the frailty of the traditions to which we all belong. The "ontology of decline" thus imposes a rejection of foundationalist expectations but also of the return to the origin and to first principles. One must look forward without excessive illusions, but also with fewer constraints. According to Vattimo, the collapse of what is "immutable" does not annul the categories of metaphysics developed in the long period spanning from Plato to Nietzsche: those categories instead remain as indelible traces of a path that to this day has no alternatives. As much as these categories may have been weakened, they cannot be renounced. One must instead remember them and demonstrate, by confronting them, the same *pietas* that is shown toward every living, finite being that withers and dies: "*Pietas* is a term which evokes, above all, mortality, as well as finitude and ephemerality: Being is not that which is but that which befalls, perhaps even in the sense that it befalls next to something; Being, insofar as it is ephemeral, is part and parcel of all representations."[19]

In Vattimo's often disenchanted reflection, there are hints of subtle melancholy, secular religiosity and a "belief in believing" which revolves around an oxymoronic, quiet but restless meditation on death, the place where "values are located." For death collects:

> the life experiences of past generations, the great people of the past with whom we wish to dialogue, as well as those whom we have loved and who are gone. Their very language, a crystallization of acts in words, of ways of experience, resides in the casket of death. That casket is also, after all, the source of the precise rules that can help us move through existence in a manner that is not cha-

---

18 Rovatti, preface to *Il pensiero debole*, p. 10.
19 Vattimo, "Dialettica, differenza, pensiero debole," p. 22.

otic and disorderly, even though we know that we are not going anywhere.[20]

Surrounded by the eventual oblivion of all things (and knowing that there have been people in this world, as Chateaubriand puts it, whom we can only remember),[21] we provisionally conserve within our mortal "casket" the fragile memory of that which has been and that which, even though it has meaning for us and for others, is exposed to loss and dissolution.

Given that history no longer seems to possess any dependable reference points, individual experience tends to de-historicize itself and to flatten every event onto a plane of a temporality which lacks depth or direction. One no longer intimately appropriates anything, and alienation is no longer revoked. Disenchantment is complete. Yet nihilism can serve as a chance to fulfill, without excessive drama, the decisive "leap into the abyss of mortality" and into a new and sensible dimension of Becoming. The acceptance of frailty–serene but not overly so–replaces history (as a key to explaining events with their own logic and their own end) with "hermeneutics," which move in an infinite circle of varied degrees of comprehension and misunderstandings and constitutes the *"shape of the dissolution of being* in the age of completed metaphysics."[22] Today, hermeneutics show the irreducible and incommensurate multiplicity of ideas, opinions and events in which reality is presented in this era of the "fairy tale" world created by the media. One could say that the power of the media has provisionally lowered the intellectual and moral level of the society it penetrates, and that it produces an unpleasant cacophony or inauthentic Heideggerian chatter. The power of the media does, however, have the advantage of bringing differences into the open and letting the voices of those formerly excluded be heard: "Once the idea of rationality as central to history fell by the wayside, the world of generalized communication exploded as a multiplicity of 'local' rationalities–ethnic, sexual, religious, cultural, or aesthetic minorities–which now had the opportunity to speak. Finally, they were no longer silenced and repressed by the idea that there is only one true form of humanity to be fulfilled, to the detriment of all particularities and limited, ephemeral and con-

---

20   Gianni Vattimo, *Al di là del soggetto. Nietzsche, Heidegger e l'ermeneutica* (Milan: Feltrinelli, 1989), pp. 10–1. See also *idem, Credere di credere* (Milan: Garzanti, 1996).

21   See François-René de Chateaubriand, *Mémoires d'outre-tombe* (Paris: Gallimard, 1951), p. 24: "I am perhaps the only man in the world who knows that these persons existed."

22   Vattimo, *Al di là del soggetto. Nietzsche, Heidegger e l'ermeneutica*, pp. 18, 128–29, 164.

tingent individualities." The means of mass communication–the perverse aspects of which are not fully perceived–allow for a type of emancipation based not "on entirely explained self-consciousness or perfect awareness of the way things are" but rather on the "erosion of the very 'principle of reality,'"[23] and the multiplication of unrelated points of view and unresolved conflicts. The individual now moves in a sphere of infinite and never complete interpretation, a reality whose incessant transformations impede any crystallization of metaphysical principles or definitive criteria of choice.

Looking Forward

These philosophies, which emphasize either permanence or Becoming–the need for certainties bound to the indestructibility of Being or the acceptance of the fragility of all life–do not constitute the theoretical coronation of the present age in Italy. They are but the most recent stops on a long and uninterrupted journey, coexisting alongside other different forms of thought and sensibility. They represent, however, a plausible seismograph of our condition inasmuch as they register, by marking the extreme margins, the oscillations on the graph of contemporary life. In other words, they elaborate conceptually the state of a world in which various factors–enigmatic evidence in plain view–oblige us either to review the scenarios and instruments of understanding or to reformulate current ethical norms. Among these factors are the crumbling of traditions; the need of individuals to lead their lives with greater autonomy; the only recently initiated encounters between the major cultures of the planet; the extreme alternatives between nihilism and fundamentalism; the collective migrations that are increasing the number of multi-ethnic societies in the West; the process of "globalization" and the concentration of riches and knowledge; and the impact of science and technology on new modes of thought and production. Philosophizing in a "shrinking world," which creates new fields of tension, is no less difficult than philosophizing in a divided world.[24]

---

23 Gianni Vattimo, La *società trasparente* (Milan: Garzanti, 1989), pp. 17, 15.
24 I am referring to the title of Gerard Elfstrom's *Ethics for a Shrinking World* (London: Macmillan, 1990). For reflections on modern ethics and more recent developments in philosophy, see my books *Geometria delle passioni* (Milan: Feltrinelli, 1994); *Se la storia ha un senso*; and *La filosofia nel Novecento* (Rome: Donzelli, 1997), pp. 170-88.

We have seen the experiments that have been conducted-with greater or lesser awareness-to make sense of the collective choices of the Italian people. The many moral traditions of the past have been refashioned over and over again in various combinations: by inserting them into the framework of values of the Catholic Church; by attributing ethical duties to the state or to the political parties of the post-war period; by gradually assigning to individuals (or unloading onto individuals) roles and obligations outside of religion and politics; by endowing women with greater freedom and dignity; by changing attitudes on sexuality, family, class divisions, work, politics and the desire for well-being and self-fulfillment. In all of its complexity, an ethos is always in motion, bubbling with life even when it seems that customs have been corrupted or that there is general disorientation with regard to what the future holds.

Looking back on the road traveled, we can perceive the great density of experiences lived by every Italian within the framework of a common history, as well as their intrinsically insatiable and necessarily open-ended character. For all of us-"dilettantes of life"-every balance is temporary and each day brings and accumulates the unexpected, shifting the horizon of understanding and evaluation. With the dawn of the new millennium, we can only wonder what Italy will be like in fifty years. But this is a desire that is impossible to satisfy, for while there may be latent seeds of the future hidden among the folds of our ideas or in the unfolding of events around us, the future does not generally proceed from the past along discernible lines, nor does it simply reveal what has always been implicit in it. It demands choices which bring newness into the world and which filter reality by condemning to oblivion those possibilities that have been discarded. Perhaps it is of some consolation that ignorance of the future has never stopped anyone from moving forward all the same.

POSTSCRIPT
Eight Years Later

Looking back on the events which have taken place over the eight years since the Italian edition of this book was published, I find it difficult to take stock. And this is not only for the obvious reason that what we have just lived through is opaque to us: as an old Chinese proverb says, "darkness reigns at the foot of the lighthouse." Indeed, time has not allowed the meaning of things to settle, and the dust storm of daily news impedes our ability to discern the main vectors history's course. There are, however, other, more specific reasons. The first is that history has never ceased to surprise us. Unexpected crises, acts of terrorism and wars have set the rhythm of our days and our concerns: after the fall of the Berlin Wall, the dismemberment of the Soviet Union and the dissolution of the Warsaw Pact, we have witnessed the events of September 11 in New York, March 11 in Madrid and a series of wars and exterminations, from Kosovo to Uganda, from East Timor to the second Gulf War. At the same time, there have also been positive surprises, like the greatly anticipated mapping of the human genome and rapid progress in technology and science in very diverse fields.

It seems that the saying of the great economist John Maynard Keynes has come true: "The inevitable never happens. It is the unexpected always." In other words, we are ever more exposed to the unforeseeable, and ever less able to formulate reliable hypotheses for the future. This is also caused – on the individual level – by the privatization of the future, an attitude that has become prevalent in the West over the last decade. The great collective expectations have faded, which until only ten years ago (when the world was still divided into two opposing political blocs) spurred billions of men – if only ideologically – toward collective freedom or social justice.

Now people are more inclined to carve out a piece of heaven on earth for themselves and build their own customized utopias at home. Fear of terrorism, exacerbation of international tensions and the need to entrench one's values may cause the gradual abandonment of this attitude, but it will not be easy to alleviate the sense of uncertainty that will continue to push men and women to occupy themselves with the immediate surroundings of their existence. The second of many reasons that render an overview of these years less clear is the partial loss, in many spheres, of the "anomalies" that had characterized the Italian situation in the past. In step with many other countries, Italy has become increasingly immersed in the processes of economic globalization; increasingly at the center of migratory flows; increasingly caught in the lagging gap between the speed of economic, social and technical transformations and the slowness of politics to keep up with them; increasingly dragged into conditions of growing complexity due to the multiplication of social actors (six billion people distributed over approximately two hundred states); increasingly affected by the volatility of the financial markets; increasingly caught in a historical situation in which the great civilizations of the planet continue not to recognize each other's respective differences sufficiently; increasingly torn between the centripetal forces of integration into Europe and the world and the centrifugal forces of local fragmentation; increasingly sharing both the benefits and the risks of the biotech revolution, such as the growing use of psychotropic drugs in the Prozac and Ritalin family that may help the conscience to adapt complacently and to absorb the relationships of domination, which, however "soft" they may be, are no less overwhelming and oppressive. While the battle for mere survival is generally over, the political use of such technologies and of the media calls into question the European humanist tradition, together with its values of dignity and freedom (enjoyed, of course, until now only by the elite). It thus threatens to introduce new forms of planned subjugation of the masses. There exists, in other words, the risk of creating specially bred men and women, by ensuring that their legitimate primary and secondary needs are satisfied – needs which for millennia were not fully met for the majority of humanity (food, sex, entertainment) – but encouraging them (with the complicity of commercial television) to think of nothing else.

Residual "Anomalies"

And yet, even within such transnational processes, some peculiarities remain. On May 1, 2004, Italy entered – together with 24 other nations – into the economic realm of the Euro, which now brings together a European Union of over 450 million inhabitants, extending from the Artic Circle to Malta, and from the Azores to Cyprus. The entry into the monetary area of the Euro was prepared during a period of great sacrifices by the center-left government to reduce the state deficit and bring it within parameters compatible with the so-called Maastricht accords (named for the Dutch city where they were signed). The advantages of the integrated market are evident, but Italy has had and continues to have some difficulties, for it can no longer resort to competitive devaluations of the lira in order to increase exports – an economic strategy to which producers had become accustomed. Moreover, the European Union, which arose as a "Hobbesian" project aimed at avoiding a war of all against all between European states, and which evolved in a "Kantian" direction to create a civil Europe that defends human rights and dignity without recourse to aggression, is now at risk of plunging back into a Hobbesian state of nature. This risk is a product both of the demands of international economic competition, which places pressure on and has eroded the guarantees of the welfare state, as well as of the military policies of the current Bush administration.

Entry into the Euro also prompted a crisis in Italy's family-based form of capitalism, which – along with many successes – witnessed the decline of the biggest privately owned Italian manufacturer, FIAT. Over the last twenty-five years, the company has lost 110,000 workers, employees and managers, and only now, after the death of Gianni Agnelli, has it embarked upon a painful program of healing. These are tumultuous times in which the entire financial and economic horizon has been spasmodically searching for new strategic alliances capable of keeping up with the competition, made much tougher by the opening of markets and the relative depreciation of the dollar. Despite the lag and tension in relation to its other European partners, even Italy has tried to reorganize itself. The perception of the European Union as an economic giant has become increasingly clear, as has its status as a political dwarf (especially after the rejection of the European constitution by France and Holland) and as a negligible military power, as far as its super-national status is concerned (this was demonstrated during the recent divisions provoked by the Anglo-American war on Iraq). It is therefore predictable that the need for greater political cohesion and strengthening of its defenses will top the agenda in coming years, requiring further transformation of the structure of the state and a massive investment in the military.

In the political sphere, the real Italian particularity, however, was the electoral victory of the center-right in May 2001, with a coalition comprised of Forza Italia, National Alliance (AN), two tiny parties of the now defunct Christian Democrats and, after a long period of stormy relations, even the Northern League. The "Berlusconi phenomenon" reflects an unforeseen reversal of the social pyramid in the voting booth. In other words, a new distribution of electoral support has taken shape: the lower-middle classes, the poorest and least educated part of the population, which traditionally voted for the left, have instead generally opted for the parties of the center-right. On the other hand, the privileged and sophisticated classes have shifted their hopes to the center-left. The idea of Berlusconi running the country has attracted many Italians: he is successful, one of the richest men in Italy and the owner of three television networks and hundreds of businesses in the field of insurance and publishing. The fact that he is a man entangled in glaring conflicts of interest has not tarnished their faith in someone who knows and ably exploits his talents as an expert communicator, addressing a public opinion that depends more on television than on newspapers and parliamentarian debates.[1] Perhaps the jurist and writer Salvatore Satta was right in 1944-1945 when he wrote – in somber tones reminiscent of Guicciardini – of the failure of the left-wing parties in the face of fascism: "It is unpardonably naïve to think that the [Italian] lower class, only because it is poor, nurses a mystic sense of hostility toward the rich, and that it is willing to crusade for the establishment of social justice as if that were the reign of God on earth. The lower class is composed of individuals, and if there is anything that they yearn for, it is to become rich themselves and replace, if need be, the rich of today. In every poor person,

---

1 On Berlusconi, his politics and electoral victory in 2001, see: Francesco Tuccari, ed., *Il governo Berlusconi. Le parole, i fatti, i rischi* (Rome-Bari: Laterza, 2002); Paul Ginsborg, *Berlusconi: Television, Power and Patrimony* (London: Verso, 2005); Federico Orlando, *Lo Stato sono io* (Rome: Riuniti, 2002).

there is a potential rich one."[2]

Is Berlusconi's appeal premised simply upon the manipulation of public opinion? The age-old idea that "the common people wish to be deceived" is as false and simplistic as the complementary notion that there is a perennial conspiracy of the powerful to deceive them. In reality, Berlusconi's appeal cannot be explained as either the result of brainwashing or a plot hatched by the powerful, but to varying degrees as a mental and political fusion of contradictory elements: the provisional acceptance of external impositions and planned intervention from above; reality and desire; the wish to implement one's desires and at the same time to be guided in this pursuit. Given that, for better or for worse, Italy has often been a political laboratory of regimes that were later established elsewhere (such as fascism and the inclusion of post-communists and post-fascists in the government), it is probable that a new model of plebiscitary democracy is being sketched in this case as well. This is a model that combines private wealth, the sophisticated and far-reaching control of the means of mass communication and a politics that employs the image in ways akin to the methods used in marketing, in order to solidify itself against social classes that are less and less involved in the administration of the *res publica* and increasingly bewitched and insecure in a "shrinking world," which brings its upsetting news into the intimacy of the home.

This new political formation has increased the level of social clashes and Berlusconi and his government now (2006) find themselves in serious difficulties and increasingly are losing support. Part of the Left, lacking credible leadership and increasingly ready to look for inspiration outside its own traditions – for example in the pontifs Pope John Paul II and Pope Benedict XVI – sought for a brief period to counter the politics of the Berlusconi government with a return to the streets, with classic rallies and "hand-holding" events in which thousands of persons join hands and encircle a building or symbolic place. These collective gatherings are organized by the unions, anti-war protesters or those opposed to the governmental reforms of the justice system, which seem to many to be *ad hoc* laws intended to guarantee impunity for corrupt officials entangled in the "Tangentopoli" trials (which unleashed further tensions between the government and the judiciary). One episode that has left a long trail of controversy was the ferocious clash

---

2   Salvatore Satta, *De profundis* (Milano: Adelphi, 1980), p. 64.

in Genoa between demonstrators and the police in July 2001 during the meeting of heads of state of the G8 countries. The police answered the violence of some fringe demonstrators, who burned cars and attacked banks and a McDonald's, by roughing up some young people who were sleeping quietly in a protestor-occupied school.

Unlike other countries, Italian society – situated in the Mediterranean between North Africa and the East – is troubled by the immigration of thousands of people who continuously land on its long coastlines, pass through its poorly secured border crossings or arrive with tourist visas in its airports. In the last decade, Italy has experienced an increasing influx of masses of illegal aliens, foreigners and refugees arriving from every corner of the world (first Albanians, North Africans and Senegalese, then more recently Eastern Europeans, Ukrainians, South Americans, Indians, Sri Lankans and Chinese). They have given up or lost their own identity and have abandoned even the minimal protection guaranteed by their previous citizenship. In doing so, they have made themselves officially invisible and impossible to find. For many Italians (especially supporters of the Northern League and National Alliance), these people seem to threaten not only the sovereignty of the host nation in establishing access to and exclusion from its territory, but also the rights, prerogatives and privileges reserved for its citizens. Yet many (especially the small-business owners in Northeastern Italy, where the Northern League is strong) recognize that the immigrants are a useful resource inasmuch as they are willing to do heavy labor, poorly paid work and dangerous or temporary jobs (limited-term and part-time employment) that Italians either no longer want or deem beneath them (because they are attached to the idea of the "*posto fisso*" or life-long employment). They also realize that the immigrants will eventually contribute to the pension fund and help pay for the retirement of an increasingly aging local population. We are thus witnessing a clash between two diametrically opposed positions: one that wishes to close the borders in order to thwart the "invasion" and the other that would open them indiscriminately, since the flow of immigrants cannot be stopped in any case. Perhaps the wisest position is that of a generous welcome, though limited out of necessity, capable of guaranteeing the progressive acquisition of the rights of citizenship to the new arrivals. There is an additional fear, shared by the spokespersons of the Catholic Church, that the massive arrival of Muslims, which have greater difficulty integrating into Italy's national traditions, could unleash phenomena of mutual intolerance and in some cases promote collusion with Islamic terrorism. Should they be proposed, integration and access to citizenship would have to be strictly political in nature. In other words, they cannot demand the renunciation of one's own ethnic and religious identity (which is rarely negotiable), but rather require only the observance of the laws of the host nation.[3] Such questions have sharpened the debate, ignited in the 1990s, on the nature of Italian identity, and have promoted a plan, especially in the Northern regions, whereby the regions are granted greater or exclusive control over matters of public health, education and public safety under the aegis of a request for greater contact between politics and citizens, and for greater security in the face of criminality.

Emigrants in Time

By re-examining the last century, another particularity can be observed in Italian history:

> Almost everything that seems worth remembering happened in the first half of the century, when Italy took part in two world wars and sought to build itself a colonial empire… But in the last fifty years the Italians have made the greatest progress in their millennial history by building a democracy and achieving prosperity. In the first part of the twentieth century, Italy sought to play a leading role; in the second half, the Italians have had more modest objectives and have brought the country into the circle of the greatest world powers. One could say that Italy has not been able to create its place in the sun, while Italians have managed to do so.[4]

Yet, restlessness and vacillation of former certainties weave through this same period of greater prosperity. This is also true because history now

---

3 There is a necessary distinction between "pluralism" (a condition for the co-existence of many cultures, where none has a political value per se, but only to the extent that it is compatible with the others; see G. Sartori, *Pluralismo, multiculturalismo e estranei* [Milan: Rizzoli, 2000]) and "multiculturalism" (in which a certain and decisive weight must be given to singular cultural identities); see Amy Gutmann, ed. *Multiculturalism and the "Politics of Recognition"* (Princeton: Princeton University Press, 1992), esp. the essays by Charles Taylor and Michael Walzer. See also Will Kymlicka, *Multicultural Citizenship* (Oxford: Oxford University Press, 1995).

4 Aurelio Lepre, *Storia degli italiani nel Novecento. Chi siamo, da dove veniamo* (Milan: Mondadori, 2003), p. 3.

seems to many to be the orphan of the intrinsic logic which was supposed to be leading toward a determined objective: progress, the reign of freedom, a classless society or, for Catholics, the Last Judgment. A culture has faded, which – thanks to the mediation of the mass "ethical parties" – induced millions to believe that events were marching ineluctably in a certain, known or predictable direction. For a long time in Italy, many – especially those of the Marxist faith – have been accustomed to believing that conscious human intervention was capable of abbreviating the time necessary for the occurrence of the inevitable, of "accelerating labor pains," or, for Christians, that it could delay the final reckoning with God. With the idea of a single over-arching history – whether sacred or profane – in disrepute (although it has not been altogether disproved), the sense of living in time seems, now more than ever, to be scattered in a plethora of uncoordinated histories (with a lowercase "h"), in personal narratives that are only tenuously connected to common endeavors and in events subject to forces beyond their control.

In recent years, Italian philosophy has reflected on these problems and has connected them with original results to questions that have been debated elsewhere, like the effects of the encounter and clash of civilizations, the impact of technology, the paradoxical articulation of rationality, the nature of community and the weight of a unredeemed past.[5] But philosophy moves out of phase with events. To borrow a geological metaphor, we could say that its vicissitudes are comparable to the recording of tectonic movements – generally slow but sometimes catastrophic – of the *globus intellectualis*, which records the movements and tremors of reality either before or after the fact. The principal task of philosophy is to critically redraw the variations in the maps of meaning, reorienting individuals with respect to continuous mutations in the balance of ideas and values, and to destroy and to expose ill-equipped, sectarian or untruthful modes of thought. This is how – more or less consciously – we register the fact that there has been a change in course for the valences traditionally associated with the future

---

5 Among other philosophical works that have had the greatest impact on the public discussion, the following should be consulted: Roberto Esposito, *Communitas. Origine e destino della comunità* (Turin: Einaudi, 1998); Roberto Esposito, *Immunitas. Protezione e negazione della vita* (Turin: Einaudi, 2002); Giorgio Agamben, *Quel che resta di Auschwitz. L'archivio e il testimonio* (Turin: Bollati Boringhieri, 1998); Umberto Galimberti, *Psiche e techne. L'uomo nell'età della tecnica* (Milan: Feltrinelli, 1999); Remo Bodei, *Le logiche del delirio. Ragione, affetti, follia* (Rome-Bari: Laterza, 2000); Remo Bodei, *Destini personali. L'età della colonizzazione delle coscienze* (Milan: Feltrinelli, 2002).

as a time of waiting, of redemption, of the imminence of the Kingdom of God or the Revolution. The image of one's own existence as a preparatory moment for another life, in the religious sense or as a secular tool for edification in a radiant future – which only our great-grandchildren will experience – has become hard to conceive of and defend. Many life situations (pain, illness, old age, death) have now been judged basically to be unredeemable, because they cannot be taken seriously either in a religious afterlife of celestial beatitude or in an earthly future in which conflicts have been harmoniously resolved. The "alchemic" transformation of the negative into the positive theorized in different dialectical scenarios, and the promises of compensation for present suffering by means of future joy seem to have suddenly become a dead letter. At times, this situation causes a sort of implosion in the arc of the individual's existence, left without hope but not without anxiety, resignation or indifference. Entire realms of experience and wide regions of meaning – first considered from the perspective of eternity or a remote future – are thereby reformulated and transcribed according to new criteria of relevance. What holds true for "negative" experiences, holds also for "positive" ones: the desire to enjoy directly, as unrepeatable gifts, love, friendship, pleasure and luxury seems to have become concentrated in instantaneous, timely, discontinuous "moments of being" of a life worthy of itself. The contraction of individual expectations in the arc of his or her mere physical existence immerses the individual evermore in the unredeemable rhythm of caducity. It forces him or her to elaborate the grief caused by the need to transplant the roots of one's "I" from the solid and immutable ground of the afterlife or the epochal rhythms of history into the crumbly and transient soil of his or her own body, his or her own biography or the entourage of persons and institutions that are closest to him or her. Today one reacts to this uneasiness through a strategy of cultivating the present, forcing it to produce fruit rapidly without worrying about what will happen in the distant future. This brings about, however, a desertification of the future and it risks creating an opportunistic and predatory mentality. But there are signs that even this attitude could be eroded by recent events, by the return of war as a possible horizon of everyone's existence, by the requirements that rise up from a society of great compactness, seriousness and individual responsibility, as well as from the ambiguous exchanges occurring between promises of greater security and requests for greater sacrifices of freedom.

What can be done? We are all emigrants in time: we move from a present that is known to us toward an unknown future – both personal and collective. Every instant serves as a bridge, and at the same time as a caesura with respect to what will occur subsequently. We need the memory of the past, which gives meaning to experience, as well as attention to the present in order to orient ourselves in the world. But in order for us to act, we also need forgetfulness, which allows us to be open toward the future and to think about the new and the possible. This is an arduous challenge, even for Italians who are known for their inventive ability to adapt to change.

www.ingramcontent.com/pod-product-compliance
Lightning Source LLC
Chambersburg PA
CBHW030522080526
44586CB00011B/290